Making
CONNECTIONS 4

Skills and Strategies for Academic Reading

Jessica Williams | Pamela Vittorio

CAMBRIDGE
UNIVERSITY PRESS

CAMBRIDGE
UNIVERSITY PRESS

University Printing House, Cambridge CB2 8BS, United Kingdom

One Liberty Plaza, 20th Floor, New York, NY 10006, USA

477 Williamstown Road, Port Melbourne, VIC 3207, Australia

4843/24, 2nd Floor, Ansari Road, Daryaganj, Delhi – 110002, India

79 Anson Road, #06–04/06, Singapore 079906

Cambridge University Press is part of the University of Cambridge.

It furthers the University's mission by disseminating knowledge in the pursuit of education, learning and research at the highest international levels of excellence.

www.cambridge.org
Information on this title: www.cambridge.org/9781108570237

First published 2016

20 19 18 17 16 15 14 13 12 11 10 9 8 7 6 5 4 3

Printed in the United Kingdom by Latimer Trend

A catalogue record for this publication is available from the British Library

Library of Congress Control Number: 2015948233

ISBN 978-1-108-57023-7 Student's Book with Integrated Digital Learning
ISBN 978-1-107-51616-8 Teacher's Manual

Additional resources for this publication at www.cambridge.org/makingconnections

Cambridge University Press has no responsibility for the persistence or accuracy of URLs for external or third-party internet websites referred to in this publication, and does not guarantee that any content on such websites is, or will remain, accurate or appropriate. Information regarding prices, travel timetables, and other factual information given in this work is correct at the time of first printing but Cambridge University Press does not guarantee the accuracy of such information thereafter.

TABLE OF CONTENTS

SCOPE AND SEQUENCE   iv
INTRODUCTION   vi
ABOUT THE AUTHORS AND CONTRIBUTORS   x

1 TECHNOLOGY   1

2 BIOMEDICAL SCIENCE   75

3 BUSINESS   149

4 SCIENCE AND ENGINEERING   227

APPENDIX 1: KEY VOCABULARY   299
APPENDIX 2: INDEX TO KEY VOCABULARY   314
APPENDIX 3: IMPROVING YOUR READING SPEED   316

REFERENCES   319
CREDITS   323

SCOPE AND SEQUENCE

UNIT	SKILLS & STRATEGIES	READINGS	READING SKILLS PRACTICE
1 TECHNOLOGY page 1	1 **Reading** Identifying Claims and Evidence page 2 2 **Vocabulary** Managing Unfamiliar Vocabulary page 28 3 **Study Skill** Annotating a Reading page 54	The Technological Age 1 "Technology and the Individual" page 7 2 "Virtual Reality and Its Real-World Applications" page 17 Data by Design 3 "Life in 3D" page 32 4 "Mapmaking in the Digital Age" page 41 Expert Text 5 "How Information Got Smart" page 58	Every reading in every unit: • Connecting to the Topic • Previewing and Predicting • While You Read • Main Idea Check • A Closer Look • Skill Review Readings 2 & 4 in every unit: • Improving Your Reading Speed
2 BIOMEDICAL SCIENCE page 75	4 **Reading** Understanding Text Organization page 76 5 **Vocabulary** Using the Dictionary to Find Word Meaning page 104 6 **Study Skill** Using Graphic Organizers page 129	Mobile Health 1 "Health and Wellness on the Go" page 82 2 "Funding Global mHealth Projects" page 92 Personalized Medicine 3 "Genomics" page 109 4 "A Case Study in Genomics" page 118 Expert Text 5 "Drug Discovery in the 21st Century" page 134	
3 BUSINESS page 149	7 **Reading** Making Inferences page 150 8 **Vocabulary** Identifying Language Chunks page 176 9 **Study Skill** Summarizing page 204	Interaction and Exchange 1 "Crowdsourcing and Crowdfunding" page 155 2 "Outsourcing: Managing Labor Needs" page 164 New Ways of Communicating 3 "The Language of Twenty-First Century Business" page 180 4 "Disruptive Innovation and the Challenges of Social Media" page 190 Expert Text 5 "New Thinking about the Right to Copy Art" page 209	
4 SCIENCE AND ENGINEERING page 227	10 **Reading** Adjusting Reading Strategies to Reading Purpose page 228 11 **Vocabulary** Retaining Vocabulary page 252 12 **Study Skill** Preparing for a Test page 277	Materials Science 1 "The Pursuit of Strength" page 233 2 "Biomimetics" page 242 The Future of Innovation 3 "Blue-sky Research" page 255 4 "Frugal Innovation" page 265 Expert Text 5 Selections from *An Engineer's Alphabet* page 282	

VOCABULARY DEVELOPMENT	CRITICAL THINKING WITH RESEARCH AND WRITING		MAKING CONNECTIONS
Activity types vary by reading but include: • Definitions • Words in Context • Synonyms • Academic Word List (after Readings 2 & 4) • Word Families • Same or Different (after Reading 5) • Disciplinary Vocabulary (after Reading 5)	**R1** Understanding Point of View **R2** Synthesizing **R3** Clarifying Concepts **R4** Synthesizing **R5** Analyzing Information	page 16 page 26 page 40 page 52 page 72	Evidence, Contrast, Detail page 73
Activity types vary by reading but include: • Definitions • Synonyms • Words in Context • Academic Word List (after Readings 2, & 4) • Same or Different (after Reading 5) • Disciplinary Vocabulary (after Reading 5)	**R1** Exploring Opinions **R2** Synthesizing **R3** Exploring Opinions **R4** Synthesizing **R5** Exploring Opinions	page 91 page 102 page 117 page 127 page 146	Correction, Cause, Contrast, Detail page 147
Activity types vary by reading but include: • Definitions • Synonyms • Words in Context • Academic Word List (after Readings 2 & 4) • Word Families • Same or Different (after Reading 5) • Disciplinary Vocabulary (after Reading 5)	**R1** Analyzing Information **R2** Analyzing Information **R3** Agreeing and Disagreeing **R4** Clarifying Concepts **R5** Agreeing and Disagreeing	page 163 page 174 page 188 page 202 page 223	Result, Solution, Detail page 224
Activity types vary by reading but include: • Definitions • Words in Context • Academic Word List (after Readings 2 & 4) • Synonyms • Same or Different (after Reading 5) • Disciplinary Vocabulary (after Reading 5)	**R1** Clarifying Concepts **R2** Applying Information **R3** Analyzing Information **R4** Exploring Opinions **R5** Applying Information	page 241 page 250 page 264 page 275 page 295	Result, Solution, Contrast, Detail page 296

Making
CONNECTIONS

MAKING CONNECTIONS 4 is an advanced academic reading and vocabulary skills book. It is intended for students who need to improve their strategic reading skills and build their academic vocabulary.

Understanding Text Organization

In most academic texts, writers use different forms of organization as they present supporting details for their ideas. They often use these different forms of organization for sections of text, paragraphs, or within individual sentences. They use formatting, specific words, or punctuation to signal these organizational structures. Becoming familiar with the most common forms of organization and their signals will help you understand academic texts.

Examples & Explanations

A New Post-Surgery **Remedy**

①After surgery, most patients just want to go home. ②Patients recover more quickly at home, so most doctors support the practice, but then they face a **dilemma**. ③If they send patients home too soon after surgery, then they may develop complications. ④It is vital to watch these patients carefully until they are out of danger. ⑤The ideal **solution** would be remote monitoring. ⑥This option has recently become available in the form of small patches that can be attached to the skin. ⑦The patches contain sensors that send information to the patient's doctor. ⑧**Several** studies have demonstrated that allowing post-surgery patients to return home with a skin patch can **result in** lower medical costs. ⑨One study showed that the patch **led to** a 25 percent drop in the number of days a patient spent in the hospital, with **similar** health outcomes to those who remained in hospital care.

The overall organization of this passage is problem-solution. However, several other forms of text organization are found within this structure.

Headings often give a clue to organization. This heading includes a word, *remedy*, which suggests a solution.

In sentence 1, the writer introduces the topic: the claim that patients do not want to remain in the hospital after they have had surgery.

In sentence 2, the writer uses the word *dilemma* to announce that the claim presents a problem.

The problem is clearly identified in sentence 3 with an *if–then* expression, which indicates cause and effect. Sentence 4 provides details.

In sentence 5, the word *solution* signals a possible resolution. Sentences 6 and 7 provide details about this resolution.

In sentence 8, the writer does several things.

a. He continues to discuss the solution, but as part of the solution, he begins a section that has cause-and-effect organization, with the signal *result in.*

b. He also makes a claim – a skin patch can result in lower health costs – leading the reader to expect some evidence for the claim.

Sentence 9 offers the first piece of evidence to support the claim. It uses both cause-and-effect organization, with the signal *led to,* and comparison organization, with the signal *similar.*

> Each unit begins with an in-depth study of key skills and strategies for reading academic texts, helping students to learn how and when to use them.

> Students learn strategies for approaching academic texts and skills for consciously applying the strategies.

In addition, writers may use formatting, such as headings, lists, and bullets, as well as punctuation, to signal text organization.

Strategies

These strategies will help you recognize and understand text organization.

- Look for signals of broader text organization, like section headings and bulleted lists while you preview or read an article.
- While you read, look for more local signals of text organization, such as words, phrases, and punctuation.
- After identifying a text organization signal, scan ahead to find information that is linked to this type of organization. For example, if the signal indicates a list, look for items in the list. If a signal indicates a problem, identify the problem and then look for a solution.
- Expect several types of text organization within a single reading. Some will structure larger portions of the reading; others will only give structure to short sections.
- Writers do not always provide explicit signals to indicate text organization. In these cases, you will need to infer how the text is organized.

Skill Practice 1

Read the following sentences. Highlight the text organization signals and check (✓) the type of organization they signal. A signal may be a single word or a phrase, and there may be more than one signal in an item. The first one has been done for you.

1 The fatal misdiagnosis of their daughter in 1993 led a British couple to develop an app to help doctors arrive at more accurate diagnoses.
   a _____ compare/contrast   b ✓ cause/effect   c _____ definition

2 The app has several components. One section provides all possible diagnoses. A second section helps the user rule out irrelevant ones and narrow down likely possibilities.
   a _____ classification   b _____ definition   c _____ problem/solution

3 Errors in diagnosis are the most serious patient safety issue. Hospitals are starting to develop systems to catch these errors before patients get hurt.
   a _____ problem/solution   b _____ cause/effect   c _____ definition

4 Many hospitals have difficulty maintaining a sterile environment.
   a _____ cause/effect   b _____ comparison/contrast   c _____ problem/solution

5 Periodic outbreaks of infections in hospitals are often blamed on bacteria and fungi that grow on walls, floors, and bedding.
   a _____ problem/solution   b _____ cause/effect   c _____ definition

FEATURES

- Critical thinking skills
- Real-time practice of skills and strategies
- Study of the Academic Word List
- Audio files of all readings available online

UNIQUE TO THIS LEVEL

Reading 5 texts are by experts in technology, science, business, and engineering.
A concluding activity targets vocabulary common to the unit discipline.

Before You Read

Connecting to the Topic

Discuss the following questions with a partner.

1 How would you describe the difference between scientists and engineers?

2 What are some major engineering failures or even engineering disasters that you know of (for example, the collapse of a bridge or building, the failure of a major project)? Describe one of them.

3 What do you think the causes of such failures might have been?

4 It has often been said that failure is the best teacher. Do you agree? Why or why not?

Previewing and Predicting

Reading the title, section headings, and the first sentence of each section can help you predict what the reading will be about.

A Read the section headings and first sentences of sections I–IV in Reading 5, and think about the title of the reading. Then read the following topics. Write the number of the section where you think each topic will be discussed.

SECTION	TOPIC
	Successful engineering projects that are built on failures
	A history of design problems based on overconfidence
	The contrasting roles of scientists and engineers on design projects
	Examples of good designs that do not need improvement
	Failures that occurred as a result of ambitious but unrealistic designs
	The importance of failure in engineering success
	Problems with pursuing perfection in designs

B Compare your answers with a partner's.

While You Read

As you read, stop at the end of each sentence that contains words in **bold**. Then follow the instructions in the box in the margin.

Predicting the content of a text is critical for reading college books, and students practice this skill extensively before beginning each reading.

Each unit contains 5 readings, providing students with multiple opportunities to practice applying the skills and strategies.

Students learn how to use the skills and strategies by applying them to each text while they read it.

READING 5

◄)) Selections from *An Engineer's Alphabet*

by Henry Petroski

I. Failure

1   Understanding the concept of failure is central to understanding engineering and the engineering design process. In fact, an operational definition of engineering could be that engineering is simply the avoidance of unintended failure. The results of the calculations engineers carry out and the data they collect and analyze in experiments would be virtually meaningless without a sense of how those results or data compare with the critical, or failure values. Whenever engineers work with a steel structure, an electronic device, or a machine, they need to know, for example, the maximum load the structure can support, the maximum current it can take, the maximum rainfall it can accommodate, or the maximum temperature at which it can operate. Without such knowledge, there is no understanding of the limits within which the system can operate without **failure.**

2   Although often associated with the catastrophic collapse of a structure or the total breakdown of a system, the term "failure" can also mean the inability of design to fulfill completely its intended function. Thus, a skyscraper that is in no danger of collapsing, yet is so flexible that the occupants of its upper floors get queasy[1] when moderate winds blow in a certain direction, could be considered a design failure. The **excessive** flexibility of the structure should have been anticipated and the design modified.

3   There is also a paradox associated with design: that failures, through the lessons learned from them, provide invaluable information on how to achieve subsequent successful designs. An example of failure leading to success is the history of the repeated failures of suspension bridges in the early nineteenth century. By studying those failures and their causes, the engineer John Roebling came to understand what was needed in the design in order to achieve a successful suspension bridge, which he did, most famously the Brooklyn Bridge that spans the East River in New York City to this day.

The Brooklyn Bridge

WHILE YOU READ ❶

As you read this paragraph, choose three words for vocabulary cards. Underline them so you can return to them when you have finished reading.

WHILE YOU READ ❷

Use context and your knowledge of word parts to guess the meaning of *excessive*. Does it mean (a) dangerous or (b) more than expected?

---

[1] *queasy:* feeling as if you are going to vomit

FROM THE SERIES AUTHORS

"Reading is an interactive process, in which readers use their knowledge of language, text organization, and the world to understand what they read."

"Reading is goal-oriented and strategic; good academic readers know when to use the right reading skills."

Skill Review

In Skills and Strategies 7, you learned that writers do not always state information directly. Sometimes a writer implies ideas or states facts from which the reader must make inferences.

A Review paragraphs 6–11 in Reading 2. Read the inference statements below based on information in these paragraphs. Then find a sentence from the paragraph in parentheses that supports the inference. The first one has been done for you.

1 **Inference:** Many Americans lost their jobs when GM moved its automotive production to Mexico. (Par.6)

   Evidence: _In the 1980s, General Motors (GM) closed 10 American factories and moved its production to Mexico._

2 **Inference:** GM's IT infrastructure was leading in inefficiency. (Par. 7)

   Evidence: _____

3 **Inference:** The insourcing process at GM is gradual. (Par. 8)

   Evidence: _____

4 **Inference:** Some of the employees at overseas call centers have lim... (Par. 9)

   Evidence: _____

5 **Inference:** Though some companies are now bringing outsourced j... headquarters, outsourcing remains a widespread practice. (Par. 10)

   Evidence: _____

B Compare your answers with a partner's. Discuss how the evide... the inference.

Students continually review the skills and strategies, helping them build up a valuable set of tools for reading academic texts.

Vocabulary Development

Definitions

Find the words in Reading 2 that are similar to the definitions below.

1 existing commonly or happening frequently (adj) Par. 1

2 to br...

3 base...

4 to ca...

5 to re...

6 a str...

7 a situ...

8 a fee...

9 some...

10 a co...

11 centr...

12 mad...

13 to ca...

14 to m...

15 anno...

Words in ...

Complet...

| consoli... |
| delegat... |

1 We r...

2 It is i... mark...

3 _____ is pr...

4 The ... busi...

5 Ther... with...

6 The ...

Students expand their vocabularies by studying key words from each reading and academic words from each unit.

7 The law requires that the company's divisions be taxed as separate _____ .

8 Good managers do not try to control everything; they _____ responsibility for different projects.

9 Careful planning ensured the successful _____ of the project.

10 The plan to move the sales and manufacturing operations to one _____ division will save the company millions of dollars in operating costs.

Academic Word List

The following are Academic Word List words from Readings 1 and 2 of this unit. Use these words to complete the sentences. (For more on the Academic Word List, see page 299.)

| advocates (n) | converted (v) | initiatives (n) | sector (n) | subsidiary (n) |
| assembled (v) | core (adj) | paradigm (n) | security (n) | valid (adj) |

1 For many consumers, patriotism is a / an _____ issue when they decide on purchases.

2 The corporation sold its _____, which was a smaller electronics company, and made a good profit.

3 In the 1990s, outsourcing became the dominant _____ for managing labor demand.

4 Local politicians are usually strong _____ of any program that promises jobs to their community.

5 In almost every business _____, examples of outsourcing can be found.

6 During times of economic uncertainty, many workers worry about the _____ of their jobs.

7 The manager presented a / an _____ argument for why he needed to hire additional employees.

8 In the early days of computers, many hobbyists _____ the machines themselves.

9 Most businesses _____ to the metric system decades ago.

10 The start-up company launched several new _____ to raise capital.

THE APPROACH

The *Making Connections* series offers a skills-based approach to academic reading instruction. Throughout each book, students are introduced to a variety of academic reading and vocabulary-building skills, which they then apply to high-interest, thematically related readings.

Beyond the Reading

Critical Thinking

Readings 1 and 2 present information about advances in mHealth and how they may improve health and wellness. Reading 2 emphasizes the positive impact these applications could have on global health and makes several recommendations about where mHealth funding and efforts should be concentrated.

SYNTHESIZING

Critical thinking includes connecting new information to information you learned in previous readings.

A Work with a partner. Consider the three health-related United Nations Millennium Development Goals (MDGs):

| 4 Reduce Child Mortality | 5 Improve Maternal Health | 6 Combat HIV/AIDS, Malaria and Other Diseases |

B Based on what you read in this unit and your own knowledge, answer the questions below. Review the readings if necessary.

1 Do you agree with the funding recommendations in Reading 2? Explain why or why not.
2 For which MDG do you think mHealth solutions will be the most useful?
3 In what situation(s) would you personally find an mHealth application useful or helpful?
4 Do you think that the application you chose in number 3 could be extended to meet any of the health-related MDGs?
5 In Reading 1, you read that mHealth solutions have been made possible by three developments: (1) more powerful sensors, (2) cloud-based computing storage, and (3) wireless data transfer. Which of these will be most important for meeting health-related MDGs and why?

Research

As you have read, many NGOs and philanthropic organizations are eager to embrace mHealth applications as a means of solving global health problems. Choose one of the MDGs and research a health problem that is not discussed in the readings. You may want to begin with the United Nations MDG website.

Choose one that you think could be improved with an mHealth application. Take notes on the problem and how an mHealth application could contribute to a solution. You do not need any technical knowledge. Assume only that the mHealth

> Each unit develops students' higher level thinking skills, such as evaluating and synthesizing information.

> Students also learn to read more quickly, a valuable skill for extended academic texts.

> The unit ends with a study of academic connectors, helping students learn how to navigate dense academic text.

MAKING CONNECTIONS

Exercise 1

Writers may connect ideas between sentences in many different ways. The second sentence may:
a describe a **result** or **effect** of what is reported in the first sentence
b provide a **solution** to a problem described in the first sentence
c provide a **contrast** to what is described in the first sentence
d add a **detail** or details to support the more general information in the first sentence

How does the second sentence in each pair of sentences below connect to the first sentence? Write *a*, *b*, *c*, or *d* on the line depending on whether it is a result, a solution, a contrast, or a supporting detail.

.... 1 Only 24 percent of the population of Sub-Saharan Africa has access to electricity. Even those fortunate enough to have such access often experience highly unreliable service with outages more than 50 days a year.

.... 2 Tariffs on power in most countries in the developing world range from U.S. $.04 to U.S. $.08 per kilowatt hour. In spite of the poor service, the cost in Sub-Saharan Africa can be more than double the rate of neighboring countries.

.... 3 Efforts to stabilize and rehabilitate dilapidated power grids and scale up power generation capacity are likely to take many years and millions of dollars. Ultimately, an alternative path – the use of leapfrog technology and the development of local solutions – may be a preferable option.

.... 4 Communities that are not connected to a power grid or have no access to a consistent source of electricity often rely on kerosene. This is hardly an ideal alternative as it is a major source of home fires, and its noxious fumes contribute to the two million annual deaths from indoor air pollution.

.... 5 Alfredo Moser, a mechanic in São Paolo, Brazil, had to endure constant power blackouts, which had a very negative impact on his business. In response, in 2002, he invented the bottle bulb – a plastic bottle of water with bleach mounted in the roof, which gives 50 watts of illumination at no cost.

About the Authors

Jessica Williams is Professor and Head of the Department of Linguistics at the University of Illinois at Chicago, where she has taught in the MA TESOL program for almost 30 years. Her research area is second language acquisition, particularly the acquisition of academic literacy. She is an author of Cambridge University Press's *Making Connections* and *Academic Encounters* series.

Pamela Vittorio is Associate Teaching Professor at the New School in New York City. She has extensive experience in ELT as a teacher, teacher-trainer, and as the author of several ELT texts. Pamela is a frequent presenter at international conferences and conducts workshops and training at various academic institutions.

About the Contributors

Dr. David Weinberger is a senior researcher at the Berkman Center for Internet and Technology at Harvard University and writes extensively about the effect of technology on ideas. He received his Ph.D. from the University of Toronto.

Dr. Brian K. Kay is Professor in the Department of Biological Sciences and Distinguished Professor in the College of Liberal Arts and Sciences at the University of Illinois Chicago. He is an expert in molecular biology. He received his Ph.D. from Yale University and did his post-doctoral training at the National Institutes of Health.

Alan Behr is a partner in the Corporate & Business Law Department and Intellectual Property Practice, and chairman of the Fashion Practice at Phillips Nizer LLP, specializing in international intellectual property, fashion, and entertainment law. He received his J.D. from the Columbia University School of Law.

Dr. Henry Petroski is the Aleksandar S. Vesic Professor of Civil Engineering and a professor of history at Duke University. He writes broadly on the topics of design, success and failure, and the history of engineering and technology. His reading in Unit 4 is from *An Engineer's Alphabet: Gleanings from the Softer Side of a Profession*, published by Cambridge University Press. Dr. Petroski received his Ph.D. from the University of Illinois at Urbana-Champaign.

1

TECHNOLOGY

SKILLS AND STRATEGIES

- Identifying Claims and Evidence
- Managing Unfamiliar Words
- Annotating a Reading

Identifying Claims and Evidence

In academic writing, an author makes claims and cites evidence to assert a thesis and support a point of view. A claim is an arguable statement; evidence is information that shows the statement to be true or untrue. To identify claims and evidence, good readers search for key words and phrases called "lead-in" or "signal" phrases. Signal phrases, such as *in the words of* or *as the author states*, are used to introduce quoted material or to paraphrase the words of another author. Writers often cite and evaluate the ideas of others to support or argue against previously stated claims. Identifying claims and evidence will help you understand and evaluate the major ideas in academic texts.

Examples & Explanations

①**There is no doubt that** new forms of technology have made a great impact on society. ②By working both independently and in teams, inventors and scientists have helped improve many aspects of our lives; not just methods of travel and communication but also in the areas of medicine, engineering, and business. ③However, *where* these specialists work plays a role that is just as important to the development of new ideas as the inventors themselves.

④Cities like San Francisco, California, or Boston, Massachusetts, attract large numbers of engineers and computer scientists with Bachelor of Science degrees from top U.S. universities. ⑤**It is reported that** there are 10 percent more technology and engineering experts working in these two areas compared to the rest of the U.S.

Writers usually make a claim first and then support it with evidence. To identify claims and evidence, good readers ask the following questions as they read a paragraph:

- *What claim does the writer make about the topic?*
- *What evidence does the writer use to support a claim?*
- *What phrases does the writer use to indicate a claim or supporting evidence?*

In this text, sentence 1 introduces *technology* as a general topic. The phrase *there is no doubt that* is used to introduce a claim the writer makes about this topic. Sentence 2 introduces several facts (general knowledge) about technological achievements before asserting the thesis. Sentence 3 then gives the writer's main claim, or thesis, about the role of the places where specialists work.

In sentence 4, the writer mentions specific cities as examples that support his thesis. In sentence 5, he gives a statistic as evidence. The lead-in phrase *it is reported that* signals that the writer will present this evidence.

⑥"Silicon Valley" in northern California stretches from the San Francisco Bay to the Santa Clara Valley and has been the home of American computer innovators and manufacturers since the 1970s. ⑦**According to** expert Enrico Moretti, author of *The New Geography of Jobs*, places like Silicon Valley are "brain hubs" – central locations where great numbers of scientists, engineers, and innovators can meet and work. ⑧In addition, Moretti **states** that workers in these fields generate five times more local jobs than other industries.

In sentence 6, the writer further supports his thesis by introducing another area where specialists create new forms of technology. In sentence 7, he uses a lead-in statement, *according to*, before citing evidence from an expert. Sentence 8 offers additional information and statistics from the expert to support the effects of brain hubs.

⑨Moretti also **analyzes** one of the most fundamental aspects of future job growth in the U.S.: the impact of education with a focus on Science, Technology, Engineering, and Mathematics (STEM) courses at the elementary and high school levels. ⑩He **claims** that STEM students are more apt to go on to college and complete studies in a STEM field. ⑪In one analytical report, **statistics showed** that these college graduates have been moving to areas like New Orleans, Louisiana; Pittsburgh, Pennsylvania; and San Antonio, Texas, among other cities, where the cost of living is not as high as it is in Silicon Valley.

In sentences 9 and 10, the writer uses the words *analyzes* and *claims* in order to make a claim about the impact of STEM courses on college education and job growth. Sentence 11 cites statistics from a report to support the claim that college graduates in science and technology fields are moving to other brain hubs across the U.S.

⑫Brain hubs play an important role in bringing together a diverse group of well-educated scientists and creative thinkers. ⑬These places have lasting effects that can influence the future of technology as well as the global workforce.

Sentences 12 and 13 contain a concluding summary about brain hubs that re-asserts the thesis and supports what the writer has stated previously in the text.

The Language of Claims and Evidence

Academic writers often present and evaluate claims and evidence from outside sources to support their own ideas. Here are some words and phrases that can signal claims and evidence.

SIGNAL VERBS AND NOUNS THAT INTRODUCE CLAIMS		SIGNAL VERBS AND NOUNS THAT INTRODUCE EVIDENCE
admit – admission *agree – agreement* *argue – argument* *assert – assertion* *believe – belief* *claim – claim*	*consider – consideration* *contend – contention* *insist – insistence* *state – statement* *suggest – suggestion*	*cite – citation* *indicate – indication* *point out/to* *prove – proof* *reveal – revelation* *show*
SIGNAL PHRASES THAT INTRODUCE CLAIMS		**SIGNAL PHRASES THAT INTRODUCE EVIDENCE**
according to *in the opinion of* *in the words of* *it is clear/likely that* *there is little/no doubt that*		*according to* *a study found/showed* *the evidence shows* *in fact* *the fact is/that* *is evidence of* *it is reported that* *statistics show*

Strategies

These strategies will help you identify claims and evidence.

- Identify the writer's main claim, or thesis, as soon as possible. It is often found in the first few paragraphs and summarized in the final paragraph of a text.

- Before you begin reading, scan the text for names, dates, statistics, key words, and phrases that help you identify claims and evidence.

- As you begin each paragraph, ask yourself: *What is the writer's point of view? What claim does the writer make? What evidence does the writer use to support the claim?*

- Identify signal verbs and phrases that a writer uses to give evidence to support a statement.

- Look for signal verbs and phrases that writers use to introduce claims or evidence from other authors or experts.

- Note the use of certain transition words like *although, despite, however, likewise,* and *similarly* that can be used to contrast or compare ideas and evidence with the claims of others.

- As you read, look for sentences that connect statements at the end of one paragraph with the next paragraph. Writers sometimes make a claim at the end of a paragraph and elaborate on or give evidence for that claim in the first sentence of the next paragraph.

Skill Practice 1

Read the following paragraphs. As you read, underline the signal verbs and phrases that introduce a claim or evidence. Then identify the statement that follows as a claim (C) or evidence (E). The first one has been done for you.

1   The expression "great minds think alike" is often used when two or more people express the same idea at the same time. Technology blogger Matt Novak believes that *C* this statement can be proven. He asserts that "the concept of the nerdy, lone inventor is a myth." Novak also states that invention is "messy" and takes a great team of developers in order for a great idea to become a reality. Whether we look at specific examples from history, like Serbian-American scientist Nikola Tesla's system for alternating electrical current or one of the many devices credited to the American inventor Thomas Edison, Novak points to the fact that none of these things were actually created by a single individual. The evidence shows that other Italian and German inventors contributed to the development of alternating current, while Edison was only one of a number of inventors of light bulbs. In fact, Novak contends that something called "simultaneous innovation" was much more common throughout history: a situation where more than one person has the same new idea at the same time and makes a great effort to develop that idea and bring it to life.

2   Matt Novak's major assertion regarding the lone inventor controversy is relevant to issues that arise today with patents for devices or ideas. For example, who invented the iPad? Novak cites court cases where "rectangular viewing devices" appeared in science fiction movies from the 1960s and 1970s, thereby "invalidating the patent of the iPad." This supports the argument that no single person came up with the idea for the tablet or iPad and that its designs were simply improvements on the next generation of an earlier concept. It is clear that no matter what they are called, these devices are actually products of "simultaneous innovation" – teams of scientists working on the same problems. Novak insists that to perpetuate and uphold the myth of the lone inventor is to ignore the diverse group that was necessary to create these devices.

Skill Practice 2

Read each paragraph and the claim that follows. Highlight the evidence that supports the claim in the paragraph. Underline any phrases that introduce the evidence.

1   Some of the best-known inventors of all time, including Alexander Graham Bell, Thomas Edison, and the Wright Brothers, began their research in some kind of home

laboratory: a basement workshop, a garden shed, or a kitchen. In the 1950s, this idea evolved into the popular notion that the lone engineer or computer technology expert "tinkered" in a garage or some other place where he could experiment with his own equipment and inventions. However, several modern technology theorists, such as physicist Eric D. Isaacs, assert that none of the greatest inventions of the past century were actually created in a garage. On the contrary, Isaacs points out that these creations were produced by research and development (R&D) teams working in spacious, multimillion-dollar laboratories. Although big companies such as Apple, Hewlett Packard (HP), Google, and Microsoft actually had their earliest origins in a garage, the fact is that their founders often used equipment provided by government or corporate money to get their start. According to tech blogger Jodi Lieberman, "all the real development work occurred in an investor- or government-funded, state-of-the-art lab." Lieberman agrees with Dr. Isaacs that Americans need to "let go of the garage myth" and embrace the fact that innovation clusters and brain hubs, where many exceptional minds work together, are the real homes of great inventions.

Claim: The greatest inventions of the last 100 years were the result of teams of scientists.

2   According to Evan I. Schwartz, in his biography of inventor and electronics wizard Philo Farnsworth, Farnsworth began "tinkering" at the age of 20 in a laboratory above his garage. Farnsworth's work started a ripple effect that would change the world forever. In 1927 he successfully demonstrated the first all-electronic television system, which was based on a design he drew in his high school chemistry class. From the late 1920s to the mid-1930s, Philo Farnsworth was engaged in legal battles with RCA, the corporate giant of the radio airwaves, to secure the rights to the *Television System*. RCA's leaders were determined to gain the rights, and employed Vladimir Zworykin to work simultaneously on a similar system. Zworykin visited Farnsworth's laboratory to view the device that Farnsworth had been tirelessly creating. Though Zworykin held patents for very similar devices, he was unable to produce a working television. After years of court cases against RCA, Farnsworth was finally granted the copyright, or patent. It was not until 1939 that RCA was able to sell their "electronic television cameras." During his lifetime, Farnsworth patented more than 130 different devices, mostly on his own. As the title of Schwartz's book implies, it is clear that Farnsworth was *The Last Lone Inventor*.

Claim: Philo Farnsworth was a lone inventor who should be credited with the invention of the modern television.

Connecting to the Topic

Discuss the following questions with a partner.

1 Look at the title. What do you think the reading will be about?

2 Do you work best in a group or on your own? Explain your answer.

3 Do individuals or teams make the best contributions to society? Explain your answer.

4 The "ripple effect" is a series of things that happen as a result of a particular action or event. How could it apply to inventions and new ideas? Give examples to support your answer.

Previewing and Predicting

You will understand a text more easily if you skim and scan for key words. Look for signal verbs and phrases like names, places, dates, or other facts. Scan for signal phrases in each paragraph.

A Read the first sentence of each paragraph in Reading 1 and scan for key words. Then read the questions. Write the number of the paragraph where you think you will find the answer to the question. The first one has been done for you.

PARAGRAPH	KEY WORDS AND PHRASES
4	Was Thomas Edison really a lone inventor?
	How did Steve Wozniak feel about working in a team?
	Did Steve Jobs think highly of customer feedback?
	What device influenced the development of the computer?
	How do technology specialists collect and measure data?
	How many cell phone and Internet users are there in the world?
	Do customers always give feedback?
	What are the origins of the Internet?
	Who invented the wireless telegraph?
	What do experts suggest is the best solution to the debate between working alone or in a team?

B Compare your answers with a partner's.

While You Read

As you read, stop at the end of each sentence that contains words in **bold**. Then follow the instructions in the box in the margin.

◀)) Technology and the Individual

I. The Ripple Effect

1   Nearly 200 years before technology wizards[1] Steve Wozniak and Steve Jobs launched the Apple computer and changed how the world communicates, inventor Charles Babbage came up with a kind of engine that could mechanically perform calculations. This primitive calculator would become the precursor to modern electronic devices. Babbage's ambitious efforts made it possible for twentieth-century computers to evolve from performing complex calculations to being a means for everything from design to communication. Two centuries later, Babbage's original design for a calculator has evolved into something that today's computer users consider a simple "app." Many experts agree that without Babbage's early work, technology of the past century may have progressed much more **slowly**. It is no surprise then, that Babbage is often called the "father of the computer."

2   Similar to Babbage's accomplishments are the innovations of Italian physicist and radio pioneer[2], Guglielmo Marconi. In 1901, Marconi discovered a way to convey information signals around the world. This transatlantic transmission of radio signals – known as the wireless telegraph – was the first ripple in a wave that would develop into the Internet. It can be said that Marconi's research continues to inspire and support advancements in the field of communication and information technology. In 2014, the Marconi Society (founded by Marconi's daughter) gave its highest prize to India-born Arogyaswami Joseph Paulraj, of Stanford University in California, for his invention of a transmission system with multiple "antennae," or receivers. This revolutionary system is at the core of high speed Wi-Fi and Broadband networks, used by billions of people **worldwide**.

3   The invention of the Internet cannot be attributed to one person. Instead, several individuals share the **credit.** While researchers were creating a special email system (Ethernet) to be used among employees at the copier company Xerox PARC, other technology experts were simultaneously developing the infrastructure[3] of the Internet. This is known as Transmission Control Protocol/Internet Protocol (TCP/IP). In simple terms, TCP is a "layer" of transmission that manages the way data files are gathered, sent, and combined to create a message. The lower layer of this system is Internet Protocol (IP). IP ensures that the message gets to

---

WHILE YOU READ ❶

Highlight a signal verb in this sentence that introduces a claim about technology.

WHILE YOU READ ❷

Look back at paragraph 2 and highlight two claims.

WHILE YOU READ ❸

The writer makes a claim in this sentence. Highlight the evidence for the claim.

---

[1] *wizard:* a genius or expert
[2] *pioneer:* a person who is among the first to develop or study an area of knowledge or scientific field
[3] *infrastructure:* the basic structure of a system that is necessary for its operation

the right destination. In the journey from wireless telegraph to wireless Internet, the inventions of Babbage and Marconi were significant and necessary steps in the process, resulting in communication systems that could function and deliver messages effectively.

II. "Sheltered Innovation" vs. "Combinatorial Creativity" – Lone Worker or Team Player?

4   Thomas Edison's name may evoke an image of the stereotypical solitary inventor, working tirelessly in a laboratory to perfect the latest version of a device. This image, however, does not reflect the reality of Edison's world. In Menlo Park, New Jersey, Edison created his own "invention factory," a concept that companies in the "brain hubs" of California's Silicon Valley – the home of all things technological – have tried to imitate in their own workspaces. Edison's work environment could be considered the first research and development lab. Though he experienced long periods of working in isolation, he also collaborated with teams of specialists from all over the world. These technicians and machinists, whom he had invited to his facility, aided Edison in the process of producing and perfecting his devices.

5   It is not uncommon for an individual scientist or engineer to work alone at some point in time. This method of working independently to produce something original is often called *sheltered innovation*. Sheltered innovation allows the inventor to be creative without the influence of other scientists' ideas, while also evoking the nostalgic[4] image of the "garage inventor." Some technologists believe that this approach toward product development allows for more creativity. Steve Wozniak, co-creator of Apple/Mac computers, felt that inventors are like artists and work best alone. In the words of Wozniak, "I don't believe anything really revolutionary has ever been invented by a committee. . . I'm going to give you some advice that might be hard to take. . . Work alone. . . Not on a committee. Not on a team." Yet despite his statements, Wozniak was an integral part of the "brain hub" of **Silicon Valley**.

6   Other Internet experts, however, like Steven Johnson, author of *Where Good Ideas Come From*, assert a different approach to creativity. Johnson contends that ideas must collide, or run into one another, which cannot happen while working **alone**. He refers to this collision of great minds as *combinatorial creativity*. This term was first defined by Margaret Boden, a pioneer researcher in artificial intelligence[5], cognitive and computer science, and psychology. She expressed combinatorial creativity as "the unusual combination of, or association between, familiar ideas. . . ." Boden, however, does not deny that working alone is significant to the creative

> **WHILE YOU READ 4**
> Highlight the transition words in this sentence that introduce evidence that contrasts with claims in the previous quotation.

> **WHILE YOU READ 5**
> Highlight a signal verb in this sentence that introduces a claim.

---

[4] *nostalgic:* feeling pleasure and sadness at the same time when thinking about the past
[5] *artificial intelligence:* the use of computer programs that have similar qualities of the human mind, such as the ability to recognize language, pictures, and learn from experience

process. Her method somehow bridges that gap between the autonomous inventor, Steve Wozniak, and team player, Steven Johnson.

III. How Are We Doing?: The Individual and Feedback

7   Whether innovative undertakings are pursued by an individual or a group, there is no doubt that the globalization of technology has created a shift in the way individuals communicate, work, socialize, and conduct business. From face-to-face meetings and telephone conversations to texting, video chats, and web-based discussions, the world wants and needs immediate access to it all. This rapid progress in technological development has an impact on people in ways that are both observable and measurable. According to a global study, while more than 90 percent of the world's population own cell phones, more than 3 billion people are Internet subscribers. And that number continues to grow. These statistics also raise a number of questions regarding the development of products or services and the individual: With such a high number of users, can an individual user affect how a new device can be improved? How do technologists get feedback from individuals, and what do they really think about it?

8   In 1997, when asked about using customer feedback, Apple co-founder Steve Jobs admitted that he viewed user feedback as an impediment to enhancing Apple products and devices, and placed little value on using focus groups. Jobs claimed that "a lot of times, people don't know what they want until you show it to them." Jobs, like his partner Steve Wozniak, was a supporter of working in isolation.

9   For users to have any influence on modifications or changes to a device, they must communicate information and opinions to the developers. This is generally done through surveys, comments, or direct communication through a company's marketing system. Most technologists get a head start on feedback by testing services or products before they are released to the public.

10   When technologists truly desire feedback from users for the development of a product or the improvement of a system, they conduct their final

Figure 1.1 Internet and Cell Phone Use

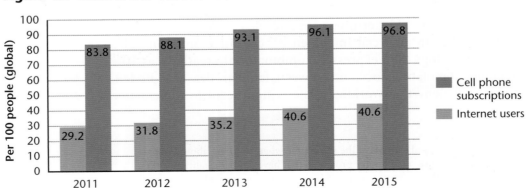

stage of product testing known as *beta testing*. Beta testing is a common term used to describe a partnership between companies and potential customers who are willing to try out the product free of charge. Beta testing exists in almost every aspect of technology and the sciences. For example, before launching a new website, a heuristic, or "rule of thumb," evaluation is established to make sure that the website meets the needs of its target audience. This process determines usability factors[6] and compares that data against certain principles. Usability testing is often conducted by interview over the phone or computer while users simultaneously test features of the website or a product. Researchers who conduct these interviews must adhere to specific guidelines to avoid influencing the user in any way. They are encouraged to remain silent, let the user speak freely, and be detached and objective during the conversation. These are the types of activities that can occur in companies located in European innovation clusters, where customers play a significant role in the R&D process.

11 Companies often invite users to participate in focus groups – small groups of people who represent a particular demographic[7] of the population – but there are advantages and disadvantages to beta testing and collecting feedback from individual users. Because of the lack of anonymity in a focus group – everyone in the group sees and hears what each participant has to say – people are not always willing to voice honest opinions. Though a focus group is generally the more reliable method, the results may be unpredictable. In addition, if people do not have an incentive, they are not always willing to participate in a focus group or answer a survey. Besides, what Steve Jobs contended has at times proven true: consumers do not always know what they want until they see the **product**.

A focus group

WHILE YOU READ ❻

What is the main idea of paragraph 11? Highlight it.

12 From computers to mobile devices, the technology we use today is the direct result of generations of engineers, inventors, and technologists. Their efforts, whether they started out in garages or developed in "brain hubs," have individually and collectively affected our lives. From the minds of these inventors to the hands of the users, from tangible[8] devices to invisible signals, the development cycle of technology ripples from the world of one to the universe of many.

---

[6] *usability factors:* characteristics of the degree to which something is easy to use
[7] *demographic:* a population's size, age, education, and other characteristics
[8] *tangible:* real and able to be shown or touched

Main Idea Check

Here are the main ideas from five paragraphs in Reading 1. Match each paragraph to its main idea. Write the number of the paragraph on the blank line.

_____ A Before a product reaches the market, objectively gathering data from customers is an important step in the research and development process.

_____ B The truth is that none of Edison's great inventions were created in a garage or exclusively by him.

_____ C The inventions of nineteenth-century scientists influenced the evolution of the Internet and computer systems.

_____ D Some scientists find the need to work independently of others at some point in their research.

_____ E Through participation of customers in face-to-face situations, companies are able to collect information about their products.

A Closer Look

Look back at Reading 1 to answer the following questions.

1 Why does the writer discuss the early work of Charles Babbage?
   a To support a claim that Babbage's research had an effect on the modern computer
   b To give evidence of how technology has evolved over 200 years
   c To offer proof that nineteenth-century devices have become useless
   d To supply background information on the computer

2 Two scientists are credited with the development of Internet Protocols. **True or False?**

3 According to the reading, which of the following is true? Choose all that apply.
   a Johnson argues that great inventors cannot work by themselves.
   b Steve Wozniak's views support the concept of _sheltered innovation._
   c Experts agree that creative ideas have been the product of teams of great thinkers.
   d Boden believes that inventors who work independently cannot produce creative ideas.

4 Steven Johnson believes that the concept of _sheltered innovation_ is better for technology than working in teams. **True or False?**

5 What is true about the globalization of technology? Choose all that apply.
   a It has changed the way people communicate.
   b Technological advancements happen too quickly to measure.
   c Many people can now use video chat instead of talking face-to-face.
   d The number of Internet and cell phone users is growing rapidly.

6 What is Steve Jobs's opinion of customer feedback?
  a He believed that people never knew what they wanted.
  b He thought that collecting surveys was a good use of his time.
  c He felt that people needed to see a device before they realized they wanted it.
  d He did not place any value on the opinions of his customers.

7 Which statement best supports the writer's point of view about technology?
  a The Internet and most devices have evolved because of Edison's early work.
  b The wireless telegraph could not have influenced how the Internet developed.
  c The best way for technology to develop is for inventors to work alone.
  d Regardless of how or where inventions are created, each discovery makes an impact on the other.

Skill Review

In Skills and Strategies 1, you learned to identify claims and evidence in a text. One way is to look for signal verbs and phrases that introduce claims and evidence. Identifying claims and evidence will help with overall comprehension of academic texts.

A Review Reading 1. Match the claim in the middle column with its evidence. Then write the number of the paragraph that contains each claim in the column on the left. The first one has been done for you.

PARAGRAPH	CLAIM	EVIDENCE
10	_d_ Technologists consider user feedback essential to the development of a product.	a In a focus group, the fact that people are seen and heard by the other participants can affect their responses.
3	_e_ Messages can be conveyed and received over the Internet.	b Scientists and researchers from all over the world worked together at his "invention factory."
7	_g_ The globalization of technology has changed how people communicate.	c Margaret Boden's theories bridge the gap between the two points of view.
5	_f_ Steve Wozniak's point of view about working alone does not reflect the reality of his business.	d Beta testing enables customers to participate in the R&D process.

11	_A_ Customers do not always provide accurate feedback.	e There are two protocol layers that make sure data is collected and sent to the right place.
4	_B_ Thomas Edison probably started the first research and development lab.	f The Apple team was located in the "brain hub" of Silicon Valley.
6	_C_ New ideas do not always happen exclusively in isolation or on teams.	g Approximately 90 percent of the world's population uses a cell phone.

B Compare your answers with a partner's. Discuss any differences you have.

Definitions

Find the words in Reading 1 that are similar to the definitions below.

1 something that comes before another and influences its development (*n*) Par. 1 *Precursor*

2 new ideas or methods (*n pl*) Par. 2 *Innovations*

3 the act of sending a signal or message (*n*) Par. 2 *Transmission, transmit*

4 groups formed from parts connected together (*n pl*) Par. 2 *Networks*

5 to say or think that something is the result or work of something else (*v*) Par. 3 *Attributed. (characteristic)*

6 existing or acting separately from other things or people (*adj*) Par. 6 *Autonomous.*

7 efforts to do a difficult job (*n pl*) Par. 7 *Undertaking.*

8 a strong effect on a situation or person (*n*) Par. 7 *Impact, effect, result*

9 something that makes progress difficult or impossible (*n*) Par. 8 *Impediment.*

10 a situation in which a person is not known by name (*n*) Par. 11 *Anonymity.*

Words in Context

Complete the passages with words or phrases from Reading 1 in the box below.

asserts	guidelines	imitate	rule of thumb	stereotypical
conveys	head start	revolutionary	simultaneously	target audience

1 The *stereotypical* concept of the lone inventor is slowly changing.

2 Automobile companies follow specific *guidelines* to ensure that a new vehicle is safe.

3 Companies should consider their *target audience* and collect feedback before launching a product.

4 Technology experts use a / an *rule of thumb* to measure results and collect data.

5 At its most basic level, wireless technology *conveys* voice and data signals without wires or cables.

6 The *revolutionary* ideas of the earlier inventors have influenced modern scientists.

7 Summer internships at local businesses can help college students get a *head start* on their careers.

8 Many technology experts were working *simultaneously* on the development of the Internet.

9 Steven Johnson *asserts* that ideas must collide, and that working alone is not productive.

10 Some scientists believe that technology developments *imitate* nature.

Critical Thinking

UNDERSTANDING POINT OF VIEW
Writers can present more than one point of view on an issue. They may explain why this point of view is preferable or leave that judgment to the reader.

In Reading 1, the writer offers various arguments for where technological innovations take place (brain hubs, innovation clusters, or garages/workshops), who created them (lone inventor or collaborative team), and how they developed (with feedback or not).

A Read the following statements. Decide whether the writer opposes, is neutral about, or supports the statement. Then put a check (✓) in the appropriate column.

STATEMENT	OPPOSES	NEUTRAL	SUPPORTS
The computer and Internet would not be possible without the work of Babbage or Marconi.			
Where an inventor creates devices is not significant to the final product.			
Steve Jobs and Steve Wozniak succeeded because they preferred working without customer feedback.			
Margaret Boden's theories on how creativity works offer the best solution to the controversy.			
Innovations in technology create a ripple effect because each one influences the other.			

B Compare your answers with a partner's. Explain your opinions.

Research

Choose an innovative idea or invention that is not mentioned in Reading 1. Find answers to the following questions:

- What is the significance of the invention?
- Who is credited with the invention?
- How was the invention or device perceived by the public?
- How did it develop over time?
- Where was the device developed?

Writing

Write two to three short paragraphs on one technological innovation or invention. Argue whether or not you think the device was created by one individual (*sheltered innovation*) or was the product of a team using *combinatorial creativity*.

Connecting to the Topic

Discuss the following questions with a partner.

1 Have you ever played an interactive video game? Which one?

2 Do you think games can be good for you?

3 What are possible reasons for playing video or online games other than entertainment?

4 What do you think "gamification" is?

Previewing and Predicting

> Scanning the first sentence or two of each paragraph for key words or phrases will help you comprehend the main idea of each paragraph as well as the overall gist of the passage.

A **Quickly read the first two sentences of each paragraph in Reading 2. Decide what the topic of the paragraph will be. Then read the following topics. Write the number of the paragraph next to the topic that best describes it. The first one has been done for you.**

PARAGRAPH	TOPIC
3	While wearing special headgear, patients are able to play games against avatars.
	Virtual reality (VR) games can be used for physical rehabilitation by people of any age.
	Immersive learning in the classroom may help students remember more than learning in traditional ways does.
	Patients who used VR games experienced positive physical and mental effects.
	People used to think that VR could only exist in a science fiction film.
	The concept of a virtual classroom has the potential to expand people's educational opportunities.
	A special space that gives its users a 3D experience has been created.

B **Compare your answers with a partner's.**

While You Read

As you read, stop at the end of each sentence that contains words in bold. Then follow the instructions in the box in the margin.

Virtual Reality and Its Real-World Applications

I. Introduction

1   Daniel is competing in a game of Ping Pong against a young woman named Angela. The sound of the ball echoes as it is volleyed back and forth. It's the final point of the match. Angela has a determined look on her face as she prepares to deliver her final serve. As she makes her last great effort, Daniel moves toward the right corner of the table to return her shot and . . . he wins! This might seem like an ordinary scenario, except for the fact that Daniel's opponent, Angela, is really an avatar[1], and Daniel is 40 years old. He has been playing in a computer-generated[2] world made possible by new technology embedded in a special pair of glasses, and his objective is to improve the range of movement in his right arm.

2   It might sound more like science fiction than fact, but the concept of "virtual worlds" has been a reality for over 20 years. This new digitally enhanced[3] universe – where the user experiences the sensation of being "inside a computer-generated environment" – is no longer limited to the entertainment industry or video games. Instead, virtual reality (VR) has "morphed" into something with multiple uses. To comprehend how VR has evolved into this new model, it is important to note the various settings in which VR now has "real world" practical applications. VR and gamification[4] are changing the way modern society approaches challenges in everything from medicine to **education**.

II. Background: The VR Environment

3   When Daniel enters the small white room, the first thing he notices is the technology-covered walls. On each side are in-sight cameras that capture motion from every angle, 3D motion controllers[5], and three wide-screen High Definition (HD) TVs that project finely detailed images. However, among these familiar items is also the latest innovation of VR: the "headset." VR headsets are based on an old concept – like the visors worn in Sci-Fi movies from the 1980s and '90s, *Tron* or *The Matrix*.

> **WHILE YOU READ ①**
>
> Look back at paragraphs 1 and 2. Highlight the sentence that best states the main claim (thesis) of the reading.

---

[1] *avatar:* a character or creature that you create to represent yourself in a computer game or on the Internet

[2] *computer-generated:* designed or produced using a computer program

[3] *digitally enhanced:* improved upon by use of technology or computer

[4] *gamification:* creation of a game-like environment in nongaming contexts to encourage users to learn or solve problems

[5] *motion controller:* a device that controls the movement of other objects

But this is neither a movie set nor an electronics showcase: This is a CAVE – a Cave Automatic Virtual Environment – located in a center for outpatient[6] rehabilitation.

III. The Cave Automatic Virtual Environment

4   In VR, <u>simulation is the ability to create an</u> environment that closely resembles the real world and allows the user to interact with that world. The user must be "immersed," much like the heroes of Sci-Fi films; as soon as the visor is placed over the eyes, the player is drawn into the computer universe. By using these special headsets or head-mounted displays (HMDs), the experience and sensations of the user are heightened. In the CAVE, a user is able to see in 3D, while observers who are not wearing visors see a typical 2D screen. Through this unique eyewear, the user perceives an "alternate world," and experiences a point of view that exists outside the real world. Though the process of immersion usually begins with physical rather than mental immersion, as seen in the following case studies, its applications are diverse and have been used successfully in both aspects.

Virtual reality headset

IV. Case Study 1: Physical Rehabilitation with Console- or Desktop-Based VR

5   First launched in 2006, the Nintendo Wii is a console-based[7] video game device that requires no special eyewear. Attached to a television monitor, the Wii offers an interactive form of technology through its gaming controls equipped with motion sensors. An occupational therapist (OT) specializes in helping patients with injuries, diseases, or disabilities through the use of everyday activities. The OT's approach is a mind-body treatment: they work with physical and psychological aspects of a patient's life. Many times the therapist will help the patient by focusing on things like motor skills and coordination. In this part of the case study, patients played games on the Nintendo Wii to work on strengthening weak muscles or improving balance. This could be accomplished through completing simple tasks like the repetitive movement of hitting a Ping-Pong ball or swinging a golf club. Patients who participated in the VR rehabilitation study were encouraged to use gaming modules, like the Wii, throughout their course of treatment at the center, as well as at home.

---

[6] *outpatient:* referring to a person who receives medical care from a hospital but does not stay there overnight

[7] *console:* a special box or cabinet that contains electronic equipment like a video game or TV

6   In the first part of the two-part study, occupational therapists interviewed ten male patients with spinal cord[8] injuries, ranging in age from their mid-twenties to mid-fifties. Three to six months after these participants had sustained[9] their injuries, the patients began a course of treatment using console-based VR games. At the end of this period, interviews were conducted with each patient via a 45-point questionnaire. The therapists were also required to complete a special survey regarding their experiences using VR with patients. Then in the second part, the study was conducted again with the same patients, but this time using personal computers (PC) as the gaming platform. The rationale for testing the VR experience on a PC was to determine whether it would be simpler or more convenient than the console-based model.

7   The results of the two-part study proved to be significant. Playing VR games not only improved the patients' endurance and physical movement, but also gave the patients a sense of motivation that they had not experienced before. Patients who had little to no knowledge of computer technology were able to learn and use the VR games quickly and with little effort. Moreover, the games did not cause the patients any added discomfort or pain, and helped them maintain a sense of **independence**. In the second part of the study, patients played PC-based VR games and completed a similar questionnaire. The results mirrored those of the console-based study except for the fact that the desktop PC was easier to operate or transport, whereas the console-based games were stationary.

WHILE YOU READ ❷

Reread the beginning of the paragraph. Highlight evidence that supports the claim in the first sentence.

V. Case Study 2: Using VR in Education

8   Imagine students all over the world, sitting in front of computers wearing VR headsets and taking a class at the same time. This desktop-based method of VR enables the learner to have a certain amount of autonomy in that each person can take the class from the comfort of home. Online learning has changed how educators think about the classroom and has afforded instructors an easy-access way to teach without having to be in the same room with their students. Yet for all its apparent contradictions, online learning also seems like the natural, next step in the evolution of **education**. The MOOC (Massive Open Online Course) is one way of making a class available to more than 100 students at a time. This takes place via a desktop-based platform and affords the students the convenience of not having to travel or change time zones: a student in Canada can easily attend a course in the U.K.

9   Developed by Linden Lab in 2003, the VR program *Second Life* allows people all over the world to join and interact in a wide variety of ways. Within the computer program, teachers are able to set up their own classrooms. Each student who wishes to join the class can design an avatar to

WHILE YOU READ ❸

Highlight an example in the paragraph that supports the claim in this sentence.

---

[8] *spinal cord:* the set of nerves inside the spine that connect the brain to other parts of the body
[9] *sustain:* to experience damage or loss

represent him- or herself. The instructor, in turn, creates a "virtual" class-room where the students' avatars enter the room, sit in class, and chat with one another. The instructor can lecture and give on-screen presentations, such as PowerPoint, and teach a class that simulates the real world. Though the technology is a bit more complicated than playing a video game on a console, the environment is vibrant and provides real-life experience for anyone who wants to study subjects like English online.

10   VR can also be useful in the physical classroom setting. Using an immersive 3D program called Chaotic Moon, students wear a VR headset and use a motion controller to experience the subjects they are studying. They can take a walk through the Amazon jungle and interact with its plants and animals, or even the people who live there. According to Chaotic Moon's CEO Ben Lamm, this is "i-learning" – immersive learning. Lamm claims that people remember 90 percent of what they do, but only half of what they hear, and 10 percent of what they **read**.

WHILE YOU READ 4

Highlight any signal verbs or phrases in paragraph 10 that introduce claims or evidence.

11   If what Lamm says is true, there will be countless opportunities for patients and learners to achieve their goals by playing VR games. Whether VR is used for rehabilitative or educational purposes, it is obvious that VR's practical applications expand far beyond entertainment. These "gam-ification" cases barely scratch the surface of the possibilities for virtual worlds in the **future**.

WHILE YOU READ 5

Reread paragraph 11. Highlight the claims the author makes about the future of VR games.

A student avatar in a virtual classroom

Main Idea Check

Match the main ideas below to five of the paragraphs in Reading 2. Write the number of the paragraph on the blank line.

_4_ A Being completely involved in a 3D game helps the user engage all of their senses.

_8_ B Online courses enable instructors to teach greater numbers of students without a physical classroom.

_2_ C Games can have uses beyond simple entertainment.

_10_ D Use of VR in a regular classroom can help expand student's abilities to retain information.

_5_ E Therapists are helping people heal by using VR and video games.

A Closer Look

Look back at Reading 2 to answer the following questions.

1 Why is Daniel playing Ping Pong with Angela?
   a He wants to play against an avatar.
   b He needs to play for health reasons.
   c He's taking part in an experiment.
   d He's playing for educational purposes.

2 What is special about the VR headset?
   a It improves the vision of the player.
   b It is just like what was used in sci-fi movies.
   c It changes the user's perception of the real world.
   d It enables the player to have a three-dimensional experience.

3 In the CAVE, a user experiences a world that looks and feels real. **True or False?**

4 The writer describes different types of games for rehabilitation. Choose all that apply.
   a Games that are used from a device connected to a computer
   b Games that make users experience and interact in a movie
   c Interactive games that are played with controllers
   d Games that can be played via the Internet

5 Teaching classes online is an interesting concept, but one that is unlikely to change traditional education. **True or False?**

6 What is true about using Second Life for teaching online classes? Choose all that apply.
   a Users can interact with each other and the instructor in a realistic environment.
   b Students can have a learning experience online similar to that of a physical classroom.
   c Online classes are usually more complicated than regular classes.
   d Teachers are still able to make presentations and talk to students.

7 What is true about the effect of immersive learning (i-learning) on individuals?

   a It enables students to be fully engaged and interact with what they are learning instead of just reading.

   b Immersive learning helps students stay focused on what they are learning.

   c Children can play games while they learn in order to remember more.

   d Students will enjoy walking in nature more if they are wearing a headset.

8 What is the writer's prediction about the future of VR?

   a It will be suitable for people who enjoy game playing when they learn.

   b We have not even begun to explore the possibilities it has for educational purposes.

   c It is likely that most people who use it will begin to remember things better.

   d It does not matter whether VR is used for educational goals or not; people will like it.

Skill Review

In Skills and Strategies 1, you learned that writers make and support claims by providing evidence in a text. Writers use signal verbs and phrases to introduce claims.

A **Reread the following paragraph from Reading 2. Choose the claim that is supported by evidence in the paragraph. Then highlight the evidence that supports this claim.**

In the first part of the two-part study, occupational therapists interviewed ten male patients with spinal cord injuries, ranging in age from their mid-twenties to mid-fifties. Three to six months after these participants had sustained their injuries, the patients began a course of treatment using console-based VR games. At the end of this period, interviews were conducted with each patient via a 45-point questionnaire. The therapists were also required to complete a special survey regarding their experiences using VR with patients. Then in the second part, the study was conducted again with the same patients, but this time using personal computers (PC) as the gaming platform. The rationale for testing the VR experience on a PC was to determine whether it would be simpler or more convenient than the console-based model.

   a Most patients lose interest in playing games after six months.

   b Male patients between the ages of 25 to 55 are more likely to play video games.

   c It is important for patients who participate in such studies to begin within a fairly short time after they are injured.

   d Whether patients who are undergoing occupational therapy play games on their own computers or a VR console does not affect them.

B **Compare your answers with a partner's.**

Definitions

Find the words in Reading 2 that are similar to the definitions below.

1 a situation or description of possible events (*n*) Par. 1 _scenario_

2 existing or firmly attached within something (*adj*) Par. 1 _embedded_

3 to change gradually in appearance or form (*v*) Par. 2 _morphed_

4 to change or develop gradually (*v*) Par. 2 _evolve_

5 uses, particularly computer-related (*n pl*) Par. 2 _Applications_

6 the process of returning someone to a healthy or normal condition (*n*) Par. 3 _rehabilitate_

7 a model of a real activity, created for training purposes (*n*) Par. 4 _Simulation_

8 complete involvement in an activity (*n*) Par. 4 _Immersion, – immerse_

9 a device used for studying movements (*n*) Par. 5 _motion sensor_

10 the ability to make all parts of the body work together (*n*) Par. 5 _Cordmation_

11 expressed or happening in the same way many times (*adj*) Par. 5 _repetitive_

12 pain, usually not severe (*n*) Par. 7 _Discomfort_

13 to make available or provide naturally (*v*) Par. 8 _Afforded_

14 things that are opposite of what is said or done (*n pl*) Par. 8 _Contradiction_

15 to deal with only a superficial part of a subject of problem (*idiom*) Par 11 _Scratch the surface_

Synonyms

A Complete the sentences with words from Reading 2 in the box below. These words replace the words or phrases in parentheses, which are similar in meaning.

| countless | echoes | mirrored | practical | stationary |
| drawn | heightened | platform | rationale | virtual |

1 The bicycle remains (in place) _stationary_, but the rider experiences the sensation of cycling through Ireland.

2 People can play video games on any type of gaming (hardware and software) _platform_.

3 During a VR experience, a user's sense of sight is usually (increased) _heightened_

4 There are (numerous) _countless_ texts and instant messages sent every day.

5 At the electronics store, the sound of six TVs playing at once (repeats) _echoes_ through the showroom.

6 There are many (useful) _practical_ applications for using VR.

7 When a student's classroom experience is (almost real) _____Virtual_____, she will still be engaged and interested in learning.

8 One of the most interesting things about using VR is that the player feels as if he has been (pulled) _____drawn_____ into the game.

9 When an instructor uses VR activities in a lab, what is on her computer is (reproduced) _____mirrored_____ on the screen in the class.

10 The (justification) _____rationale_____ for teaching online is to make classes available to more people all over the world.

Academic Word List

You have already studied the words in the box in Vocabulary Development exercises in Readings 1 and 2 of this unit. These are particularly important words to study because they come from the Academic Word List – a list of words that frequently appear in academic texts. Use these words to complete the sentences. (For more on the Academic Word List, see page 299.)

Steps, Rules.

attributed (v)	guidelines (n)	innovations (n)	scenario (n)	transmission (n)
evolve (v)	impact (n)	networks (n)	simulations (n)	undertaking (n)

1 The success of most technological _____innovations_____ is often due to the efforts of an R&D team.

2 Managing online classes via the Internet is a serious _____undertaking_____ for any teacher.

3 NASA astronauts practice flight _____simulations_____ before heading into space.

4 The invention of the world wide web (www) is _____Attributed_____ to Tim Berners-Lee.

5 To beta test new products, technologists follow certain _____guidelines_____ to ensure that data is objective.

6 The number of mobile _____networks_____ worldwide is not increasing as fast as the number of cell phone users.

7 It is not hard to envision a / an _____scenario_____ where viewers can interact with TV programs and commercials.

8 Cell and mobile towers are responsible for the _____transmission_____ of signals to a phone.

9 The "ripple effect" implies that ideas, designs, and products _____evolve_____ over time because one influences the other.

10 The usefulness of VR and its educational purposes are likely to have a / an _____impact_____ on future generations.

Critical Thinking

SYNTHESIZING

Critical thinking includes connecting new information to information you learned in previous readings.

Reading 1 presents perspectives about how we have perceived the development of technology and different points of view about inventors, inventions, and the places where ideas come to life. In Reading 2, you discovered innovative applications of Virtual Reality and gaming.

Based on what you read in this unit and your own knowledge, answer the questions below. Discuss with a partner.

1 How has technology shaped the way we learn, find restaurants, get directions, and shop?
2 Can you think of other ways to make use of technology such as apps, gaming, or virtual reality?
3 Do you think brain hubs might influence how quickly new devices and games get created? Why or why not?

Research

Investigate new developments or innovations in technology and how they are used for more than entertainment purposes. These can be mobile apps, devices, or computer software programs.

- Who developed or created the innovations?
- How do they work?
- Who do you think will benefit the most from them? Why?

Writing

Your assignment is to write a short essay on innovations in technology. Discuss who came up with a new way to use an app or gaming for more than entertainment and describe how these innovations change the way we work, manage our health care, exercise, or learn.

A Preparing to Write

1 Look over your notes from your online research.
2 Review Readings 1 and 2. Highlight any information you think you would like to include in your report.
3 Organize your notes from your research and any information from Readings 1 and 2.

B Writing

1 Write an introductory paragraph about an innovation and include background information on its inventor.

2 Explain how you think this new technology might be used and who will benefit from it.

3 Include examples and evidence or arguments from your research to support your arguments.

4 Conclude with the supporting evidence and a restatement of your perspective about the innovation.

5 When you have finished your report, check it for grammar and spelling errors.

Improving Your Reading Speed

Good readers read quickly and still understand most of what they read.

A Read the instructions and strategies for Improving Your Reading Speed in Appendix 3 on page 316.

B Choose one of the readings in this unit. Read it without stopping. Time how long it takes you to finish the text in minutes and seconds. Enter the time in the chart on page 317. Then calculate your reading speed in number of words per minute.

Managing Unfamiliar Words

Good readers have strategies for managing unfamiliar vocabulary they encounter in both academic and general texts. They do not stop at every unknown word or phrase as this will slow down their pace and interfere with their ability to comprehend the overall meaning of a text. Instead, they skip or make educated guesses about certain vocabulary and apply useful strategies when encountering other unknown words. Recognizing roots or parts of words they already know, using context clues, identifying special punctuation, and noticing repeated words are valuable techniques all readers can utilize.

Examples and Explanations

①Can you imagine buying a car that was created by a 3D printer and then being driven in that same car by a computerized **chauffeur**? With the power of "**additive** manufacturing" (3D printing) and computer-driven automobiles, this is now possible.

Skip unfamiliar words: The word **chauffeur** may be unfamiliar to you, but knowing the meaning of this word is not important for overall comprehension. You can probably guess that a chauffeur is a synonym for "driver."

Look for roots or parts of words that you recognize: You know the word *add* and can guess from the *-ive* form that this is an adjective.

②It took years to design, but only 44 hours to print. Called Strati, this innovation is a two-seat electric car that travels at 40 miles per hour (64 km/h). The design for this **prototype** was created in Italy.

Look for context clues, such as examples or images: Sometimes there are clues to the meaning of an unknown word in the surrounding context. In paragraph 2, you can make an educated guess that the word *prototype* means almost the same thing as *first model* in the following sentence (paragraph 3).

③The types of materials used to print the first 212-layered model range from **thermoplastic** – a type of plastic that becomes **pliable** at a high temperature but returns to **solid** form after it cools – to carbon fiber, which has properties such as low weight and high strength. Except for the glass windshield, engine, and other electrical components, the rest of the car's interior and exterior were the products of an extremely large 3D printer.

Look for special punctuation and a definition: Writers often define technical or specialty words. Look for commas, long dashes, or parentheses, which are used to draw attention to a definition. In paragraph 3, the word *thermoplastic* is a technical term, so the writer included its definition between long dashes for the reader's benefit. Writers can also use examples and images to help define abstract or unfamiliar terms.

Look for comparison or contrast: In paragraph 3, the contrast signal *but* and the word *solid* imply the opposite of *pliable*, so you can determine that *pliable* means *bendable*.

④Another 3D-printed car is the Urbee 2. Unlike the Strati, it took 2,500 hours to print Urbee 2's panels and features. In addition, the Urbee 2 is a **hybrid,** though it relies mainly on electric current to operate.

⑤In a study conducted in California, data showed that Google's **autonomous** Prius and Lexus cars offer smoother rides than cars that were controlled by people. These self-driving cars steer themselves safely and can stop in time to avoid an accident.

In paragraph 4, there is a comparison and a contrast between the Strati and another 3D-printed model, the Urbee 2. From the context you can guess that a *hybrid* is a car that uses a combination of two types of fuel.

Look for repeated words or synonyms in previous or subsequent sentences: When writers repeat a word, it means that word has importance. However, to avoid redundancy, writers often use a synonym for a previously used word. In paragraph 5, the word *autonomous* is rephrased as *self-driving*.

Strategies

These strategies will help you manage unfamiliar vocabulary.

- If you encounter an unfamiliar word, ignore it, and continue reading until the end of the sentence or paragraph.
- If an unfamiliar word looks like a word you already know, use that knowledge to guess the meaning of the unknown word.
- Look for context clues, such as examples, images, and a special font (italics) or punctuation (commas, long dashes, parentheses, and quotation marks) used for important words and definitions, to help you identify and figure out the meaning of unknown words and phrases.
- Look for comparisons or contrasts to help you understand the context and guess the meaning of an unknown word or phrase.
- Look for repeated words that indicate key words or important concepts.
- Look for synonyms – noun or adjective phrases that the writer uses to avoid redundancy.
- Remember that to comprehend a text, you do not have to understand every word or phrase, and you can combine strategies to guess meaning.

Skill Practice 1

As you read the following sentences, think about whether you need to understand the words and phrases in bold in order to understand the sentences. If you do not need to understand the words or phrases, write *A* on the blank line. If you need to understand the words or phrases, write *B* on the blank line. Then highlight any

context clues that helped you determine their meaning. **The first two have been done for you.**

A = I can generally understand the sentence, so I can ignore the word(s) in **bold**.

B = Context clues can help me understand the meaning of the word(s) in **bold**.

__A__ 1 Urbee 2's creators claim that it can make a 2,500 mile trip on 10 gallons of **bio-fuel**.

__B__ 2 The materials used to print the first 212-layered model range from thermoplastic – a type of plastic that becomes **pliable** at a high temperature but returns to solid form after it cools – to carbon fiber, which has properties such as low weight and high strength.

_____ 3 Except for the glass **windshield**, engine, and other electrical components, the rest of the car's interior and exterior were the products of an extremely large 3D printer.

_____ 4 In addition, the Urbee 2 is a hybrid, though it relies mainly on **electric current** to operate.

_____ 5 This self-driving car **steers** itself safely and can stop in time to avoid an accident.

_____ 6 According to manufacturers, a customer can choose the **configuration** of the car that they prefer, in layouts ranging from convertible to four-seater.

_____ 7 The Strati's engine **propels** it at a speed of 40 miles per hour for a range of 120 miles.

_____ 8 The manufacturers believe that eventually anyone can **custom fit** the car to conform specifically to his or her shape.

Skill Practice 2

Look back at the sentences in Skill Practice 1. Which strategies helped you guess the meanings of any unknown words and phrases in bold? Fill in the chart below for sentences 1–8 from Skill Practice 1. Put a check (✓) next to the strategies that helped you. You can check more than one strategy.

STRATEGY	1	2	3	4	5	6	7	8
Skipped this word								
Recognized a root (or part) of the word								
Found examples								
Found punctuation and definition(s)								
Found a comparison or contrast								
Found synonyms								

Skill Practice 3

The following sentences contain words in **bold** that you may not know. Use the strategies you have learned to try to figure out their meanings. Write your answers on the blank lines. The first one has been done for you.

1 Government institutions and social networking sites now have exceptional **biometric** facial recognition programs that can identify people from a photo.

   using detailed information about a person's body, like eye color, to prove who they are

2 Facebook's software development team does not consider *verification,* or matching two images to the same face, to be the same thing as *recognition* – identifying a person in a new photo and matching it to a user.

   _____

3 In **cinematography,** the use of computer-generated effects in films enables the editor to work in the studio to add digital and animated features to the movie.

   _____

4 Though the movie *Tron* utilized more 3D effects than any other film in the 1980s, Hollywood film companies were **reluctant** to embrace the new technology at that time.

   _____

5 Animation is actually the movement of models that have been created on computers in 3D through a **predefined,** or preset, path.

   _____

Connecting to the Topic

Discuss the following questions with a partner.

1 How long has three-dimensional design existed?

2 What are some ways that we use 3D design in technology?

3 What are the benefits of using computer technology for drawing or designing objects? Explain your answer.

4 Do you think robots or human-like robots are useful to society? Why or why not?

5 What types of things could be useful to print on a 3D printer? Why?

Previewing and Predicting

Looking for key words and phrases can help you predict what a text will be about. Scan the text for key words that the writer uses more than once. Words that appear to be repetitive are often important concepts or terms that the writer wants the reader to know.

A Read the following sentences from Reading 3, and look at the key words or phrases in **bold**. For each key word or phrase, highlight the punctuation that signals a definition. Underline words and phrases that are definitions, synonyms, or context clues.

1 This **juxtaposition**, or contrast, of light and shadow tricks the observer's eye into seeing multiple planes and dimensions.

2 The complexity of 3D design also corresponds to Leonardo's early drawings of **polygons** – flat shapes with three or more straight sides – and **polyhedrons** – highly constructed geometrical shapes containing more than four sides.

3 Leonardo applied mathematical theories to his drawings in terms of **proportion**, known as the "Golden Ratio," as evident in his famous drawing *Vitruvian Man*.

B Compare your answers with a partner's.

While You Read

As you read, stop at the end of each sentence that contains words in **bold**. Then follow the instructions in the box in the margin.

◀)) Life in 3D

I. The Art of Geometry

1   The earliest three-dimensional representation of the human body was an innovation of Renaissance master Leonardo da Vinci's constant experimentation with the quality of light in his work. Leonardo was likely the first artist to render the human figure with contours – angles, curves, and shadows – which he applied to give the *Mona Lisa* artistic perspective unlike any painting of its **time**. This juxtaposition, or contrast, of light and shadow tricks the observer's eye into seeing multiple planes and dimensions. The third dimension is not only characteristic of the realism portrayed in modern art, but is also an important element in mathematics and physical science. The difference is that mathematics is easy to observe while physical science is more theoretical.

2   The complexity of 3D design also corresponds to Leonardo's early drawings of polygons – flat shapes with three or more straight sides – and polyhedrons – highly constructed geometrical shapes containing more than four sides. Leonardo applied the mathematical theories regarding proportion known as the "Golden Ratio" to his work, as evident in his famous drawing *Vitruvian Man*. Without these theoretical applications, contemporary designers would struggle to interpret and represent the objects around us. Solid geometry explores the space in which we live. 3D designers take a simple two-dimensional shape – a circle, square, or triangle – and by adding depth or width, create a sphere, cube, or **pyramid**. These 3D shapes have volume and surface area, but can also have multiple sides. The resulting structures are intrinsic to the 3D work done by computer graphics programmers, designers, and robotics engineers.

WHILE YOU READ ❶

Look back at this sentence. Highlight the punctuation that introduces context clues that help you understand the meaning of *contours*.

WHILE YOU READ ❷

Look back at this sentence. Highlight the words that are examples of two-dimensional shapes.

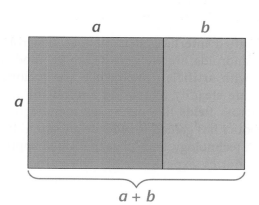

Vitruvian Man

The Golden Ratio

II. Expanding Our Visual Capabilities

3   When a CGI (computer-generated imagery) programmer creates an object or an avatar in 3D for a film or video game, he uses special software that plays a critical role in conveying the final object on the screen. From a simple 2D sketch of a woman's face to an image of her head that he can rotate 360 degrees, the software enables the programmer to manipulate the image on-screen. 3D objects are rendered by a multistep process: First, they are drawn and designed. Next, their data is entered into a computer software program, which then alters an object from a 2D to a 3D representation. This process also entails scanning and modeling. Polygonal design, like the polygons drawn by Leonardo da Vinci, can be used to represent the human face. This is basically a process of drawing intersecting points in 3D space called *vertices*. Design software programs like AUTOCAD and 3DFACE allow the programmer to use these vertices to create complex 3D structures. Faces can be created from 2D photographs that have been uploaded to the computer program. Designers can also apply a drawing or photo to this polygonal mesh, and the resulting image is very realistic in appearance. The programmer can control age, gender, race, and many other features of the face in this way. This type of computer visualization of three-dimensional design paves the way for many practical applications.

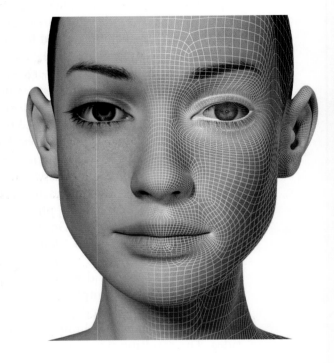

III. From Avatar to Android

4   In robotics, the concept of "Human Machine Interaction" (HMI) is one of the most important fields of study. HMI involves how humans and machines communicate and interact with each other through a very refined and limited interface. It is obvious that robots, or human-like robots such as androids, are the next step in 3D modeling – these human-like androids with artificial intelligence are no longer science fiction. Robotics jobs are steadily increasing around the world. With multiple applications across fields like medicine, manufacturing, and aerospace industries, robotics has gained worldwide attention. Its effects can be seen in all aspects of technology, and it has unlimited **applications**.

5   Japanese robotics expert Hiroshi Ishiguro, a professor at Osaka University's Department of Systems Innovation, has been developing robots for over two decades. The result of his work is an android that mimics human behavior and facial expressions. Ishiguro has created three different types of androids that resemble a human adult, teen, and child. Each android was created with special material that makes them look and feel real, and each can perform certain human-like tasks, which the

> **WHILE YOU READ** ③
> What is the main idea of paragraph 4? Highlight the sentence that expresses it.

robotics research teams can then evaluate. The first one, the *otonaroid*, resembles an adult Japanese female and is so well designed that in photographs, it is hard to distinguish the android from the person on whom its features are based.

Otonaroid speaks with other robots at a press conference in Tokyo, Japan.

6   Cumulative data collected from the androids helps the engineers to conduct further research and expand the android's potential. The otonaroid was designed to interact with humans and adapt its behavior based on an algorithm in its programming. The otonaroid, in particular, is called a "robot science communicator." The android adjusts its behavior based on input and interaction with its human observers. For example, it can turn its head and blink while conversing with a visitor.

7   At the heart of Ishiguro's design lie questions about what it means to be human. He invites observers to do the same as they communicate with the androids. The process of designing and building these robots is part of his investigation of how humans express emotions. And, at the core of this component of HMI, there is a highly sophisticated mapping system.

IV. Just the "FACS" – Facial Action Coding System

8   In order to understand how to construct "humanoids," engineers and artists must first analyze human facial expressions and gestures, which they then map to points on the mechanisms of the android's face, as well as its mechanical, internal structure. This mapping system is what enables the android to mimic or imitate human expressions and body language. Each point on the face of the android represents a muscle of the human face.

9   The Facial Action Coding System (FACS) is a critical tool for any CGI designer or robotics engineer. This is a system where the work of psychologists and physiologists plays a role in the development of the android's human-like face. The FACS is integral to the design of a 3D image because it is a system of coding and mapping a person's facial expressions – those small movements made by human faces. There are 43 muscles in the human face and six "groups" of emotional responses that people typically express. The designer must understand the psychological implications as well as the anatomical and physiological structure of the human face in order to accurately render the physical features of the **android**. These are key factors in the mechanical design of a human-like robot. In turn, the robot is equipped with cameras in each eye and tracks the movement of objects and the humans who interact with it, thereby collecting information and learning to "adapt." As researchers gather more data on how androids and complex computer systems interact with humans, these details become more important. The more human-like the robot or android is, the more likely people are to react positively toward it.

WHILE YOU READ ④

Look back at this sentence. Highlight the word that means *draw* or *design*.

V. 3D Printing – The Shape of the Future

10   Although the average person does not have the capability to build an android, the idea of manufacturing lifelike 3D models of oneself is not implausible. A company in China can do just that: Its 3D printer measures over 6 feet (1.8 meters) high and can reproduce a life-sized wax replica of any individual.

11   The work of engineers and technologists in robotics and 3D computer-generated imagery has also made other forms of 3D modeling possible. Additive manufacturing, or 3D printing from digital design, is rapidly changing the world of possibilities for manufacturing industries. Using special complex plastics, resins[1], and polymers[2] that can be conveyed in powder mixed with a liquid binder, the 3D printer slowly deposits thin layers of the material in succession until a solid 3D object **emerges**. This process was used in 2013 by a team of French researchers who successfully printed a robot from a 3D printer. Anyone can purchase the kit to print the robot, "Poppy." Poppy resembles a human skeletal system and lacks the appearance and sophistication of the otonaroid. However, Poppy has biological research at the foundation of its design, which allows it to walk and interact with its owner.

12   Twenty-first-century technology is the driving force behind a new "Renaissance" for 3D design. It spans from aeronautics and automotive manufacturing to biomedical sciences to robotics. From a simple tea-cup to artificial limbs[3] to automobiles, the applications of 3D printing are astounding, and its uses are limitless. 3D printers are the wave of the future.

> **WHILE YOU READ** ⑤
>
> Highlight any words or phrases in this sentence that can help you determine the meaning of the word *binder*.

---

[1] *resins:* a clear, yellow, sticky substance produced by some trees and plants and used to make varnish, medicine, or plastics, or a similar substance produced chemically
[2] *polymer:* a natural or artificial substance made from many smaller molecules
[3] *limb:* arm or leg

Main Idea Check

Here are the main ideas for five of the paragraphs in Reading 3. Match each paragraph to its main idea. Write the number of the paragraph on the blank line.

_____ **A** 3D software enables designers to accomplish more now than in the past.

_____ **B** The materials used in 3D printing allow for a variety of objects to be created.

_____ **C** Leonardo da Vinci used mathematical concepts to give his drawings proportion.

_____ **D** Exploration of human nature has given androids more realistic qualities.

_____ **E** Android creation has evolved because scientists have incorporated facial expressions in the androids' designs.

A Closer Look

Look back at Reading 3 to answer the following questions.

1 What does the writer imply about artists during the fifteenth century?
   a Leonardo da Vinci was a master artist.
   b Most artists represented the human body in three dimensions.
   c Most of the artists at that time did not use the same techniques as Leonardo da Vinci.
   d Artists experimented with light to make the observer see things that were not there.

2 What factors do 3D designers need to consider to render 2D shapes into 3D shapes? Choose all that apply.
   a Math theories   c Surface area
   b Proportion   d Depth

3 Indicate the correct order of steps that a CGI programmer uses to turn a 2D image into a 3D avatar. Write the correct letter in each box.

   A The image is rendered into a three-dimensional object.
   B An image is sketched or designed.
   C The designer adds data to the software to manipulate facial features.
   D The sketch or photograph is uploaded to the software program.

4 Computer-generated "robot communicators" can interact with people via 3D monitors. **True or False?**

5 The FACS was designed with the help of which professionals? Choose all that apply.
   a Psychologists   c Physiologists
   b Therapists   d Robotics specialists

6 When a 3D printer creates a model based on a digital design, the final product immediately emerges as a complete form. **True or False?**

Skill Review

> If you encounter unfamiliar words, skip them if you can understand the main idea. Look for comparisons or contrasts, context clues, definitions, repeated or redundant words, and synonyms to help you manage unknown vocabulary.

A Read the following sentences from Reading 3. Write *CC* if you use context clues to understand the meaning, *D* if the word is defined, or *SYN* if there is a synonym near the word.

_____ 1 The earliest three-dimensional **representation** of the human body was an innovation of fifteenth-century Renaissance master Leonardo da Vinci's constant experimentation with the quality of light in his work.

_____ 2 Da Vinci was likely the first artist to render the human figure with **contours** – angles, curves, and shadows – which he applied to give the *Mona Lisa* a perspective unlike any painting of its time.

_____ 3 The third dimension is not only characteristic of the realism portrayed in modern art, but is also an important element in the mathematical and physical sciences. The difference is that mathematics is easy to observe while the physical science is more **theoretical**.

_____ 4 **Polygonal** design, like the polygons drawn by Leonardo da Vinci, can be used to represent the human face.

_____ 5 The FACS is integral to the design of a 3D image because it is a system of coding and mapping a person's **facial expressions** – those small movements made by human faces.

_____ 6 Poppy resembles a human **skeletal** system and lacks the appearance and sophistication of the *otonoroid*.

B Reread paragraph 6. Look at the six words in **bold**. On the blank line next to the line of text, write *S* if you should skip the word, *C* if you should look for a context clue, or *R* if the word is an important technical term that is throughout the text.

_____ **Cumulative** data collected from the androids helps the engineers to conduct further
_____ research and expand the android's **potential**. The otonaroid was designed to interact
_____ with humans and adapt its behavior based on an **algorithm** in its programming. The
_____ otonaroid, in particular, is called a "robot science communicator." The **android** adjusts
_____ its behavior based on **input** and interaction with its human observers. For example, it
_____ can turn its head and **blink** while conversing with a visitor.

C Compare your answers with a partner's.

Definitions

Find the words in Reading 3 that are similar to the definitions below.

1 the method used to give objects drawn or painted on a flat surface the appearance of depth and distance (*n*) Par. 1

2 the placement of people or things next to each other in order to compare them (*n*) Par. 1

3 flat, two-dimensional surfaces (*n pl*) Par. 1

4 to control something by using one's hands or by using a machine (*v*) Par. 3

5 to change a characteristic or cause a change to happen (*v*) Par. 3

6 crossing at a point or set of points (*adj*) Par. 3

7 to make it possible or easier for something to follow (*v phrase*) Par. 3

8 a set of mathematical instructions that are followed in a fixed order and help calculate an answer (*n*) Par. 6

9 one of the parts of a machine, piece of equipment, or concept (*n*) Par. 7

10 to appear by coming out of or from behind something (*v*) Par. 11

Words in Context

Use context clues to match the first part of each sentence to its correct second part and to understand the meaning of the words in bold.

_____ 1 The designer renders an image on the computer screen

_____ 2 Twenty years ago, the thought of androids

_____ 3 When a person enters a virtual world,

_____ 4 The latest 3D printers are equipped with

_____ 5 Some birds, like parrots, have the ability to imitate sounds,

_____ 6 With a special 3D printer, an individual can now create

_____ 7 The oversized head of the android was strangely

_____ 8 A clever painting technique used by artists

_____ 9 The idea of androids that can drive our cars seems

_____ 10 The job description of a 3D designer

a **entails** having artistic abilities as well as knowledge of many software programs.

b **tricks** the eye into seeing three dimensions.

c which is why they easily **mimic** the human voice.

d there is a high level of sensory **input** that makes the experience seem real.

e out of **proportion** to its body.

f with **artificial intelligence** seemed like science fiction.

g a 3D **replica** of him- or herself.

h feed **mechanisms** that deposit layers of plastics, resins, and polymers.

i almost **implausible**, but it is now very possible.

j that **corresponds** almost exactly to the artist's 2D sketch.

Critical Thinking

Reading 3 discusses three-dimensional design from its origins to its multiple applications. The writer uses certain technical terms to describe aspects of 3D design and how it is used. If a writer believes that some terms might be unfamiliar to a reader, those terms are explained. However, there are some concepts that the writer might not explain fully. In that case, it is important that the reader is able to do research to become better informed about the topic.

> **CLARIFYING CONCEPTS**
>
> Critical thinking involves thinking carefully about important topics that the writer has not completely explained.

In a small group, discuss the following topics:

- What impact do you think the "Golden Ratio" had on the use of proportion?
- Are proportions seen in nature? Give some examples.
- The word *technology* comes from Greek word *techne*, which actually means "useful art." With this in mind, what do you think Aristotle (the Greek philosopher) meant when he said that "technology imitates nature." How do you think computer programmers or modern graphic art professionals have implemented this? Explain your answers.

Research

In Reading 3, you read about new creations made possible by 3D design. Research one of the topics below to get more information about it.

- Computer-generated imagery (CGI) (for example, computer animation on green screen in cinematography)
- Facial recognition program software
- Human-like androids and their uses in society
- The multiple benefits of 3D printing

Writing

Write a three-paragraph report on the topic you researched. The first paragraph will explain the background or historical information on the topic. The second paragraph will describe its uses by individuals or society. The conclusion will be a summary of what you have stated.

Connecting to the Topic

Discuss the following questions with a partner.

1 When you visit a new city or place, do you use a paper fold-out map or a GPS map on your cell phone to figure out directions? Explain your choice.

2 How are maps made? What do you think map makers used in the fifteenth century? What tools do you think map makers use today? Explain your answers.

3 Have you ever seen an antique map of the world? How old was it? Did the continents look the same as on modern maps? Are the boundaries of countries the same? Describe this map to your partner.

Previewing and Predicting

Writers often include graphics, charts, maps, and other images to provide a visual reference for unfamiliar words or abstract concepts. Look carefully at the images that are used to illustrate unfamiliar terms.

A Read the title and the first sentence of each paragraph in Reading 4. Look at the images in the reading. Put the number of the paragraph next to the sentence that best suits the image.

_____ A Some antique maps may need correcting.

_____ B Symbols on the map indicated direction.

_____ C Signals are sent back to Earth with details of specific locations.

_____ D Technological devices and applications allow for more accurate data.

_____ E Special instruments helped sailors measure and estimate place and distance.

B Compare your answers with a partner's.

While You Read

As you read, stop at the end of each sentence that contains words in **bold**. Then follow the instructions in the box in the margin.

◄)) Mapmaking in the Digital Age

I. Old Ways of Mapping the New World

1   In 1929, when Topkapi Palace in Istanbul, Turkey, was being converted into one of the world's premier museums, a mysterious map was found, hidden among a forgotten bundle of old maps. This unique map was painted on special parchment[1] in 1513 by Hadji Muhiddin Piri Ibn Hadji Mehmed, known as "Piri Reis." What is left of the original map is just a fragment. Yet, it serves as a fascinating glimpse into a time when transatlantic voyage was still in its infancy and the shapes of the continents around the globe were amorphous. Due to its highly fragile nature, the 500-year-old map has only been displayed to the public once (in 2013), for a period of just 20 days. Most of the time, it remains safely preserved in the archives of the museum.

2   Piri Reis (1465–1533) had been an admiral and intelligence officer in the navy during the Ottoman Empire, which reigned from 1299 to 1922. Reis, an expert navigator and cartographer, or mapmaker, created the oldest known map of the New World: North and South America. He had accomplished the Herculean[2] task of combining the work of about 20 earlier mapmakers – many of whose identities he would not disclose. Modern cartographers speculate that his map included the works of Arab and ancient Greek cartographers, as well as those of other explorers from his era like Vasco da Gama and Christopher Columbus. The result of this peculiar mix was a remarkable *portolan chart*. A portolan chart does not rely on lines of latitude and longitude (North-South and East-West measurements around the **globe**). Instead, cartographers of this chart, typical of their time, used compass roses[3] to draw attention to key points on the map. Each point on the compass rose indicates an approximation of the true direction (N, S, E, and W). Reis eventually reproduced this map in a book called *Book of the Mariner*, or *The Naval* **Handbook**.

3   What is most striking about Reis's map is not only its detail, but also how Reis drafted it with such accuracy despite the simple tools of technology available in the sixteenth century. The outlines of the continents on the Reis map are more accurate than those of any of his predecessors. With so few tools, Piri Reis had created a masterpiece.

4   In the early to mid-twentieth century, mapmakers performed aerial surveys from balloons or airplanes to take photographs of the places they

WHILE YOU READ ❶

Look back at this sentence. Highlight the definition of *latitude* and *longitude*.

WHILE YOU READ ❷

Look back at paragraph 2 and find the word *portolan*. Is it necessary to know its definition in order to understand the meaning of the paragraph?
a) Yes
b) No

---

[1] *parchment:* antique paper made from dried animal skin
[2] *Herculean:* requiring great strength and determination
[3] *compass rose:* a figure on a map used to show latitude and longitude (North, South, East, and West positions) and the points in between them

A portolan chart

A satellite map

wanted to **map**. Today, satellites now accomplish this task very easily. The process still requires the mapmaker to designate coordinates for locations with points, colors, lines, and symbols to show how each area is marked. Now, with the capability of computer imaging, a person can use interactive computerized systems like Google Maps or Google Earth to see exactly where they are going and what the surroundings look like.

5   The question arises: with millions of people around the world using GPS – Global Positioning System, or satellite navigation – can individuals contribute to one unified map in the same way that Piri Reis combined the work of 20 other mapmakers?

II. Pioneers of a New Navigation System

6   To many, the concept of carrying an old fold-out paper map around while touring a new city is becoming outdated. Naturally, many people still use paper maps, but more often, it seems tourists use their cell phones to help them figure out directions. This change can also be seen in people who have GPS devices in their cars – it's a whole new way to approach navigation. In the twenty-first century, this new tactic in travel has taken over: it is a form of "virtual navigation," using GPS and GIS (Geographic Information System)[4]. The satellite or "satnav" systems employed by GPS have given rise to a new way to map the world, and from this new system, mapmakers are able to integrate these two technologies in order to create a more accurate map or chart. Using GIS, mapmakers are able to visually understand, analyze, and interpret the data **acquired.**

7   However, regardless of available technology, mapmaking is still a unique combination of science and artistry. Computer-based programs that utilize digital mapping, such as Google Earth, dominate the field. New technology and special software allow consumers to do things like superimpose maps of the present onto maps of the past and see the world in a very different way.

---

[4] *Graphic Information System (GIS):* a computerized data management system used to capture, store, manage, retrieve, analyze, and display information about spaces that are represented on paper maps

A compass, a sextant, and a telescope

A satellite orbiting Earth

8   Where telescopes, compasses, and sextants[5] were used by early cartographers to measure positions for a 2D map, satellites with cameras now enable us to see the 3D geographical landscape of any area we are searching for. The combination of art, technology, science, and graphic design has greatly expanded the possibilities of mapmaking. Yet, just as the maps of Piri Reis and his contemporaries had been, today's computer-generated 3D maps are as visually appealing as they are informative. It is possible today to create multiple layers of information for the user to access: natural and topographic[6] features of land, man-made structures, and historical contexts; the list goes on. Currently there are thousands of beta testers using new GPS apps to help contribute to better representations of remote areas of France, with the goal to improve the overall effect and accuracy of the **maps**.

9   In addition, many users of maps are now direct contributors to mapmaking, a development that has become pervasive in modern cartography. The participation of multiple users in testing GPS apps and using GIS to mark geo-location points via social media is contributing to innovations in mapping. It is now possible to improve upon what is known about Earth because apps and software programs are able to collect much more data.

III. Collaborative Mapping

10   Collaborative mapping is a new trend. Today's mapmakers may be more architect and designer than they are cartographer. They are also specialists in digital technology who can use software that can incorporate data from multiple sources into one. We can now do something we could not accomplish in the past – map a city in real time. The result of this has turned consumers into "prosumers," meaning, people can correct the errors they

WHILE YOU READ ⑤

Look back at paragraph 8. Highlight a sentence that makes a positive comparison between maps of the past and maps of today.

---

[5] *sextant:* a device used on ships or aircraft for measuring angles between stars or Sun and Earth
[6] *topographic:* natural shapes of land and the science related to mapping its features

find on maps as they arrive at specific physical locations. For example, the New York Public Library's Historical GIS program uses "georectification[7]," which allows citizens to look at a building on a map and digitally align it with what exists in real life. Users enter data into the computer to verify whether the architecture of that building is different from what is on the map. Did mapmakers make mistakes in the past? Certainly, but consider that people were willing to accept a certain margin of error since there was no other way of checking the work of traditional surveys. This is where "old school" meets new technology – and the way we interpret our past. Users feel more encouraged to become involved if they can see **real-time** results; it is a form of instant gratification.

11   This is a contemporary cartographer's connection to Piri Reis – combining centuries of knowledge, science, and art into one great, innovative world map: a New World, all from a digital point of view.

WHILE YOU READ ⑥

Find and highlight a synonym for *real-time* in this sentence.

---

[7] *georectification:* the adjustment and addition of a place or location to a known coordinate system by identifying a set of points in the image for which the latitude and longitude are known and superimposing them onto a map

Main Idea Check

Here are the main ideas for five of the paragraphs in Reading 4. Match each paragraph to its main idea. Write the number of the paragraph on the blank line.

_____ A Despite the limitations of fifteenth-century navigation instruments, Reis was able to create a map that was very accurate.

_____ B People all over the world can contribute to the creation of today's maps.

_____ C Interactive computerized systems have revolutionized the art of mapmaking by making places much easier to identify.

_____ D In many ways, contemporary mapmakers have to be better at design than they are at cartography.

_____ E Though many people carry paper maps, virtual navigation seems to be the preferred way of figuring out directions.

A Closer Look

Look back at Reading 4 to answer the following questions.

1 What does the writer mean by "just a fragment"?
   a We do not know what the original map looked like.
   b Part of the original map is missing.
   c The map has several small pieces.
   d The map is difficult to handle.

2 What are the most logical explanations for the fragile condition of the Reis map? Choose all that apply.
   a It is more than 500 years old.
   b It breaks into fragments after 20 days.
   c It was created on a very delicate type of paper.
   d It had been forgotten until the early twentieth century.

3 What does the writer say about the 20 predecessors of Reis?
   a They did not want to tell Reis their names.
   b We have no clues to their identities.
   c Most of them were close friends of Reis.
   d Reis would not reveal all of their names.

4 All of the maps that existed before 1513 had accurately represented the New World. **True or False?**

5 Put the events in chronological order from the 1500s to today to indicate how the process of mapmaking has evolved. Write the correct letter in each box.

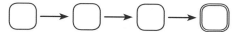

   A Mapmakers began to involve groups of people by using apps and computer programs.
   B Navigators used sextants and other instruments to measure distances.
   C Cartographers took measurements and images during air travel.
   D The use of satellite systems gave mapmakers more precise images.

6 Maps are the result of a cartographer's artistic ability combined with scientific knowledge. **True or False?**

7 The phrase "Reis's contemporaries" refers to which group?
   a All 20 other mapmakers
   b Cartographers who lived from 1299 to 1922
   c Christopher Columbus and Vasco da Gama
   d Ancient Greek and Arab cartographers

8 In what ways is today's process of mapmaking similar to mapmaking before the twentieth century? Choose all that apply.
   a Mapmakers can still use aerial surveys.
   b GPS and GIS technology are important tools.
   c Paper-based maps are still produced and used by consumers.
   d Cartographers may combine or integrate information from multiple maps.

Skill Review

In Skills and Strategies 2, you learned to focus on key vocabulary and skip over unknown words or phrases that are not crucial to your understanding of a text. You also learned that it is important to use a combination of strategies in order to manage unfamiliar words. Reading without interruption will help you better understand academic texts.

A The following sentences are from Reading 4. Use what you learned in Skills and Strategies 2 to determine the definition that matches the word in bold.

_____ 1 Yet, it serves as a fascinating glimpse into a time when transatlantic voyage was still in its **infancy** and the shapes of the continents around the globe were amorphous.
   a being or behaving like a baby
   b in early stages of development

_____ 2 Due to its highly **fragile** nature, the 500-year-old map has only been displayed to the public once (in 2013), for a period of just 20 days.

    a easily destroyed or damaged

    b emotionally weak

_____ 3 Piri Reis (1465–1533) had been an admiral and intelligence officer in the navy during the Ottoman Empire, which **reigned** from 1299 to 1922.

    a had dominant feelings

    b ruled a country or area

_____ 4 Modern **cartographers** speculate that his map included the works of Arab and ancient Greek cartographers, as well as those of other explorers from his era like Vasco da Gama and Christopher Columbus.

    a explorers of maps

    b mapmakers

_____ 5 Users enter data into the computer to **verify** whether or not the architecture of that building is different from what is on the map.

    a prove if something is true

    b change or make something different

_____ 6 However, regardless of available technology, mapmaking is still a unique combination of science and **artistry**.

    a having special art or design skills

    b the skill of painting

B Writers often use synonyms to avoid repetition or reinforce meaning. Read the sentences from Reading 4. Find the word or phrase in each sentence that is closest in meaning to the word or phrase in **bold** and write it on the line below.

1 Today's mapmakers may be more architect and designer than they are **cartographer**.

_____

2 The question arises: with millions of people around the world using GPS – Global Positioning System, or satellite navigation – can individuals contribute to one unified map in the same way that Piri Reis **combined** the work of 20 other mapmakers?

_____

3 The **satellite** or "satnav" systems employed by GPS have given rise to a new way to map the world, and from this new system, mapmakers are able to integrate these two technologies in order to create a more accurate map or chart.

_____

4 It is possible today to create multiple layers of information for the user to access: natural and **topographic** features of land, man-made structures, and historical contexts; the list goes on.

_____

Definitions

Find the words in Reading 4 that are similar to the definitions below.

1 best or most important (*adj*) Par. 1

2 a small piece or part of something broken off (*n*) Par. 1

3 a brief look at someone or something (*n*) Par. 1

4 having no clear form, or of undetermined shape (*adj*) Par. 1

5 to give new or secret information to someone (*v*) Par. 2

6 a sheet of paper containing organized information (*n*) Par. 2

7 to show or signal a direction to make something clear (*v*) Par. 2

8 something made or done with great skill, especially an artist's greatest work (*n*) Par. 3

9 of, from, or in the air (*adj*) Par. 4

10 to be the most important person or thing (*v*) Par. 7

11 to put a picture or words on top of something so that what is underneath can still be seen (*v*) Par. 7

12 present or noticeable in every part of a thing or place (*adj*) Par. 9

13 to include something within something else (*n*) Par. 10

14 the amount by which a set of data or facts might be inaccurate (*n phrase*) Par. 10

15 a feeling of pleasure after immediately getting what you want (*n phrase*) Par. 10

Word Families

Word families are different *parts of speech*, or word forms, that have similar meanings. Some parts of speech are *verbs, nouns, adjectives,* and *adverbs*. When you learn a word, learn the other words in its word family, too.

A The words in **bold** in the chart are from Reading 4. The words next to them are from the same word family. Study and learn these new words.

ADJECTIVE	NOUN	VERB
approximate	**approximation**	approximate
collaborative	collaboration	collaborate
-----	**gratification**	gratify
navigable	**navigator**	navigate
speculative	speculation	**speculate**

B Choose the correct form of the words from the chart to complete the following sentences.

1 The _____ changed the course of the ship and headed south.

2 Innovative 3D simulation programs attempt to _____ the need of a user to experience realistic sensations.

3 Scientists can only _____ about the reasons for Piri Reis's secrecy.

4 The _____ efforts of interested amateur mapmakers may produce more accurate results.

5 Viking artifacts found in the state of Maine in 1957 are the source of _____ about the earliest discoveries of North America.

6 The date of the map is a / an _____ and cannot be determined with accuracy.

7 Scientists do not experience a sense of _____ unless they can prove a theory with supporting evidence.

8 Leif Erikson is believed to be the earliest captain to _____ to the North American shore.

9 Mapmakers today understand the importance of _____ and the use of all the technological tools that are available.

10 It is not uncommon to estimate a / an _____ time, place, or location by using GPS or other forms of technology.

Academic Word List

The following are Academic Word List words from Readings 3 and 4 of this unit. Use these words to complete the sentences. (For more on the Academic Word List, see page 299.)

alter (v)	component (n)	error (n)	indicates (v)	mechanisms (n)
chart (n)	emerge (v)	incorporated (v)	margin (n)	perspective (n)

1 The _____ used by Leonardo da Vinci in his paintings was unlike most great artists of his time.

2 The Wu Xian Star Map, which dates from 1000 BCE, is the earliest _____ of the night sky and includes 141 stars.

3 An important _____ of the Strati 3D printed car is its unique bio-fuel system.

4 The programmer has to compensate for a computer _____ by adjusting the data.

5 There are several _____ in the android's face that allow it to smile or look serious.

6 When the facial recognition software analyzes data from photographs, patterns begin to _____ .

7 It is possible to _____ a person's physical appearance in a photograph by using software programs like Photoshop.

8 Reis _____ a compass rose and other navigation symbols into his work, thus enabling him to render a highly accurate map of early North America.

9 The new software program has a greater profit _____ with companies that sell to government institutions like the FBI.

10 The ability of the android to interact with its observers _____ a high level of programming and technological innovation.

Critical Thinking

Reading 3 discussed how early drawing techniques helped 3D design from computer programs to androids and 3D printing. Reading 4 explains how early mapping techniques are still relevant for modern map makers.

Using what you have learned in the two readings and your own knowledge, answer the questions below with a partner. Review the readings if necessary.

> **SYNTHESIZING**
>
> Critical thinking includes connecting new information to information you learned in previous readings.

1 What are some benefits of using collaborative mapping techniques?

2 How do historians or researchers use tools like 3D design and GPS to improve on our present knowledge of past events?

3 Why are old maps still important? Explain your answer.

Research

Research one of the following topics and gather information, opinions, and other important data about using collaborative tools.

1 Google Maps/Google Earth: Search for background information on Google Maps or Google Earth. Find out how they incorporated old map making with 3D views and GPS. What innovations did they use for rendering 3D views of locations? How is this new technology helpful for both tourists and historians?

2 Ecological and Environmental Impact: Read the information from the U.S. Environmental Protection Agency and how they are using maps to collect data about problems with climate change and environmental issues around the U.S.

3 Archaeological Interpretation: Look up the U.S. National Park Service's National Archaeological Database (NADB-Maps). How can digital mapping change what we know about the past? How do they use their database to help find cultural and geographical information across the U.S.?

Writing

Your assignment is to analyze and synthesize the points of view of one or more researchers in the fields of collaborative mapping or historical mapping. Write three paragraphs. Make an assessment of a program that is used to create or improve upon map making.

Ⓐ Preparing to Write

1 Look over your notes from your research.

2 Review Readings 3 and 4. Highlight any information you might like to include in your essay.

3 Gather relevant information from at least three different sources (blog, article, or video) and take notes.

4 Organize your notes into an outline for an essay that will include a paragraph of each of the following sections:

- a short background of the system or program
- the benefits or disadvantage of using this program
- the differences among the various programs that are currently being used for mapmaking

B Writing

1 Write your three-paragraph analysis.

2 Begin each paragraph with a general sentence that tells your reader what the paragraph will be about.

3 When you have finished, check your writing for grammar and spelling errors.

Improving Your Reading Speed

Good readers read quickly and still understand most of what they read.

A Read the instructions and strategies for Improving Your Reading Speed in Appendix 3 on page 316.

B Choose one of the readings in this unit. Read it without stopping. Time how long it takes you to finish the text in minutes and seconds. Enter the time in the chart on page 317. Then calculate your reading speed in number of words per minute.

Annotating a Reading

Annotation is the process of highlighting and adding notes or comments to a text or a drawing. It is an important skill to use while you read, particularly if you are reading a longer text. Good readers usually highlight and underline key words, explanations, and definitions, and write in the margins of the text. Annotating helps you understand organization, main ideas, and claims and supporting evidence, as well as manage unfamiliar words in a text.

Examples & Explanations

①Files, tables, codes, and bytes are just a few of the many components of digital computer *data*. ②Information systems specialist Paul Beynon-Davies distinguishes between data and *information*: "data is a series of symbols, while information occurs when the symbols are used to refer to something." ③After more than half a century of collecting, processing, and analyzing data's smallest parts, society has swung to the other extreme: We are now inundated with an excess of information.

Definition of what makes up digital computer data

Here are details about data and information.

The main idea is that we have too much information.

④Government agencies all over the world collect data. ⑤Businesses and institutions also accumulate a lot of data and facts on their employees and their customers or clients. ⑥Employee data used to be stored in folders in the employer's Human Resources office, but now it is all accessible on computer. ⑦The government acquires data in many forms, media, email, GPS locations, etc., and uses it to manage everything from birth, marriage, and death records to taxes and voting rights. ⑧Even the average person collects a large amount of data – and it might be anything – from a document or email or a photo to a spreadsheet. ⑨But what happens when there is too much data for the average person to process? *Information Overload.*

Writer make claims about places that acquire data for certain purposes.

Examples of kinds of data

Definitions of information overload

The student has:

- **identified** the definition of an important term [sentence 1]

- **noted** important details [sentence 2]

- **highlighted** the main idea [sentence 3]

- **identified** claims and evidence to support the writer's argument [sentences 4 and 5]

- **noted** important examples [sentence 7]

- **identified** a definition [sentences 9 and 10]

⑩Information overload is a <u>pervasive</u> <u>problem that affects the lives of everyone</u> <u>both at home and at work.</u> ⑪Some cognitive scientists call it the "dark side" of the technology revolution.

⑫Though on the one hand, people enjoy all the benefits and flexibility of technology, all the excessive input that people are exposed to on a daily basis can disrupt the way the human brain functions. ⑬From email to texts and social media accounts, individuals have to divert their attention and "multitask" – or, do too many things at once. ⑭When there are too many demands on the human brain, much like a computer's processing system, it can get overwhelmed if it does not find the <u>right balance.</u>

Unfamiliar word

New term – multitask

Writer claims that society has too much data and information. Technology is good but has a dark side. It can overload our brains.

- **encountered** an unfamiliar word, and can skip it or look it up later [sentence 11]

- **noted** new vocabulary by punctuation [sentence 13]
- **summarized** the conclusion of the text and underlined key words that support the author's argument [sentence 14]

Strategies

These strategies will help you annotate a text.

- Decide which items you will highlight, circle, draw a box around, underline, etc., and be consistent.

- Use different colored highlighters, pencils, or pens to distinguish between items.

- Use large brackets next to sections or paragraphs that are essential to the major ideas of the text.

- As you read, write in the margins. Identify key words and unfamiliar vocabulary, and note repeated patterns of key words and phrases. Identify and question claims and evidence. Include your opinion about the writer's claims. Write down your reactions or comments. Analyze the arguments. Summarize information.

- Highlight and make notes on subheadings in the text, which act as guides for topic shifts and the overall organization of the text.

Skill Practice 1

Read the following paragraph. Then read a student's margin notes about the paragraph and match them to the correct sentences in the first column. Then put a check (✓) in the box below the annotation strategy or strategies used in the margin note. The first one has been done for you.

①Data collection can be a big challenge for any company. ②It is the process of gathering information in particular areas of interest to potential users and organizing it in a systematic way. ③Methods for data collection can vary depending on the type of company or business. ④Some companies collect all forms of data from customers or users that might be useful in the future; however, this can be problematic. ⑤Studies have shown that the quality and accuracy of information collected are more important than how much data a company has acquired; errors might occur when people fill out surveys or enter data incorrectly. ⑥Before businesses begin collecting data from customers, good systems of "querying" (gathering information) and a process for organizing the data need to be in place so that fewer errors will occur.

SENTENCE	MARGIN NOTES	KEY WORDS-DEFINITIONS	STATE YOUR OPINION	IDENTIFY CLAIMS AND EVIDENCE	ANALYZE ARGUMENTS	SUMMARIZE
5	Strong point about the relation between the amount of data collected & accuracy. Good example of potential problem.			✓	✓	
	Definition of <u>data collection</u>					
	Too much data can cause problems. How? Is there evidence?					
	Different businesses might use different ways to collect data from customers. Banks v doctors?					
	Definition of <u>querying</u>. The writer suggests that companies must improve their surveys & organization systems to make data collection work.					
	The writer makes a general claim about data collection. Probably true.					

Skill Practice 2

Read the following sentences and match each sentence to the correct description of the annotation. The first one has been done for you.

___d___ **1** Big Data leads to more accurate analyses of users' online activity. }

a The reader is highlighting an unfamiliar word.

_____ **2** The speed of data creation and how it streams over the Internet, or its velocity, is a challenging but important component of real-time management of Big Data.

b This is a summary of a section.

_____ **3** What Peter Drucker and W. Edward Deming say is true, "You can't manage what you don't measure." Therefore, it makes sense that companies like Walmart would collect 2.5 petabytes (or 2.5 quadrillion bytes) of data from its customers every hour.

c The reader has noted a pattern of repeated key words.

_____ **4** Information Overload and Its Problems

d The reader has bracketed a section of information that is essential to the main idea.

_____ **5** The writer is saying that information overload can occur from trying to multi-task or doing too many things at once.

e This is an example of a claim and evidence highlighted by the reader.

_____ **6** Volume is another factor of Big Data. Along with velocity and variety, volume can be structured or unstructured. Social media is typically unstructured.

f This is a subheading and introduces a new topic.

Connecting to the Topic

Discuss the following questions with a partner.

1 When did scientists begin using computers? What do you know about them?

2 What do you think "information science" is? Explain your answer.

3 How do Internet companies collect information about users?

4 What is Big Data? Have you heard this term before? Where?

Previewing and Predicting

> When you preview a reading, look to see if the writer has divided the text into sections. This can help you anticipate topics and vocabulary. Look to see if the sections have headings. Read the headings and think about why the writer has divided the text.

A Read the title and section headings in Reading 5. Then decide what content will be in each section. Write the number of the section (*II–VI*) next to the topic that best describes it. The first one has been done for you.

SECTION	TOPIC
VI	Certain factors may get in the way of our ability to measure Linked Data and make progress toward its acceptance.
	The word *information* has a modern meaning in which messages can be reduced to a series of ones and zeroes.
	Linked Data allows researchers to look at the big picture in terms of how it relates to a person's activity on the Internet and how computers can track that information.
	Data collection, looking at patterns and correlating data, are essential to understanding how Big Data actually works.
	Inventing browsers, marking up text, tagging, and creating hyperlinks are among many of the ways that the pioneers of the World Wide Web made it easier for computers to understand and analyze data.

B Compare your answers with a partner's. Then with your partner, discuss some examples that might be included in each section.

While You Read

As you read, stop at the end of each sentence that contains words in **bold**. Then follow the instructions in the box in the margin.

◀) How Information Got Smart

by Dr. David Weinberger

I. Introduction

1   When computers became a part of our lives in the 1950s, they were widely viewed as oppressive machines that not only reduced what we knew to what could fit on punch cards[1], but treated people as if they were simply numbers. At the time, that cultural critique was correct. The constraints on computer memory and processing power required users to keep the amount of information that they dealt with to an absolute minimum. However, the capacity of computers has increased exponentially over the past 50 years. They are now connected by a powerful network – the Internet – and information is becoming not only far more abundant, it is changing its nature. It is becoming smarter.

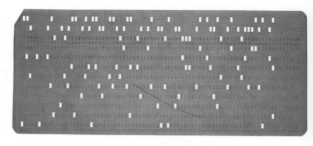

A punch card

II. Information at Its Start

2   The term *information* received its modern meaning in a 1948 paper, "A Mathematical Theory of Communication," by Claude Shannon, who initiated what we now call information science. As a researcher at Bell Labs, Shannon developed a way of measuring the capacity of any medium for transmitting what he called "information." To do this, he reduced messages to their simplest form: a series of units that can be either on or off. Those on-offs – sometimes represented as ones or zeroes – are known as bits. Shannon's complex math let him measure the capacity of a medium for moving those bits.

3   Bits are the "stuff" of computers, and even the most complex photographic image or the richest orchestral sound is stored in a computer as a series of ones and zeroes – billions and billions of them. So, from the beginning, information reduced such rich phenomena into the simplest of measurable elements.

Bits represented as 1's and 0's

---

[1] *punch card:* a stiff piece of paper that contains a system of hand-punched holes to represent data

4   When the first practical business computers became available in the 1950s, businesses had to engage in reduction at another level as well. Computer memory was so expensive and computer processing speeds were so slow that for decades, computer programs pared information down to strictly what was needed. For example, if you were designing a program for use by the Personnel Department to track employee information, it had fields to record an employee's name, job title, and salary, but would not include less relevant fields like hobbies, pets, or favorite sports teams. Keeping information to a minimum was just good business practice. As a result, for the first four decades of the Computer Era, contrary to the widespread belief that computers would create "information overload," computers actually were about strictly limiting the amount of information they **handled**.

WHILE YOU READ ❶

Find the contrast marker in this sentence. Then highlight the two claims that are being contrasted.

III. Big Data

5   After many decades of making information small, something happened around the turn of the millennium. Information started to get big – very big. This occurred because computer storage and processing power dropped dramatically in cost, and because computers started becoming connected through high-speed networks. Thus, computers rapidly went from being able to handle megabytes[2] to gigabytes[3] to terabytes[4], each increment representing approximately a thousand-fold increase.

A computer data center

6   At the same time, the number of sources of information increased dramatically. Sensors to measure environmental factors were placed around the earth, gathering streams of data. From thermostats to pedometers, more and more devices became computerized and networked. Companies on the Internet started tracking their users' every click, compiling vast databases of behavioral data.

7   This exponential increase in data was tantamount to inventing a new scientific instrument. It has opened up new areas of research, just as the

---

[2] *megabyte:* 1 megabyte = 1,000,000 bytes (a byte is a computer unit used for measuring the amount of information that the computer can store)
[3] *gigabyte:* 1 gigabyte = 1,000 megabytes
[4] *terabyte:* 1 terabyte = 1,000 gigabytes

microscope once made it possible for us to examine our world on a different **scale**. Here are just a few current examples:

- The European Organization for Nuclear Research, CERN[5], is using the processing power of thousands of computers at more than 150 different centers to analyze the massive amount of data it generates.
- Every heartbeat and breath of each at-risk infant is being analyzed, in an attempt to find patterns that correlate with data gathered from babies who previously contracted diseases within 24 hours of birth.
- High-frequency trading systems[6] are making investment decisions based not only on massive amounts of financial information, but also on real-time monitoring of social networking sites.

WHILE YOU READ 2

Read the beginning of paragraph 7 again and highlight the comparison the writer makes about data.

8   Perhaps most dramatically, Big Data is enabling researchers to study human behavior in ways that previously would have been thought impossible, and it turns out that we are more predictable than we used to think. For example, by amassing enough data about the daily movements of enough people, researchers can predict with a surprising degree of accuracy where any particular individual will be at any time the following day. You can get a sense of how predictable Big Data makes us by visiting a retail website like Amazon and seeing how accurate their recommendations for you are.

9   Big Data does all this simply by looking for correlations in data. Often the algorithms do not have to know what the data stands for. As a result, Big Data sometimes discovers correlations that are real but inexplicable to us. For instance, Big Data has found that in certain communities, if one person gained weight, other people in his or her social network were also likely to gain weight. Big Data by itself doesn't tell us *why* weight gain can propagate through a community the way an infectious[7] disease does, but this is, in fact, an advantage of Big Data: it can uncover facts that we might not even have thought to ask about. These new capabilities have arisen primarily because the capacity of computers has changed dramatically. The nature of information has not.

IV. The Semantic Web

10   At its most atomic level, the Internet uses bits to move information around. But as this global network has become more widely used, additional layers have been added that allow us to think about information in richer ways. One of the most important of these layers is the World

---

[5] *CERN:* European Organization for Nuclear Research, which operates the world's largest particle physics laboratory

[6] *high-frequency trading system (HFT):* a sophisticated system of technological tools and algorithms used by financial traders, particularly for rapidly trading securities or stocks

[7] *infectious:* spreading quickly

Wide Web, invented in the early 1990s by Tim Berners-Lee, an engineer at CERN. To make it easier for scientists to share their research, Berners-Lee developed a simple way for authors to create clickable hyperlinks[8] in their papers. He also had to invent a browser that could display a paper and react appropriately when a user clicked on one of the hyperlinks. So, to make these "web pages" easier to read, he created a simple set of "tags" that tells the browser how to format text in the paper. HTML (HyperText Markup Language) was what he called this set of tags. For example, if you wanted to indicate that a line of text in your paper is a subhead, you would put it between a "<H2>" and a "</H2>" tag. When the browser sees those tags, it knows to display the text between them in a larger typeface and in bold font. Alternatively, the tag "<li>" indicates the text should be displayed as an item on a list: indented and prefaced with a bullet or a **number**.

11   While that process is helpful, it also ignores important, useful information. For example, a list in one document might be a list of instructions for installing a refrigerator fan, while a list in another might be a list of ingredients in a recipe. HTML could instruct browsers to format them the same way, but had no way of capturing the fact that the lists are *about* different things.

12   Suppose you are creating an online cookbook and want to compile a list of all the ingredients used in the "Cakes" section. A computer would have no easy way to distinguish the lists of ingredients from the lists of instructions from the lists of related recipes since all those lists use the "<li>" tag. And the problem is compounded if you want to compile ingredients from multiple online cookbooks.

13   This, to Berners-Lee, looked like a missed opportunity. Therefore, in 2001, he started writing about what it would take to enable the Web to express what pages are about, in a way that would enable computers to make sense of them. He called this "The Semantic Web," that is, a web that makes the *meaning* of its content clear to computers.

14   Berners-Lee proposed that information visible only to computers be added to web pages. For example, an author might add the label "ingredient" to a "<li>" tag. That works, but this easy idea quickly gets complicated. Suppose you want to write an application that will collect scheduling and price information from local bus and train services so that a user can see which type of transportation to use for a trip. If every transportation company uses different labels to talk about the same thing, computers won't be able to make sense of the labels. For example, suppose the bus company's data expresses New York City as "NYC" and the train's as "New York City." Then imagine that the bus line labels departure times as "dep." and the train as "leaves." Computers are too literal to know that these schedules are

WHILE YOU READ 3

Look back at paragraph 10. Highlight the words and phrases that help you understand the meaning of *browser*.

---

[8] *hyperlink:* a word, phrase, or image on a website or in a document that you click on in order to go to a different website or different part of the document

talking about the same things, and this is a very simple example. In real life, data and their metadata[9] are often far more complex.

15   To address this, Berners-Lee proposed that people should write *ontologies*: formal expressions of the terms used within a domain and their relationships. In a transportation ontology, there would be **entities** such as buses, trains, travelers, and cities. There are relations among these entities: as an example, both buses and trains travel to or from cities and carry passengers. An ontology, therefore, would specify the identifying terms to be used and how these pieces of information would go together. Sites that wanted to participate effectively in the Semantic Web would use standard ontologies to express their data.

WHILE YOU READ **4**

Highlight the examples of *entities* in this sentence.

16   It is a magnificent vision, and it has had success in many areas, but ontologies can be very difficult to write because human domains are complex and messy, and groups within a domain often find it hard to agree on the details. So, in 2006 Berners-Lee lowered some of the hurdles.

V. Linked Data

17   Transportation schedules are good examples of the sort of data computers easily accommodate: they have lots of data that share the same, simple metadata. That's why they can be expressed in tables, with each column representing one type of data (e.g., departure time or destination).

18   Unfortunately, not all human knowledge fits in tables. Some items have rich sets of relations with other items. A classic book, for instance, touches our culture in many different ways, but what matters about the person who reads it does not fit within a table.

19   Linked Data, which Berners-Lee started promulgating in 2006, is a system that enables organizations to express more of that sort of contextual, relational information in a way that lets computer applications make it more discoverable and usable by humans. There are two key features of Linked Data. First, Linked Data is generally expressed in "triples" that consist of a subject, an object, and their relation to each other. "New York City is a city" is one triple – "New York City" is the subject, "a city" is the object, and "is" defines their relation. Some other triples are:

- New York City is in New York State.
- There are theaters in New York City.
- Plays are performed in some New York City theaters.
- Plays have **actors**.

20   Based on these triples, a computer could determine that there are actors working in New York State. If we were then to mash up this data with Linked Data from other sources, our computer program might even be able to create an interactive map of cultural attractions in New York state.

WHILE YOU READ **5**

Read paragraph 19 again and highlight the definition of *Linked Data*.

---

[9] *metadata*: information that is given to help you describe or find other information

21   Triples, therefore, have two benefits. First, they provide an open-ended way for information to be traversed. Second, they enable computers to make simple inferences, sometimes deriving relationships humans might have missed.

22   The second key feature of Linked Data is that it consists of links. This helps overcome one of the inhibitors of the growth of the Semantic Web: computers cannot tell the difference between "NYC" and "New York City." With Linked Data, each of the three elements ought to be a link to some public Web resource that defines them. For example, instead of using the letters "NYC," a triple could point to the Wikipedia page for New York City. Likewise for "theater" or "actor." Even the relationships should link to a page describing it, probably on a specialized website designed for such a use. That way, if a computer comes across two triples from different sources pointing to the same page, it knows that they are talking about the same **thing**.

WHILE YOU READ 6

Read this paragraph again and highlight the writer's statement about why links help Linked Data. Then highlight the writer's examples.

23   Ultimately, Linked Data is an important evolutionary step in the history of information because it enables information to be expressed by and for computers in a form that more closely matches how we humans think of it – not because it is in the unnatural form of triples, but because it lets information become complexly interrelated. This is what information looks like when it is shaped less by computers and more by the Network **itself**.

WHILE YOU READ 7

Look back at paragraph 23. Highlight the writer's opinion about the importance of Linked Data.

VI. The Future

24   It seems likely that information is only going to get smarter in both directions: bigger and more **linked**. Information will get bigger not only as the capacity of computers increases, but as we are able to join together more and more data sets over the Internet. New algorithms for discovering unexpected correlations across these data sets will also be invented. In addition, information will become more networked as more institutions put what they know into Linked Data to capture more of the relationships among the pieces of human knowledge. These developments make the network itself smarter, with more data and more relations among the pieces.

WHILE YOU READ 8

Highlight the signal phrase that introduces a claim in this sentence.

25   But there are impediments to the progress we have been making. There are already projects that are gathering so much data that it is difficult to move the data to other sites that want to process it. For example, in the field of astronomy, the Large Synoptic Survey Telescope in Chile will produce massive amounts of scientific data. The networks carrying Internet traffic need to become faster and more capacious if we are to make full use of new tools and resources.

26   There are significant **barriers** to the further adoption of Linked Data as well. Because of the complexity of Linked Data, we need better tools and more experts to deal with it. Perhaps most importantly, we need greater agreement about how to express data in compatible ways if we are to get to the common ground that multiplies the value of each institution's Linked

WHILE YOU READ 9

Look back at paragraph 25. Find and highlight a synonym for the word *barriers*.

Data by connecting it to other Linked Data collections. For information to truly reach its potential, we must encourage more people to declare their information and ideas reusable without having to ask permission for the use of those ideas.

27   Finally, for both Big Data and Linked Data, we need more people who can contribute to the information, note and correct errors, create their own algorithms, and put all this information to use in creative ways that advance our common good. **This** is imperative because in making our information smarter, we are making ourselves – now connected to one another around the world – smarter, too.

WHILE YOU READ 10

What does *this* refer to in paragraph 27? Highlight your answer.

Main Idea Check

For sections II–V of Reading 5, match the main ideas to the correct paragraphs in each section. Write the number of the paragraph on the blank line.

SECTION II: Information at Its Start

_____ A At one time, the cost of increasing computer memory and slow processing speeds meant that information had to be kept to a minimum.

_____ B Bits can be represented by sounds, images, or other documents that are stored in a computer.

_____ C Claude Shannon's early work on information science allowed for the reduction of messages to their simplest form – expressed as "bits."

SECTION III: Big Data

_____ A As the number of sources of information increased, companies began to track every click made by the user to compile behavioral data.

_____ B Although Big Data may not tell us exactly why certain patterns emerge, it can look for correlations among those data patterns and make accurate recommendations.

_____ C Over a very short period of time in the early 2000s, information went from being reduced to its smallest part to increasing in capacity.

SECTION IV: The Semantic Web

_____ A Ontologies help organize data processing and the retrieval of that information by correlating how pieces of information would go together.

_____ B Computers do not know how to differentiate between lists of different items using just an <li> tag.

_____ C There are layers in the World Wide Web that enable programmers to think about information and make the meaning of its content clear to the computer.

SECTION V: Linked Data

_____ A Organizations can express contextual information because of Linked Data.

_____ B The fact that Linked Data consists of links allows for data to be connected because when two triples point to the same page, it means the information is the same.

_____ C When data is shaped more by networks than computers, it is more closely matched to how people think.

A Closer Look

Look back at Reading 5 to answer the following questions.

1 The writer attributes the fact that computers are becoming smarter to which factors? Choose all that apply.

   a Information is becoming more abundant.
   b The Internet is a powerful network that has increased processing capacity.
   c There are no longer any limits to computer power and memory.
   d Computers no longer treat people like numbers.

2 Which of the following people or things initiated information science?

   a Claude Shannon
   b A paper about mathematical theories
   c Messages that were reduced to their simplest forms
   d Research that was conducted at Bell Labs

3 What examples does the writer provide to support his claim about increase in data and inventions? Choose all that apply.

   a Scientists are using data for research at nuclear facilities.
   b Traders can make financial decisions based on big amounts of data.
   c People can watch what others are doing on social networks.
   d Physicians and medical researchers can collect data about diseases in infants.

4 The Semantic Web is about clarifying the content of the web to its users. **True or False?**

5 By creating "Linked Data," what was Tim Berners-Lee able to do?

   a Clean up the messy details of several websites
   b Help people get over hurdles in writing code
   c Make sure that train and bus schedules were coordinated
   d Allow Internet users to find information on web pages more easily

6 Which of the following is an inhibitor of the growth of the Semantic Web?

   a Computers cannot manage links.
   b Algorithms on computers cannot understand what humans want.
   c Linked Data consists of links and connections.
   d Computers cannot distinguish between certain elements of a "triple."

7 Experts expect that new algorithms will be created that will probably allow corporations or businesses to understand customers' needs. **True or False?**

8 In the last paragraphs of the reading, what does the writer claim about the future of Linked and Big Data?

   a We need to find better ways to manage and improve how we collect information.
   b People should link all their data to Big Data collections.
   c Everyone needs to adopt the process of linking to Big Data.
   d Finding and noting errors does not impact data.

Skill Review

In Skills and Strategies 1–3, you learned strategies to identify and analyze claims and evidence, manage unfamiliar words, and annotate readings. Using these strategies will help you read, understand, and analyze academic texts better.

Read the highlighted and underlined phrases from two paragraphs in Reading 5. Then look at the reader's margin notes. Choose two skills from the box that the reader used when annotating and write the answers on the lines below.

> a. Finding the main idea
>
> b. Analyzing a claim and evidence
>
> c. Noting important details

_____ 1 When the first practical business computers became available in the 1950s, businesses had to engage in reduction at another level as well. Computer <u>memory</u> was so <u>expensive</u> and computer <u>processing speeds</u> were so <u>slow</u> that for decades computer programs pared information down to strictly what was needed. For example, if you were designing a program for use by the Personnel Department to track employee information, it had fields to record an <u>employee's name, job title, and salary, but would not include less relevant fields like hobbies, pets, or favorite sports teams</u>. Keeping information to a minimum was just good business practice.

Memory was expensive & speeds were slow, so Personnel Dept. tracked only employee names, jobs, and salaries.

_____ 2 When the browser sees those tags, it knows to display the text between them in a larger typeface and in bold font. Alternatively, the tag "<li>" indicates the text should be displayed as an item on a list: <u>indented and prefaced</u> with a bullet or a number. While that <u>process is helpful</u>, it also <u>ignores important, useful information</u>. For example, a list in one document might be a list of instructions for installing a refrigerator fan, while a list in another might be a list of ingredients in a recipe. HTML could instruct browsers to format them both as lists, but <u>had no way of capturing the fact that the lists are about</u> different things.

Making lists in a specific format is helpful but ignores some important info: e.g., lists, instructions, or recipes. But HTML can't distinguish between those lists.

Definitions

Find the words in Reading 5 that are similar to the definitions below.

1 making uncomfortable (*adj*) Par. 1

2 a careful analysis or judgment in which an opinion is expressed (*n*) Par. 1

3 moving or growing quickly (*adv*) Par. 1

4 to reduce to a level at which only the necessary parts are left (*phrasal v*) Par. 4

5 existing or distributed over many places or among many people (*adj*) Par. 4

6 an excess of information that prevents understanding or decision-making (*n phrase*) Par. 4

7 equal to something (*adj*) Par. 7

8 to connect between two or more things (*v*) Par. 7

9 to catch or become ill (*v*) Par. 7

10 to gather or collect large amounts of something, over time (*v*) Par. 8

11 to make something worse by increasing or adding to it (*v*) Par. 12

12 to spread beliefs or ideas among many people (*v*) Par. 19

13 to combine information from different sources (*phrasal v*) Par. 20

14 without an end date or planned way of ending (*adj*) Par. 21

15 having a lot of space and able to contain a lot (*adj*) Par. 25

Synonyms

Complete the sentences with words from Reading 5 in the box below. These words replace the words or phrases in parentheses, which are similar in meaning.

absolute	discoverable	increment	inhibitors	relevant
constraints	imperative	inexplicable	interrelated	traversed

1 The lack of universal Internet access is often the result of financial, not technological, (limitations) _____ .

2 It is important for corporations to collect information that is (related) _____ to their business needs.

3 Each (increase) _____ in the number of bits by the thousands is known as a byte.

4 The reasons users make purchase decisions is often (unexplainable) _____ .

5 Using features on a computer or cell phone like "Bluetooth" makes other devices (easily found) _____ .

6 The businessman quickly (moved through) _____ the station to catch his train.

7 There are often (impediments) _____ to managing large amounts of data.

8 The analyst could easily see that the information regarding the user's purchases and what she had searched for was (correlated) _____ .

9 At some point, the computer reached its (total) _____ capacity of processing power.

10 Understanding the ways that data increases exponentially and how it can be used are (crucial) _____ to the future of Big Data.

Same or Different

The following pairs of sentences contain vocabulary from all the readings in this unit. Write S on the blank lines if the two sentences have the same meaning. Write D if the meanings are different.

_____ 1 There are many forms of 3D imaging software that work across different **platforms**.

There are many **practical applications** of 3D design and imagery.

_____ 2 Brain hubs allow inventors to meet and work together on their latest **innovations**.

Brain hubs have enabled teams of inventors to **collaborate** in productive ways.

_____ 3 It is possible to **input** information into a 3D printer to create parts of a car.

The 3D printer can be used to create automobile **components**.

_____ 4 As mapping technology continues to **evolve, virtual** tourism is becoming a reality.

Map apps have **altered** the way a large **proportion** of tourists get around new cities.

_____ 5 Thanks to technology, companies are now able to **amass** far more customer data than in the past.

Improved **algorithms** now allow online businesses to track and predict customer behavior with a smaller **margin of error** than a few years ago.

_____ 6 According to a number of experts, the **impact** of big data on the way businesses operate has not yet reached its height.

Many experts **assert** that companies are just beginning to **scratch the surface** of big data's potential to change the way they do business.

_____ 7 Sophisticated equipment is necessary in order to **navigate** the new satellite **transmission** system.

The new **network** uses several satellites and towers in order to send signals.

_____ 8 The way the artist's point of view is **conveyed** in the painting appears to provide an added dimension.

The **perspective** in the painting is almost three-dimensional.

Disciplinary Vocabulary

The following words are from all the readings in this unit. Research shows that they frequently appear in academic texts related to technology. Complete the sentences with these words.

algorithms (*n*)	constraints (*n*)	infrastructure (*n*)	phenomena (*n*)	protocol (*n*)
compatible (*adj*)	domain (*n*)	mechanism (*n*)	potential (*adj*)	simulation (*n*)
complexity (*n*)	elements (*n*)	model (*n*)	process (*v*)	theory (*n*)

1 Ontologies are the formal expressions of the terms used within a / an _____ and their relationships.

2 Many companies would like to be able to collect information on consumers without any _____ .

3 The _____ by which the computer operates is a system of zeroes and ones.

4 Inventors and researchers are fascinated by the scientific _____ they discover.

5 Big Data analysts have to compile data from many sources and then _____ that information using analytic tools.

6 Most software is _____ with either a PC or Mac platform.

7 Analytic tools are constantly working and deriving new equations and _____ based on data input.

8 John McCarthy had a _____ that computers would be more productive than humans.

9 The _____ problems with Big Data may be outweighed by its benefits.

10 The android demonstrates a high level of _____ in its behavior and ability to process information.

11 After astronauts use computer _____ programs, they are better prepared for the real-life experience.

12 Internet _____ is the method by which data is sent from one computer to another.

13 In order to collect Big Data, businesses and health care institutions must consider several _____ of data collection that could cause problems.

14 The _____ of the Internet is the foundation of the network that allows computer users to perform activities such as send messages, share data, or stream video.

15 A computer _____ is a program designed to represent something that happened or might happen.

Critical Thinking

In Reading 5, you learned about Big Data and how information science works.

> **ANALYZING INFORMATION**
>
> Critical thinking involves thinking critically about important topics that the writer has not completely explained.

A Read the following claims and concerns about Big Data. Do you agree or disagree with the statements? Why?

1 Online retail companies need to collect as much data on customers as possible so they can market directly to the customer's need.

2 Inaccuracies, misspellings, and missing information that might impact data analysis are usually due to human error.

3 Telecommunication companies collect and store a smartphone user's texts, phone calls, video, and social media interactions, and can use that information for business purposes.

B Compare your opinion with a partner's. Then choose one of the claims or concerns to discuss. Use evidence from the reading and your own ideas to support it.

Research

Research one company that collects Big Data. What do you think are the most important factors in data collection, and how do you think corporations use this information? Does this data collection affect people in a positive or negative way?

Choose from among the following types of companies:

- Online-only "shops" such as Amazon
- Social Media sites like Facebook, LinkedIn, Pinterest, Twitter, or Qzone
- Stores that have a physical and online presence: BestBuy, Walmart, or Target
- Online "companies" such as Google, MSN, or Yahoo

Writing

Write two paragraphs about your research. The first paragraph will describe the way the company collects data and what their demographic is, and the second will explain how they use it. Include your opinion about the effectiveness of how companies collect Big Data.

Exercise 1

Writers connect ideas between sentences in many different ways. The second sentence may:

a contain **evidence** that supports a **claim** made in the first sentence

b provide a **contrast** to what is described in the first sentence

c add a **detail** or details to support the information in the first sentence

How does the second sentence in each pair of sentences below connect to the first sentence? Write *a, b,* or *c* on the line depending on whether it is evidence that supports a claim, a contrast, or an added detail.

_____ 1 Big Data analytics is not without problems and inaccuracies. Scenarios can arise, such as students figuring out how computer-graded essay programs work, which skew the results.

_____ 2 If Big Data that has a lot in common is analyzed, more correlations are apparent than if the analyzed information is vastly different. Medical data, however, is often full of things like misspellings, abbreviations, and even unreadable handwriting, which makes analysis challenging.

_____ 3 If a physician forgets to write down patient information, no amount of correction or "cleaning up" of the data is going to make an impact on the results because the computer cannot replace missing information. Furthermore, doctors use a lot of jargon, shorthand, or abbreviations that the computer cannot decipher.

_____ 4 Some people believe that artificial intelligence is "taking over" the jobs that people used to do. On the other hand, data entry is still conducted by humans.

_____ 5 Medicine seems to have the biggest obstacles with using Big Data. The fact is that most patients' health records have never been digitized, leaving an information gap in what Big Data results can tell doctors about diseases.

Exercise 2

Make a clear paragraph by putting sentences A, B, and C into the best order after the numbered sentence. Write the letters in the correct order on the blank lines.

1 The story of "Big Data" is messy and full of controversy. _____ _____ _____

A Over the past decade, Big Data has evolved from something general to something more specific, like the ability to estimate if people have the flu by analyzing how many people have read Wikipedia articles on the illness.

B Some researchers claim that the concept of "Big Data" is one of hubris, i.e., excessive overconfidence, because it does not consider the inaccuracies of analyzing numbers.

C Attempting to correlate the number of times a web page was accessed to the actual number of people suffering from the flu proved to be an inaccurate way of predicting flu outbreaks.

2 There are some big drawbacks to collecting Big Data. ___ ___ ___

| **A** Though the point of collecting and analyzing data is to get as much information as possible, including personal information on consumers, this has decreased the sense of trust that online customers have. | **B** Experts suggest that marketers for online companies focus on specific data rather than trying to identify the customer. | **C** One of the issues with data mining, according to researchers, is that it imposes on people's privacy. |

3 In 1963, John McCarthy founded the Stanford Artificial Intelligence Laboratory.

___ ___ ___

| **A** One of his earliest predictions was that the capabilities of artificial intelligence – computers – would surpass that of humans in 10 years. | **B** This is an ethical issue that in many ways has confirmed McCarthy's prediction, and designers have to strongly consider what it means to be human. | **C** Some tasks that were once performed by people are now accomplished by computers. |

4 Many hospitals and health care institutions are now digitizing patient records and building applications and analytical tools that will help physicians. ___ ___ ___

| **A** An algorithm is then created from the combination of data sets to provide the best source of evidence. | **B** Physicians are now making treatment decisions based on the best scientific evidence available. | **C** One way they can accomplish this is by collecting sets of data on individuals and analyzing those sets. |

5 Other than patients' records, there are various types of data that can be acquired about patients in order to benefit companies. ___ ___ ___

| **A** This form of data collection has been controversial, and health care plans are concerned about maintaining a patient's privacy. | **B** These types of activities are collected in "data pools" by health care institutions to be sold to pharmaceutical or other companies. | **C** The collection process includes gathering patient behavior and sentiment data – from recording the purchase of running shoes to measuring when users go running in those shoes. |

2

BIOMEDICAL SCIENCE

SKILLS AND STRATEGIES

- Understanding Text Organization
- Using the Dictionary to Find Word Meaning
- Using Graphic Organizers

Understanding Text Organization

In most academic texts, writers use different forms of organization as they present supporting details for their ideas. They often use these different forms of organization for sections of text, paragraphs, or within individual sentences. They use formatting, specific words, or punctuation to signal these organizational structures. Becoming familiar with the most common forms of organization and their signals will help you understand academic texts.

Examples & Explanations

A New Post-Surgery **Remedy**

①After surgery, most patients just want to go home. ②Patients recover more quickly at home, so most doctors support the practice, but they face a **dilemma**. ③If they send patients home too soon after surgery, then they may develop complications. ④It is vital to watch these patients carefully until they are out of danger. ⑤The ideal **solution** would be remote monitoring. ⑥This option has recently become available in the form of small patches that can be attached to the skin. ⑦The patches contain sensors that send information to the patient's doctor. ⑧**Several** studies have demonstrated that allowing post-surgery patients to return home with a skin patch can **result in** lower medical costs. ⑨One study showed that the patch **led to** a 25 percent drop in the number of days a patient spent in the hospital, with **similar** health outcomes to those who remained in hospital care.

The overall organization of this passage is problem-solution. However, several other forms of text organization are found within this structure.

Headings often give a clue to organization. This heading includes a word, *remedy*, which suggests a solution.

In sentence 1, the writer introduces the topic: the claim that patients do not want to remain in the hospital after they have had surgery.

In sentence 2, the writer uses the word *dilemma* to announce that the claim presents a problem.

The problem is clearly identified in sentence 3 with an *if–then* expression, which indicates cause and effect. Sentence 4 provides details.

In sentence 5, the word *solution* signals a possible resolution. Sentences 6 and 7 provide details about this resolution.

In sentence 8, the writer does several things.

a. He continues to discuss the solution, but as part of the solution, he begins a section that has cause-and-effect organization, with the signal *result in*.

b. He also makes a claim – a skin patch can result in lower health costs – leading the reader to expect some evidence for the claim.

Sentence 9 offers the first piece of evidence to support the claim. It uses both cause-and-effect organization, with the signal *led to*, and comparison organization, with the signal *similar*.

[10]Another study showed significant **savings** by utilizing the skin patch. [11]The skin patch, which required no in-house or in-hospital care, cost one hospital about $1,600 per patient per year. [12]**In comparison**, in-home care cost the hospital $13,000 per patient per year, and in-hospital care was over twice that at almost $78,000 per patient per year.

Sentence 10 provides the second piece of evidence for the claim.

Sentences 11 and 12 provide details for the second piece of evidence. They show a compare/contrast organization, using the signal *in comparison*.

The Language of Text Organization

The charts below show the signals of organization that writers often use in academic texts.

CAUSE AND EFFECT		
Nouns	**Verbs / Verb Phrases**	
benefit *influence*	*to affect*	*to contribute to*
cause *origin*	*to attribute to*	*to have a role in*
consequence *outcome*	*to be a factor in*	*to lead to*
effect *purpose*	*to be associated with*	*to play a part in*
factor *reason*	*to be responsible for*	*to produce*
impact *result*	*to benefit from*	*to promote*
	to blame	*to result from*
	to cause	*to trigger*
To Introduce a Phrase	**To Connect Clauses**	**To Connect Sentences**
as a result of [+ cause]	*as* [+ cause]	*As a result,* [+ effect]
because of [+ cause]	*because* [+ cause]	*Consequently,* [+ effect]
due to [+ cause]	*if* [+ cause] (*then*) [+ effect]	*For this reason,* [+ effect]
thanks to [+ cause]	*since* [+ cause]	*In an effort to* [+ effect]
	so that [+ effect]	*So,* [+ effect]
		Therefore, [+ effect]

COMPARISON		CONTRAST	
To Introduce a Phrase	**To Connect Sentences**	**To Introduce a Phrase**	**To Connect Sentences**
in comparison with / to	*in comparison,*	*despite*	*although*
like	*likewise,*	*in contrast to*	*even though*
similar to	*similarly,*	*in spite of*	*however,*
		instead of	*in contrast,*
		unlike	*nevertheless,*
			whereas
			while
			yet

DEFINITION
Verbs / Phrases
is / are
is / are called
is / are defined as
is / are known as
is / are referred to as
in other words
mean(s)
that is

CLASSIFICATION			
Verbs	**Nouns**		**Other**
to be based on	*category*	*part*	*based on*
to categorize	*class*	*section*	*depending on*
to classify	*component*	*set*	*including*
to consist of	*form*	*sort*	
to divide (into)	*group*	*type*	
to group	*kind*		
to include			

PROBLEMS			SOLUTIONS	
Nouns		**Verbs**	**Nouns**	**Verbs**
barrier	*failure*	*to damage*	*relief*	*to address*
challenge	*hardship*	*to endanger*	*remedy*	*to catch*
concern	*issue*	*to fail*	*resolution*	*to cope with*
conflict	*lack*	*to harm*	*response*	*to deal with*
crisis	*obstacle*	*to risk*	*solution*	*to ease*
damage	*problem*	*to threaten*		*to overcome*
danger	*risk*			*to relieve*
difficulty	*setback*			*to remedy*
dilemma	*shortage*			*to resolve*
dispute	*threat*			*to respond to*
error	*trouble*			*to solve*
				to tackle

In addition, writers may use formatting, such as headings, lists, and bullets, as well as punctuation, to signal text organization.

Strategies

These strategies will help you recognize and understand text organization.

- Look for signals of broader text organization, like section headings and bulleted lists while you preview or read an article.
- While you read, look for more local signals of text organization, such as words, phrases, and punctuation.
- After identifying a text organization signal, scan ahead to find information that is linked to this type of organization. For example, if the signal indicates a list, look for items in the list. If a signal indicates a problem, identify the problem and then look for a solution.
- Expect several types of text organization within a single reading. Some will structure larger portions of the reading; others will only give structure to short sections.
- Writers do not always provide explicit signals to indicate text organization. In these cases, you will need to infer how the text is organized.

Skill Practice 1

Read the following sentences. Highlight the text organization signals and check (✓) the type of organization they signal. A signal may be a single word or a phrase, and there may be more than one signal in an item. The first one has been done for you.

1 The fatal misdiagnosis of their daughter in 1993 led a British couple to develop an app to help doctors arrive at more accurate diagnoses.

   a _____ compare/contrast   b ✓ cause/effect   c _____ definition

2 The app has several components. One section provides all possible diagnoses. A second section helps the user rule out irrelevant ones and narrow down likely possibilities.

   a ✓ classification   b _____ definition   c _____ problem/solution

3 Errors in diagnosis are the most serious patient safety issue. Hospitals are starting to develop systems to catch these errors before patients get hurt.

   a ✓ problem/solution   b _____ cause/effect   c _____ definition

4 Many hospitals have difficulty maintaining a sterile environment.

   a ✓ cause/effect   b _____ comparison/contrast   c _____ problem/solution

5 Periodic outbreaks of infections in hospitals are often blamed on bacteria and fungi that grow on walls, floors, and bedding.

   a _____ problem/solution   b ✓ cause/effect   c _____ definition

6 For years, scientists have been trying to find a way to minimize the risk that these microorganisms pose to patients' health and safety.

   a _____ cause/effect   b ✓ problem/solution   c _____ classification

7 Covering surfaces with an antimicrobial film has resolved the problem to some degree.

   a _____ comparison/contrast   b _____ classification   c ✓ problem/solution

8 However, the film cannot be spread uniformly across soft and irregular surfaces. High cost is also an obstacle to its widespread use.

   a _____ cause/effect   b _____ classification   c ✓ problem/solution

9 A new product has just come on the market, which, unlike its predecessor, works effectively on soft surfaces like bedding and curtains.

   a _____ definition   b ✓ comparison/contrast   c _____ problem/solution

10 It consists of titanium oxide and copper.

   a ✓ classification   b _____ comparison/contrast   c _____ cause/effect

Skill Practice 2

Read the following passages. Determine what type of text organization is used in each passage and write it on the line. Highlight the signal(s) that indicates the type of text organization. The first one has been done for you.

1 The Quantified Self (QS), a program that uses technology to analyze all aspects of our daily lives, is growing in popularity.

   Definition

2 Declining costs of analysis have enabled ordinary people to participate in this kind of self-tracking. In addition, there have been improvements in two types of technology that are essential to the QS program:

  • Sensors, monitors, computer programs, and phone apps make it simple to track every possible metric.

  • Powerful computing tools have made it equally easy for anyone to break down the results to see patterns in their own behavior.

   Classification

3 When these apps first emerged, it was not possible to track blood sugar levels or examine the microbes in intestines at a reasonable price. In contrast, the cost to perform such functions today is relatively inexpensive.

   Contrast

4 There are many types of QS apps, but three categories are the most popular: The most frequently downloaded apps are related to diet and fitness. Diet apps maintain a record of the calories ingested as well as the carbohydrates, fats, and proteins consumed. Fitness apps are also popular. They monitor how users move, how far they walk, and the number of calories they burn. Finally, many QS enthusiasts have downloaded sleep apps, which monitor their sleep activity.

Classification

5 One other major type of QS app is the mood monitor. Unlike the wellness and sleep apps, mood monitor apps are more subjective. Instead of facts and data, they require opinions and emotions as data.

Contrast

6 Most users adopt QS for self-improvement. Enthusiastic supporters report that their experience using the QS app has been positive. One person wanted to lose weight. She tracked her food consumption and activity. She believes this record contributed to her weight loss – 25 pounds (11 kilos). Another person with lung disease improved his lung capacity by 30 percent. He attributes these results to the detailed record of his breathing that he kept with the QS app.

Cause and effect

7 Thanks to the growing popularity of QS, there has been a steady increase in business opportunities for app developers and marketers. There are numerous businesses that are ready and eager to sell the public the tools they need to track, analyze, and share just about any possible metric.

Cause / effect

Connecting to the Topic

Discuss the following questions with a partner.

1 The terms *health* and *wellness* have similar meanings, but they are not exactly the same. How do you think they differ?

2 Do you or members of your family rely on technology to manage your health?

3 Do you or members of your family use any technology to keep track of what you eat, how much you exercise, or what medicine you take?

4 How do you communicate with your doctor? In person? Phone? Text? Email?

Previewing and Predicting

> You will understand a reading more easily if you form an idea about its organization and content before you start reading. One way is to read the first sentence in each paragraph. This method can help you predict what the reading will be about.

A Read the title and first sentence of paragraphs 2–8 in Reading 1. Then read the following topics. Write the number of the paragraph next to the topic where you think it will be discussed.

PARAGRAPH	TOPIC
5	Controlling the spread of disease with mHealth devices
8	Attitudes of health-care professionals to mHealth
7	mHealth for healthy people
6	Providing health care in locations far from hospitals
2	Details of how mHealth devices operate
3	The role of mHealth devices in managing health-care problems
4	Improving communication with patients with mHealth devices

B Compare your answers with a partner's.

While You Read

As you read, stop at the end of each sentence that contains words in **bold**. Then follow the instructions in the box in the margin.

◀» Health and Wellness on the Go

1   Marie Jesperson is 92 and is beginning to have significant health problems that require a variety of medications, but occasionally she forgets to take them, or she confuses the days or dosage[1]. Caroline Silva is pregnant for the second time and has serious health concerns. She lost her first baby, so her pregnancy is considered high risk, requiring weekly visits to a clinic for check-ups. Her doctor has informed her that she will need to spend the final weeks of her pregnancy in the hospital connected to a fetal[2] heart monitor that can detect whether her baby is in distress. Zhang Bao has cardiovascular disease; his heart is weak, and many of his arteries are **blocked**. This condition requires medication, as well as frequent blood tests and electrocardiograms[3] to monitor his cardiovascular health. Unfortunately, there is no hospital near his home, so he has to take time off from work to go to a hospital in another town. If the tests indicate there is a problem, Zhang must make a second trip to consult with a doctor and adjust his medication. For all of these patients, the current medical care is both inconvenient and expensive, and in some cases, not as safe as their doctors would like. In the coming years, however, this situation is likely to change for the better.

For people who has health problems.

WHILE YOU READ 1

Look back at this sentence and find context clues that help you guess what *cardiovascular* means. Underline these two words.

---

2   This transformation is coming in the form of mobile health care, or mHealth, which is defined as all forms of health care that take advantage of mobile devices. The development of mHealth solutions is possible because of a combination of technological advances: smaller, more powerful sensors; increased, cloud-based[4] computing power and storage; and wireless data transfer capabilities. All of this technology has become available within a single device – the mobile phone, or, in some cases, a device that works in conjunction with a mobile phone. These powerful devices are capable of providing and transmitting health information on the go. In the past, this could be done only in doctors' offices and hospitals. As of 2013, there were nearly 100,000 health-related apps for mobile phones. Patients can download an app, and the phone transforms into a health-care **device**.

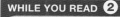

WHILE YOU READ 2

Look back at paragraph 2. Highlight a signal of definition in the paragraph and underline the definition.

I. Developments in mHealth for Patients and Practitioners

3   Although there are many new and prospective roles for mHealth, it is currently most widely used in the monitoring and management of health

---

[1] *dosage:* a measured amount of medicine
[2] *fetal:* related to an unborn baby
[3] *electrocardiogram:* a record of the electrical activity of the heart
[4] *cloud-based:* related to computer use and storage delivered from a remote location rather than a desktop

Figure 2.1 Global Mobile Sensing Health and Fitness Sensor Shipments (2012–2017)

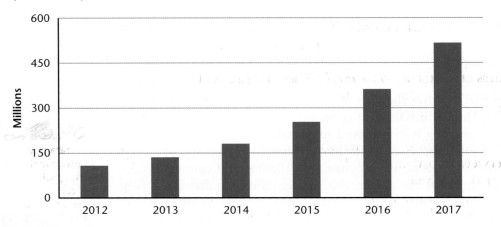

problems, particularly those associated with chronic disease. Monitoring comes in two primary forms and operates in two **directions**. In one form, patients wear sensors on their bodies, for example, on a watch or skin patch. These devices can measure and record a wide range of physiological functions, such as body temperature, respiration, and blood pressure, or, for pregnant women, fetal heart rate. This information is transmitted continuously and wirelessly to a laboratory or health-care provider, so at the first sign of trouble, often before patients themselves are aware that anything is wrong, the provider can take action. This action could be anything from adjusting medication to admitting a patient to a hospital. Such continuous monitoring minimizes the need for patients to come in for frequent tests and, more importantly, can avert a major health crisis by providing an early warning. The sale of these mobile sensors is growing dramatically. (See Figure 2.1.)

4   Mobile sensors worn on the body go in one direction, transmitting vital information from patients to health providers, whereas a second form of monitoring – a lower-tech mHealth solution – works in the other direction, from doctors to patients. When doctors prescribe medication, it can be difficult to ensure that patients comply accurately or completely with the doctor's instructions. The second form of monitoring is ideal for addressing this problem. Automated SMS text messages can be sent by health-care providers to patients, reminding them of which medications to take and when to the take them.

5   Patient compliance is also crucial with communicable diseases, such as tuberculosis[5], which are difficult to treat because of the complex and extended therapy they require. In order to cure patients' tuberculosis and,

WHILE YOU READ 3

Highlight two words in this sentence that indicate classification into categories. Scan paragraphs 3 and 4 and highlight the two noun phrases that introduce these two forms of monitoring.

---

[5] *tuberculosis:* a dangerous lung disease

equally important, to ensure that the disease does not spread, compliance is essential. However, because the therapy takes many months and involves multiple medications, many patients begin treatment but never finish it, or they skip doses. This kind of noncompliant behavior can promote drug-resistant strains[6] of communicable diseases, which can then quickly spread. mHealth programs that utilize automated reminders can increase the effectiveness of treatment considerably. They can also lead to huge savings in health-care costs. One estimate suggests that advances in mHealth could save almost 200 billion dollars over the next 25 years in the United States **alone**.

6   Advances in mHealth devices are also allowing health-care workers to provide services to patients who do not have easy access to a doctor's office or hospital. In China, there is increasing concern about cardiovascular disease, which kills three million people a year. Many of these deaths could be prevented with adequate monitoring, a practice that is difficult to sustain, particularly for patients who live outside of urban centers. Today nurses and local health-care workers in China are responding to this public health challenge by using a handheld device to collect patient data. It records thirty seconds of cardiac data and transmits it to a central facility in Beijing. There, doctors and technicians analyze the data and can then provide an immediate diagnosis and recommend a treatment plan. The program is already having a major impact on the annual heart attack rate in China. One analyst estimates that if the incidence of heart disease declined by just 1 percent over the next 30 years, China could save more than $10 trillion in health-care **costs**.

II. Personal Wellness

7   The growth of mHealth is not limited to the sick and elderly; healthy people are also using a wide range of mobile devices and apps to monitor and maintain their health. In general, the goal of these wellness mHealth devices and apps is to promote self-awareness and self-improvement. Mobile apps allow individuals to track a variety of physiological metrics, such as heart rate and body temperature, which in the past, could only be monitored by a health-care professional. People can also track their activities: how far they walk, how many calories they burn, how many hours and how deeply they sleep. These metrics are recorded by wearable sensors, while other apps require input from users; for example, users can enter what they eat, and the app tells them how many calories or how much fat they have eaten. The recorded data can be stored, analyzed, and even shared through social media.

8   In general, health-care professionals have accepted these health and wellness apps. Other mHealth apps that provide self-diagnosis, in contrast,

WHILE YOU READ 4

In paragraph 5, the author makes the claim that patient compliance is crucial. What evidence does the author provide to support that claim? Highlight the sentence(s) of support.

WHILE YOU READ 5

Look back at paragraph 6. Highlight the signals of problems and solution.

---

[6] *drug-resistant strain:* a type of bacteria that does not respond to medication

have received a more cautious reception from doctors. **Melanoma**, a dangerous and often deadly form of skin cancer, can start as small lesions[7] on the skin. Dermatologists[8] can evaluate these lesions to determine if they are cancerous. The skin cancer diagnosis app allows people to do this themselves by taking photographs of their skin lesions. The photographs are then compared to a library of images stored in the app. The results suggest whether a person's lesion may be cancerous. Health-care professionals remain skeptical of such apps. They worry that these apps may not be accurate enough to lead to early detection and are concerned that they might become an unwise substitute for consulting a doctor. Because these self-diagnosis apps are relatively recent, this question remains open.

9   It is likely that the role of mobile devices in promoting individual and community health will continue to expand throughout the twenty-first century. Annual expenditures on mHealth and wellness apps alone are expected to exceed 25 billion dollars in just a few years. At the same time, mHealth is expected to save billions of dollars and improve the lives of thousands of patients, like Marie Jesperson, Caroline Silva, and Zhang Bao.

WHILE YOU READ 6

Use punctuation clues to find the definition of *melanoma*. Underline the definition.

---

[7] *lesion:* a sore or an injury to a part of the body
[8] *dermatologist:* a doctor who treats diseases of the skin

Main Idea Check

Match the main ideas below to five of the paragraphs in Reading 1. Write the number of the paragraph on the blank line.

___3___ A mHealth devices send patient information to health-care providers.

___5___ B mHealth devices can help stop communicable diseases from spreading.

___8___ C The value of some mHealth apps has not yet been decided.

___2___ D Advances in technology have enabled the growth of mHealth.

___6___ E mHealth can extend the geographic reach of patient care.

A Closer Look

Look back at Reading 1 to answer the following questions.

1 What do the three patients in Reading 1 have in common?
 a They all need more intensive health-care solutions.
 b They have all benefited from developments in mHealth.
 c Their health care could be improved through mHealth.
 d They will all have better health care in the future.

2 What development(s) in technology have allowed mHealth to grow so rapidly? Choose all that apply.
 a Apps for mobile phones are now widely available.
 b It has become easier to send information wirelessly.
 c The cost of mobile health care has dropped dramatically.
 d Computers are much smaller than in the past.

3 In what ways are mHealth applications ideally suited for the management of chronic disease? Choose all that apply.
 a They are cheaper than visits to a doctor's office.
 b They can measure several different body functions.
 c They are more convenient for the patients' doctors.
 d They can provide constant monitoring.

4 Monitoring devices remain limited because they can only send information in one direction. **True or False?**

5 How can automated SMS messages improve health care? Choose all that apply.
 a They can improve individual health care by increasing patient compliance.
 b They can improve community health care by increasing compliance of patients with dangerous diseases.
 c They can remind patients about important health-care information.
 d They can increase the compliance of health-care practitioners with new laws for mHealth.

6 mHealth devices allow doctors to visit patients who live in remote locations. **True or False?**

7 How can mobile wellness apps help users? Choose all that apply.

　　☒ They allow users to keep a record of their behavior.

　　☒ They make users aware of their own behavior.

　　c They indicate what medication that users need.

　　d They notify the users' doctors about their behavior.

8 Why are some doctors hesitant to accept health care apps?

　　a They are afraid that some of their patients will stop coming to their offices.

　　b They are concerned that patients will be frightened by what they learn.

　　c They believe that patients should not have this kind of information.

　　☒ They are afraid that they will lead to a misdiagnosis.

Skill Review

> In Skills and Strategies 4, you learned that writers usually use a variety of text types within a single piece of writing. They often, though not always, signal the type of text organization with formatting, nouns, verbs, and connectors.

Ⓐ Reread the following paragraph from Reading 1. Then answer the questions.

　　Marie Jesperson is 92 and is beginning to have significant health problems that require a variety of medications, but occasionally she forgets to take them, or she confuses the days or dosage. Caroline Silva is pregnant for the second time and has serious health concerns. She lost her first baby, so her pregnancy is considered high risk, requiring weekly visits to a clinic for check-ups. Her doctor has informed her that she will need to spend the final weeks of her pregnancy in the hospital connected to a fetal heart monitor that can detect whether her baby is in distress. Zhang Bao has cardiovascular disease; his heart is weak, and many of his arteries are blocked. This condition requires medication, as well as frequent blood tests and electrocardiograms to monitor his cardiovascular health. Unfortunately, there is no hospital near his home, so he has to take time off from work to go to a hospital in another town. If the tests indicate there is a problem, Zhang must make a second trip to consult with a doctor and adjust his medication. For all of these patients, the current medical care is both inconvenient and expensive, and in some cases, not as safe as their doctors would like. In the coming years, however, this situation is likely to change for the better.

1 What type of text organization is used in this paragraph?

　　problem / solution.

2 Highlight the words or features in the paragraph above that signal this type of organization. _Problems, concern, high risk, distress_

B The primary text organization of Reading 1 is cause and effect. Read the following sentences from paragraph 5 of this reading. In each sentence, highlight the signal(s) of cause and effect, and then underline the phrases that show either cause or effect. Write *C* before phrases that are causes and *E* before those that are effects. The first one has been done for you.

1 *E* Patient compliance is also crucial with communicable diseases, such as tuberculosis, which are difficult to treat *C* because of the complex and extended therapy they require.

2 However, because the therapy takes many months and involves multiple medications, many patients begin treatment but never finish it, or they skip doses.

3 This kind of noncompliant behavior can promote drug-resistant strains of communicable diseases, which can then quickly spread.

4 mHealth programs that utilize automated reminders can increase the effectiveness of treatment considerably. They can also lead to huge savings in health-care costs.

Vocabulary Development

Definitions

Find the words in Reading 1 that are similar to the definitions below.

1 to get information from an expert (v) Par. 1 *Consult.*

2 ability; capacity (n) Par. 2 *Capability.*

3 working together with (prep) Par. 2 *In conjuction with.*

4 continuing for a long time, especially for diseases (adj) Par. 3 *Chronic.*

5 to reduce to the lowest level (v) Par. 3 *Minimize.*

6 to obey an order or request (v) Par. 4 *Comply – Compliance.*

7 to record behavior or development over time (v) Par. 7 *Track, monitor.*

8 the discovery and identification of a problem – usually of a medical problem (n) Par. 8 *Diagnosis, Diagnoses. Detect (v).*

9 the way that someone reacts to information (n) Par. 8 *reception.*

10 to go beyond; to be more than (v) Par. 9 *Exceed.*

Synonyms

Complete the sentences with words from Reading 1 in the box below. These words replace the words or phrases in parentheses, which are similar in meaning.

avert	distress	monitor	prospective	transformation
detect	incidence	promote	sustain	transmit

1 There is a new product that (encourages) *promotes* hair growth in men who are bald.

2 If the business does not begin to make a profit soon, we will not be able to (continue) *Sustain* our operations.

3 As part of an economic (change) *transformation* after the war, thousands of people moved from farms to cities.

4 The government will (check) *monitor* the impact of the new tax law to see if it has a negative effect.

5 We need to act immediately if we want to (avoid) *avert* a disaster.

6 Dogs can (sense) *detect* a wider range of sounds and odors than humans.

7 I am sure that this beautiful home will appeal to many (potential) *prospective* buyers.

8 Mobile phones (send) *transmit* signals to towers in the network whenever you make a call.

9 From the expression on her face, it was clear that she was in extreme (trouble) *distress*.

10 The (occurrence) *incidence* of crime is usually higher in cities than in the countryside.

Thinking

Reading 1 discusses the potential of mHealth to transform health care and personal wellness. It presents a generally positive outlook.

A Read the following list of mHealth functions you have learned about in Reading 1. If necessary, review the text. Then with a partner, discuss whether these mHealth responses to health-care problems may have any negative outcomes.

1 Patient compliance
   a To maintain individual health
   b To prevent the spread of communicable diseases

2 Home monitoring for chronic disease and high-risk pregnancy

3 Mobile diagnostics outside of a health-care facility

4 Personal health and wellness apps
   a Sensors that automatically collect data
   b Apps that require users to input data

B As a class, discuss whether the usefulness of these mHealth applications outweighs any potential negative outcomes.

Research

You have read about the growing popularity of personal health and wellness apps. Research this topic and choose an app that you think would be useful for you. Find answers to the following questions.

- What is the purpose of this app?
- How does it work?
- How is this app useful?
- How could this app improve users' health or change their behavior?
- Would you recommend it for others?

Writing

Write a short report on your research. Write two paragraphs about the app you have chosen. The first paragraph will describe the app and how it works. The second paragraph will describe in detail why you have chosen this app out of the many apps available, as well as the impact you think it could have on your health and wellness.

Connecting to the Topic

Discuss the following questions with a partner.

1 What do you think the world's most serious health problems are?

2 Where do you think the most serious health problems exist?

3 What are some of the obstacles to solving these problems?

4 Could technology be a solution to any of them? Explain your answer.

Previewing and Predicting

Writers can indicate text organization by the using special formatting, such as numbered or bulleted lists. They may use other treatments for this purpose as well. For example, certain sections of a reading may be separated from the rest of the text by the use of headings, subheadings, or phrases in italics.

A Read the title of Reading 2, the sentences that are introduced by numbers or bullets (•), and the words that are in *italics*. Then put a check (✓) next to the topics you think will be included in the reading.

_____ A How mHealth can help people who live far from cities

_____ B How overpopulation affects global health

_____ C Solving today's most serious global health problems

_____ D Recommendations for mHealth projects

_____ E The role of mHealth in education

_____ F Profits from mHealth devices

_____ G Health problems that affect mothers and young children

B Compare your answers with a partner's.

While You Read

As you read, stop at the end of each sentence that contains words in **bold**. Then follow the instructions in the box in the margin.

Funding Global mHealth Projects

Executive Summary

1   As the cost of mobile technology drops and mobile phone networks expand, philanthropic[1] and non-governmental organizations (NGOs) have rushed in to fund mobile health (mHealth) projects in the developing world. Of particular interest to many NGOs are those mHealth projects designed to meet the health-related United Nations Millennium Development Goals (MDGs):

- Reduce child mortality[2]
- Reduce maternal mortality and improve maternal health
- Combat HIV/AIDS, malaria, and other **infectious diseases**

This report provides a context for funding opportunities in mHealth, including profiles of some currently funded mHealth projects in the developing world. It also explores some of the challenges and limitations that other NGOs have encountered in the implementation of these projects. Finally, it makes preliminary recommendations for funding future mHealth projects based, in part, on lessons learned.

> **WHILE YOU READ** 1
>
> Try to guess the meaning of *infectious diseases* from the examples the author gives. Underline the examples and write a definition: _____

I. Putting the Health Problems in Context

2   There are numerous challenges in global health, but the following concerns are among the most significant.

1   Children born in developing countries are 33 times more likely to die before the age of five than children born in industrialized countries. Often the cause of death is a preventable and/or treatable disease.

2   One woman dies every minute as the result of the complications of pregnancy or childbirth. Every year, nearly 10 million more suffer a serious pregnancy-related injury or infection.

3   Approximately 2.3 million people became infected with HIV in 2012. The same year, more than eight million people contracted tuberculosis and about 200 million contracted malaria.

II. The Promise of mHealth Projects

3   mHealth programs have been heralded as transformative, with the potential to bring basic health care to geographically or socially isolated populations that often have minimal educational and financial resources. It is these populations that are the target of the MGDs and that are likely

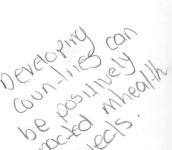

(handwritten margin notes: "Challenges in global health" and "Developing countries can be positively impacted mhealth projects.")

---

[1] *philanthropic:* charitable
[2] *mortality:* death

to derive the greatest benefit from mHealth initiatives. Studies show that in the developing world, mobile phones are far more prevalent than televisions, radios, or computers, thus facilitating their use as the primary form of communication and vehicle for the delivery of services in public health **initiatives**.

III. Current mHealth Projects

4   Currently funded mHealth projects have a broad set of goals:
Building health awareness and providing health information
    In some projects, patients and their families initiate communication with health-care providers. The predominant example of this is the call center. For a small fee, or in some cases, for no fee, members of the public can call and obtain answers to questions on a range of health issues, including **prenatal** care, immunizations[3], and disease prevention. Other mHealth initiatives operate in the other direction, with messages that are disseminated widely to the public, as in campaigns to promote immunization. In others, such as a program for pregnant mothers in Bangladesh, messages are more targeted. In this project, trained health-care workers visit expectant mothers and register them for regular health reminders by voice or text during and after their pregnancy. (See Figure 2.2.)

5   *Collecting information on public health and tracking the spread of disease*
    One of the most important mHealth functions is the tracking of infectious diseases. It is difficult for officials to respond to a public health crisis if they don't know where it is. A program in Cambodia is tackling

WHILE YOU READ ❷
Highlight the signal phrase that the author uses to present evidence for this claim.

WHILE YOU READ ❸
Use your knowledge of word roots and parts of words to guess the meaning of *prenatal*. Does it mean (a) before marriage, (b) women's health, or (c) before birth?

Figure 2.2 Sample Text Messages Between Health-care Workers and Expectant Mothers

> Mrs. <name>, thank u for registration.

> U will receive periodic advice for safe pregnancy.

> ≥60 to ≤90 days: Mrs. <name>, every pregnant mother should consult a health worker or doctor at least 1 time in 1st 3 months. If you did not consult yet, do it now & follow advice.

> Your probable date of deliver is dd/mm/yy.

> Type "No" & send to <xxxx> to cancel registration. - By Ministry of H&FW.

> Take rest. Avoid heavy work. Start saving money for child delivery. - By Ministry of H&FW

Source: World Health Organization

---

[3] *immunizations:* protection against future disease, often by injection

this problem by using SMS messages to track and report twelve diseases, including cholera, measles, and dengue fever. If local health workers become aware of outbreaks of these diseases, they send a text message to a central office, which compiles similar information from all over the country. When the number of cases of any of these diseases exceeds an established threshold, this triggers an emergency response, and a team of health professionals is sent to the area.

6   *Monitoring patient health and compliance*

This function is particularly important for managing chronic **disease**. Programs in Thailand and the Philippines have been using SMS messaging to remind tuberculosis patients to take their medication. A much more efficient and cost-effective[4] approach than home visits, these programs have achieved 90 percent patient compliance.

7   *Providing diagnosis and treatment in geographically remote areas*

Mobile phones can extend the reach of health care by empowering local health-care workers with the tools to diagnose and treat patients. In many remote areas, community health workers, not doctors, are the primary care providers. They can treat routine cases; however, they may lack the expertise for more complex cases. With mobile technology, they can rely on diagnostic and treatment guides available on their phones, eliminating the need to contact a doctor. Australian researchers are working on a project for health workers in Mozambique, creating reference materials and analytical tools that are stored on their phones.

IV. Challenges and Limitations in mHealth

8   Although the potential benefits of mHealth in the developing world are enormous, there are also significant challenges that funders[5] should not overlook.

Evaluation: Many mHealth projects never progress beyond the pilot stage[6]. Most of these have been evaluated in terms of feasibility, rather than their impact on health.

Scale: Even projects that pass the feasibility test often fail when they attempt to operate on a larger scale. What is effective in a small corner of the country may not work on a regional or national scale.

Integration: If an mHealth project fails to take into account systems that are already in place, it can be difficult to integrate the mHealth project into the existing systems. Sometimes the obstacles to success are obvious but not easy to overcome. Projects that rely on SMS messages will not work if the target population is not literate[7], if the messages are in a language that the target population does not understand, or if the patients do not trust the messenger.

WHILE YOU READ 4

What evidence does the author provide for this claim? Underline the evidence.

---

[4] *cost-effective:* producing good value for the amount of money
[5] *funders:* people or organizations who provide money for a specific purpose or cause
[6] *pilot stage:* the beginning phase of a project during which ideas are tested
[7] *literate:* able to read and write

Strategic planning: The most basic problem of all is reaching the target population. A project aimed at promoting maternal and fetal health, for example, will be most effective if the mobile phones are in the hands of women. If men control phone use, a different strategy is required.

Economic barriers: Finally, even if initiatives are considered low cost by funders, local users may not share this perspective. A subscription to an SMS health message service may cost users only a few cents, but this money may be needed for food or other essentials. Most projects that do not move beyond the pilot stage fail because these local concerns are not considered fully as part of the planning **process**.

V. Recommendations

9   Based on a review of past and current mHealth initiatives, we offer the following general recommendations:

WHILE YOU READ 5

Reread section IV and highlight the signals used to indicate problems.

1 Employ the simplest possible technology. Seventy-five percent of people in developing countries have access to basic mobile phones. Although the capabilities of smart phones make them more powerful, at this time, it is not advisable to base any project on their availability.

2 Plan a project that has the broadest possible impact. Although there are many worthy projects, those aimed at maternal-fetal health may have the greatest and most immediate potential to save lives and improve health. Providing prenatal and postnatal care need not be expensive or complicated but can make a huge difference in health outcomes.

3 Take local context and stakeholders[8] into account during the planning stage. First, funders must understand the existing public health structure and determine if and how their proposal can be integrated into it. If it cannot be, the chances for the long-term success of the project are remote. Second, it is crucial to understand the local culture. Who will patients trust for health advice and treatment? Pregnant women may prefer to hear advice from a woman, but it must also be someone they respect as knowledgeable about health issues. What language should be used in health messages? Would written or oral messages be more effective for the target population?

4 Keep costs low, both for the infrastructure and for users. To ensure the long-term success of the project, it must be possible for either the government or organizations in the host country to assume responsibility for the cost of the project once the pilot stage is over. Equally important, users must be able to participate in the program at either no cost or at a very low cost.

---

[8] *stakeholder*: a person who has an interest in the success of a program

Main Idea Check

Here are the main ideas of five of the paragraphs in Reading 2. Match each paragraph to its main idea. Write the number of the paragraph on the blank line.

__7__ A mHealth programs can bring health care to people in remote areas.

__1__ B Organizations are interested in mHealth projects for their potential to meet the UN Millennium Development Goals for health care.

__9__ C Successful mHealth programs must understand and integrate local concerns.

__3__ D A rapid increase in access to mobile phones has increased the potential of mHealth initiatives.

__5__ E mHealth projects can help monitor and prevent the spread of disease.

A Closer Look

Look back at Reading 2 to answer the following questions.

1 Reading 2 is an executive summary. What purposes does it serve? Choose all that apply.

  a It provides background information on global mHealth projects.
  b It explains reasons for the health problems of the developing world.
  c It makes funding recommendations for mHealth programs.
  d It compares health problems in the industrialized and developing world.
  e It explains the United Nations MDGs.

2 What makes mHealth particularly well suited to address global health problems?

  a mHealth solutions are particularly appropriate when primary care providers are not doctors.
  b The UN Millennium Development Goals are targeted at health problems in the developing world.
  c The wide availability of mobile phones makes the delivery of services cost-effective.
  d The Internet is giving people access to a wider range of health-care options.

3 At the core of many mHealth programs is communication and the exchange of information. In the chart below, for each program, write a check (✓) to indicate the direction in which information goes.

	PATIENTS TO PROVIDERS	PROVIDERS TO PATIENTS
Call centers	✓	✓
Immunization campaigns		✓
Prenatal health for expectant mothers in Bangladesh		✓
Patient compliance programs	✓	✓

4 How can mHealth programs slow the spread of infectious diseases? Indicate the order of the events. Write the correct letter in each box.

A Community health workers send information about the number of cases to a central office.
B An outbreak of disease occurs.
C When a predetermined level of infection is reached, health workers are sent to assist the community experiencing the outbreak.
D A central office tracks the number and seriousness of the outbreaks.

5 How can mHealth improve health care for communities in remote areas?
a Mobile phones make it easier for local health-care workers to communicate with medical experts.
b New technology allows experts in central locations to access the medical histories of patients in remote areas.
c Access to technology has meant that fewer people need to leave their communities to seek health care.
d Materials available through mobile technology can upgrade the skills and knowledge of community health workers.

6 Global mHealth projects often fail because of inappropriate evaluation. **True or False?**

7 Why should stakeholders be consulted during the planning stages of any mHealth initiative according to the Executive Summary?
a They have the most knowledge of what will work in their community.
b They can tell funders how much money mHealth projects are likely to cost.
c They can continue the project even if the funders stop their support.
d Other people trust them.

Skill Review

In Skills and Strategies 4, you learned that writers usually use a variety of text types within a single piece of writing. They often, though not always, signal the type of text organization with formatting, nouns, verbs, and connectors. You also learned that a text may have one overall type of organization but that sections within the text may contain signals of other types of organization.

A Review Reading 2. Then answer the questions below.

1 What is the organization of the text as a whole?

_____

2 What type of text organization is used in the section **Current mHealth Projects**?

_____

B Reread paragraph 5 below. Then answer the questions that follow.

Collecting information on public health and tracking the spread of disease

One of the most important mHealth functions is the tracking of infectious diseases. It is difficult for officials to respond to a public health crisis if they don't know where it is. A program in Cambodia is tackling this problem by using SMS messages to track and report twelve diseases, including cholera, measles, and dengue fever. If local health workers become aware of outbreaks of these diseases, they send a text message to a central office, which compiles similar information from all over the country. When the number of cases of any of these diseases exceeds an established threshold, this triggers an emergency response, and a team of health professionals is sent to the area.

1 This paragraph includes two different forms of text organization, one in the first half and another in the second half. What are they?
  a first half _____
  b second half _____

2 What signals does the author use to indicate the text organization?

	LIST OF SIGNALS
First half	
Second half	

Vocabulary Development

Definitions

Find the words in Reading 2 that are similar to the definitions below.

1 the process of putting a plan into action (n) Par. 1 *Implementation, implement (v)*

2 to say that something new is good and important (v) Par. 3 *herald (good announcement)*

3 to get; obtain (v) Par. 3 *Derive*

4 common or happening frequently (adj) Par. 3 *Prevalent*

5 to make something easier (v) Par. 3 *Facilitate*

6 something used as a way of achieving something (n) Par. 3 *Vehicle*

7 to cause something to begin (v) Par. 4 *Initiate*

8 most noticeable; largest or most common (adj) Par. 4 *predominant*

9 to give out; spread (v) Par. 4 *dissemiate*

10 the point at which something starts (n) Par. 5 *threshold (level)*

11 to cause a series of events to begin, often suddenly (v) Par. 5 *trigger (cause, start)*

12 to not notice or not recognize the importance of something (v) Par. 8 *overlook*

13 likelihood that something will be successful (n) Par. 8 *Feasible, Feasibility*

14 to combine two or more things to make them more effective (v) Par. 8 *Integrate*

15 the basic structures that an organization, country, etc., needs for its operation (n) Par. 9 *Infrastructure*

Words in Context

Complete the passages with words from Reading 2 in the box below.

assume	eliminated	isolated	outbreaks *occurence*	preliminary
compiling	fund *provite*	obstacle	outcome	routine

1 Although the final report will not be issued until next week, a _Preliminary_
report of Global Health Watch indicates that many people in _Isolated_
communities lack access to _routine_ health care. This situation can lead to
periodic _outbreaks_ of more serious diseases and is a major _obstacle_
in the pursuit of global health-care goals.

2 Our office is __Compiling__ information on the number of people in the country with the Ebola virus. Because there are so few local health workers who are trained to deal with this deadly disease, our organization will __assume__ responsibility for staffing hospitals in the areas. We believe that we have __eliminated__ most of the sources of infection in the local health-care facilities. We are confident that this operation will have a positive __outcome__. To help __fund__ this project, please make a donation on our website.

Academic Word List

The following are Academic Word List words from Readings 1 and 2 of this unit. Use these words to complete the sentences. (For more on the Academic Word List, see page 299.)

~~compiled~~ (v) *produce*	eliminate (v)	implementation (n)	outcome (n) *(result)*	promote (v)
~~consult~~ (v)	exceed (v)	minimize (v)	preliminary (adj)	~~transmit~~ (v)

1 If everyone wears protective clothing, we can __minimize__ the risk of infection.

2 Travelers who have suitcases that __exceed__ the weight limit for this aircraft will have to pay extra.

3 The __implementation__ of this project will have to be delayed until we receive additional funding.

4 A / An __preliminary__ evaluation indicates that a program has been very successful, but the final report will have more complete information.

5 The government has __compiled__ and published a list of hospitals that provide emergency health care.

6 You should __consult__ a doctor before you begin this diet.

7 The __outcome__ of the election will have important consequences for the nation.

8 GPS satellites __transmit__ information in the form of radio waves.

9 The new medication will __eliminate__ the need for surgery for many patients.

10 A warm, moist environment will __promote__ the growth of bacteria.

Critical Thinking

Readings 1 and 2 present information about advances in mHealth and how they may improve health and wellness. Reading 2 emphasizes the positive impact these applications could have on global health and makes several recommendations about where mHealth funding and efforts should be concentrated.

A Work with a partner. Consider the three health-related United Nations Millennium Development Goals (MDGs):

4 Reduce Child Mortality

5 Improve Maternal Health

6 Combat HIV/AIDS, Malaria and Other Diseases

B Based on what you read in this unit and your own knowledge, answer the questions below. Review the readings if necessary.

1 Do you agree with the funding recommendations in Reading 2? Explain why or why not.

2 For which MDG do you think mHealth solutions will be the most useful?

3 In what situation(s) would you personally find an mHealth application useful or helpful?

4 Do you think that the application you chose in number 3 could be extended to meet any of the health-related MDGs?

5 In Reading 1, you read that mHealth solutions have been made possible by three developments: (1) more powerful sensors, (2) cloud-based computing storage, and (3) wireless data transfer. Which of these will be most important for meeting health-related MDGs and why?

Research

As you have read, many NGOs and philanthropic organizations are eager to embrace mHealth applications as a means of solving global health problems. Choose one of the MDGs and research a health problem that is not discussed in the readings. You may want to begin with the United Nations MDG website.

Choose one that you think could be improved with an mHealth application. Take notes on the problem and how an mHealth application could contribute to a solution. You do not need any technical knowledge. Assume only that the mHealth app will be a mobile phone with the capabilities listed in question 5 of the Critical Thinking activity.

- You can research a real mobile phone app.
- Or, you can use your imagination in describing an mHealth app that you think would be useful. It does not have to be one that already exists, but it should be consistent with the level of technology that you have read about in the readings.

Writing

Your assignment is to make funding recommendations for mHealth similar to the ones in Reading 2.

Ⓐ Preparing to Write

1 Look over your notes from your research.
2 Review Readings 1 and 2. Highlight any information you think you would like to include in your report.
3 Organize your notes into an outline for the report. It should include the following sections:

- A description of the health problem – what makes this problem particularly challenging?
- A description of the mHealth app
- An explanation of how the app can contribute to solving the health problem

Ⓑ Writing

1 Write your report. Write one paragraph for each of the points in your outline.
2 Begin each paragraph with a general sentence that tells your reader what the paragraph will be about.
3 Conclude your report with a short recommendation for your app.
4 When you have finished your report, check it for grammar and spelling errors.

Improving Your Reading Speed

Good readers read quickly and still understand most of what they read.

Ⓐ Read the instructions and strategies for Improving Your Reading Speed in Appendix 3 on page 316.

Ⓑ Choose one of the readings in this unit. Read it without stopping. Time how long it takes you to finish the text in minutes and seconds. Enter the time in the chart on page 317. Then calculate your reading speed in number of words per minute.

Using the Dictionary to Find Word Meaning

In Skills and Strategies 2, you learned that good readers decide what strategy to use when they encounter unfamiliar words. In some cases, they can use context clues to figure out the meaning of these words while they are reading. However, sometimes there is not enough information in the context to figure out the exact meaning of a word.

When you come across a word you don't know and you can't determine the meaning from the context, you will need to use a dictionary. Many words have more than one entry in a dictionary, so you will have to choose among two or more meanings. You can use your own knowledge and clues in the text to narrow down your choice. Be careful to read all the meanings of the word and choose the one that best fits the context.

Examples & Explanations

1. *His years in prison **exacted** a heavy toll on his health.*

exact – *v* (obtain) to demand and obtain something, sometimes using threats or force: *The girl's family will surely exact revenge for this crime.*
exact – *adj* (correct) in perfect detail; complete and correct: *The exact distance is 3.4 miles.*

Some words look and sound alike, but they have completely different meanings and are often different parts of speech. They will appear as separate entries in the dictionary. Use grammatical clues such as articles for nouns and tense endings for verbs to decide on the correct part of speech. Then choose the meaning. In sentence 1, the -*ed* ending clearly indicates that *exact* is a verb.

2. *The public needs to **recognize** the challenges we face in terms of the increasing cost of health care.*

recognize – *v* (know) to know someone or something because you have seen or experienced that person or thing before: *I recognized my old high school teacher from the photograph.*
recognize – *v* (accept as true) to accept that something is true or important: *We recognize the problems you have faced.*

Some words have multiple meanings but are the same part of speech. The meanings may be very different, or they may be related and the differences are more subtle. Dictionaries have different ways of dealing with this situation. In learner dictionaries, different meanings may appear in separate entries with a general category of meaning in parentheses. Or, they may appear as a separate, numbered definition within the same entry. In sentence 2, substitute the general meaning in parentheses into the original sentence. Although the two meanings are close, the meaning *accept as true* is a better fit than *know*.

3. *The government needs to provide more oversight of hospitals.*

oversight – *n* (management) management of an operation or process: *The army provided technical expertise and general oversight to the investigation.*

oversight – *n* (mistake) a mistake caused by a failure to notice or do something: *Because of a bank oversight, the money had not been sent to my account.*

Context clues in the original sentence and example sentences in the definition can help you choose the correct meaning. The example sentences in the definition often use other words that commonly occur with it. In sentence 3, the word *provide* is a common collocation with the first meaning of *oversight*.

4. *He has enough money to weather this period of unemployment.*

weather – *n* Weather is what it is like outside at a specific time, for example, it is raining or snowing.

weather – *v* If you weather a difficult situation, you get through it even though it was hard.

Some dictionaries provide contextual definitions; that is, instead of a formal definition, they show how the word is used. These can be helpful especially when the word is familiar but is used in a very unfamiliar way. This kind of definition can help you decide which sentence is more like the use of the word in your sentence. In sentence 4, the *period of unemployment* is similar to "a difficult situation."

Strategies

These strategies will help you use the dictionary effectively.

- When you read an unfamiliar word, use what you learned in Skills and Strategies 2 to decide which strategy to use.

- If you think a word is important but you cannot guess its meaning, finish reading and then consult a dictionary.

- If there are entries in the dictionary for more than one part of speech, go back to the reading and look for clues such as verb endings or noun forms that will help you choose the correct one.

- If the dictionary provides more than one meaning for a word, go back to the reading to look for clues in the context, such as collocations.

- Substitute each meaning for the word in the original sentences. Decide which one makes more sense.

- Check the examples in the dictionary entry. See if one of the examples uses any of the same words as the original sentence. If the sentences include the same collocation, this may indicate that the original sentence and the dictionary example are related in meaning.

Skill Practice 1

The following sentences contain a word in bold that has more than one meaning. Read the sentences and the dictionary entries that follow. Look for clues that help you decide which definition best fits the meaning of the bold word. Highlight the clues. Then choose the correct definition.

1 The first page of the document gives a general description of the disease, and the following pages offer a **breakdown** of the symptoms and treatment options.

  a *n* (division): a division of information into parts that belong together
    We need a breakdown of the statistics into age groups.

  b *n* (failure): a mechanical failure or a failure in a system or relationship
    A breakdown in communication led to an inaccurate report.

2 After the accident, the driver was taken to a hospital, but the hospital **denied** him treatment.

  a *v* (claim not true): to say that something is not true
    She denied all of the charges that the government has brought against her.

  b *v* (refuse): to refuse something or refuse to allow someone to do something
    I asked for a little more time to complete the task, but my request was denied.

3 In his speech, the president **appealed** directly to the voters for their support.

  a *v* (attract): to be interesting or attractive
    This music will appeal to both younger and older listeners.

  b *v* (request): to make a serious and formal request
    After the earthquake the Red Cross appealed to the public for blood donations.

4 The committee quickly **dismissed** the plan as expensive and impractical.

  a *v* (not consider): to decide that something is not important and not worth considering
    Let's not dismiss this idea without discussing it first.

  b *v* (send away): to formally ask to leave
    The teacher dismissed the class early for the holiday weekend.

5 I'll finish painting the bedroom when I have some **spare** time.

  a *v* (avoid): to avoid or save something
    If you follow the directions carefully, it will spare you a lot of trouble.

  b *adj* (extra): not being used, more than is usually available
    I keep my spare keys in my desk.

6 My uncle is in the hospital with a heart **condition**.

  a *n* (state): the state that someone or something is in
    I bought the car because it was in good condition.

  b *n* (state): a state that is bad or not working
    She was born with a life-threatening condition.

  c *n* (limitation): something that must exist or occur before something else can happen
    He agreed to the arrangement, but he had several conditions.

Skill Practice 2 ✳

The following sentences contain a word in **bold** that has more than one meaning. The dictionary definitions that follow are in a contextual format. Based on these contextual definitions, decide which definition matches the word in the sentence.

1 I hate it when doctors **patronize** their patients.
   a When you patronize people, you appear to be friendly, but you really think you are better than they are.
   b If you patronize a store, you shop there and give the store your business.

2 All of the newspaper stories on the election seem **slanted**.
   a If something is slanted, it is points at an angle, not horizontally or vertically.
   b If information or a report is slanted, it deliberately favors a particular group or point of view.

3 Going to college was the **realization** of all her hopes and dreams.
   a A realization of a situation is an awareness and understanding of it.
   b The realization of a goal or a plan is the achievement of it.

4 As soon as it was light, we **scrambled** down the hill.
   a When you scramble across the ground, you move quickly often using your hands to help you.
   b If you scramble something, you mix it up.

5 The first item that the committee will discuss **concerns** the latest development in educational research.
   a When an issue or story concerns something, it tells something about it or involves it.
   b If something concerns you, it troubles you or causes you anxiety.

Skill Practice 3

The following sentences contain a word in **bold** that has more than one meaning. Use a dictionary to figure out the meaning of the words as they are used in the sentence. Use the strategies you have just learned to decide which meaning is correct. Write the definition on the blank lines. Check your answers with a partner.

1 He failed to **grasp** the reasons for this decision.

_____

2 The president **issued** a statement about the economy.

_____

3 This seems like a very **rash** decision.

_____

4 Don't **bother** reading the rest of the story.

_____

5 I am going to **defer** to you on this matter.

_____

6 The new **measure** is intended to decrease crime.

_____

7 We need **tougher** rules.

_____

8 The children were not able to **contain** themselves.

_____

9 This recipe needs another **dash** of vinegar.

_____

10 I don't like the **tone** of his message.

_____

Connecting to the Topic

Read the definitions of *genetics* **and** *genomics,* **and then discuss the following questions with a partner.**

Genetics refers to the study of individual genes, which are specific sequences of DNA, and their role in inheritance.

Genomics is the study of an organism's entire set of genetic information as well the ways in which it can be regulated.

1 What is the relationship between genes and health?

2 How do you think genetics and genomics might be useful in treating disease?

3 How many genes do you think are in a human genome?
  a about 2,000
  b about 20,000
  c about 2 million

Previewing and Predicting

Reading the section headings and the first sentence in each paragraph can help you predict what a reading will be about.

Ⓐ Read the section headings and the first sentence of each paragraph in Reading 3. Then read each question in the chart below, and write the number of the section (I–IV) where you expect to find the answer. The first one has been done for you.

SECTION	QUESTION
II	Why is it important to understand the structure of the human genome?
	What role does genomics have in preventing disease?
	How will genomics change the treatment of disease?
	What are some of the biggest problems in medicine today?
	How exact is the treatment of disease?
	How might genomics change medicine in the future?
	How can knowledge of the human genome help doctors decide on the right medicine?

Ⓑ Compare your answers with a partner's.

While You Read

As you read, stop at the end of each sentence that contains words in bold. Then follow the instructions in the box in the margin.

Genomics

Camila → 106, 154,
cepho → 125, 154,

I. Current Models of Medicine

1   The focus of modern medicine has been primarily to diagnose and cure disease. Doctors perform diagnostic tests to determine the cause of their patients' symptoms, and based on the resulting diagnosis, they suggest medication, behavioral changes, or perhaps even surgery. For serious diseases, such as many cancers, this **intervention** may occur when the disease is fairly advanced because it is only at this stage that patients begin to have the symptoms that motivate them to see their doctors.

2   This model of medical care is imprecise; it involves considerable guesswork. Based on an initial examination, doctors generally consider a range of possible causes of the patient's illness before making any decisions. First, the doctor may order imaging[1] or lab tests, the results of which often rule out some of these possibilities. Using this often lengthy process of elimination, doctors arrive at the most likely diagnosis. The next step is treatment, which can be similarly imprecise. Treatment practices are based largely on statistical data rather than on the facts of individual cases: For example, if fifty percent of patients with a particular disease have responded positively to a specific drug, doctors will begin by treating all patients with that drug.

3   There are obvious problems with this model of health care. Its imprecision is both expensive and labor-intensive. In addition, since each human being is unique, errors in both the diagnosis and treatment inevitably occur. If only fifty percent of patients with the same disease respond positively to a drug, then obviously, fifty percent do not. Some will undoubtedly receive ineffective treatment; indeed, in some cases, the treatment may even be harmful. What if we could change the focus of health care to one based on the characteristics of individual human beings, rather than on statistical probabilities? What if we could concentrate our efforts on prediction and prevention, rather than simply on diagnosis and treatment? Current medical research is taking promising steps in these directions, propelled by the research findings of a new area of biomedical science called *genomics*.

II. The Human Genome

4   Humans have 23 chromosomes[2], each of which contains hundreds of thousands of genes. These genes contain DNA, made up of approximately 3 billion pairs of chemical molecules (labeled A and T; C and G), called base pairs. Together, these base pairs make up the human genome, which contains a complete set of "genetic instructions needed to develop and direct

WHILE YOU READ ❶

Can you guess the general meaning of *intervention* from context? Highlight the examples that provide clues.

WHILE YOU READ ❷

The author makes the claim that the current model of health poses problems. What evidence does the author provide to support that claim. Highlight the sentence(s) of support.

---

[1] *imaging:* medical tests that use computers to produce pictures of the inside of the body
[2] *chromosome:* a structure that carries the genetic code for life

the activities of every organism" (genome
.gov). In 1998, scientists set out to sequence
the entire human genome, in a project
that spanned 13 years and cost close to
U.S. $3 billion. It determined the sequence
of base pairs in a healthy human being,
which established a baseline[3] reference for
subsequent research. Every human genome
is slightly different. Many genes have
mutations, or variations, most of which are
inconsequential. Other mutations, however,
result in life-threatening conditions, such as
cystic fibrosis, developmental disorders, and

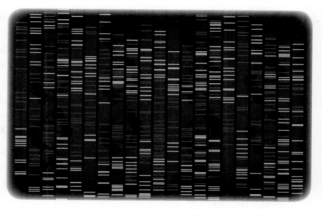

The human genome

various types of cancer. Analysis of individual genomes, and the mutations
they contain, has led to a deeper understanding of these genetic diseases.
Genomics researchers have even higher aspirations for this work: that it
can lead to individualized forms of disease prevention and treatment. In
other words, a person's genome will, in part, determine the course of his or
her health care.

III. Genomics in Treatment

5   Genomic research has already resulted in some successes in treatment,
even on diseases at an advanced stage. One example is melanoma, the
most dangerous form of skin cancer. If not detected at an early stage, it
can metastasize[4], causing tumors[5] in other parts of the body, and resulting
in almost certain death. However, melanoma is a complex disease, and its
trajectory may differ from one patient to another. As might be expected,
not all melanoma patients have an identical response to treatment. To be
effective, cancer therapy requires a detailed understanding of how specific
cancers develop. The only way to discover a cancer's precise structure is
to sequence its genome. Sequencing the genomes of different melano-
mas has revealed that certain types of melanoma have
specific mutations of a gene on chromosome 7, called
BRAF. This mutation results in a defective protein
that causes uncontrollable cell division, in other words,
cancer. In clinical trials, researchers have been testing
a drug that binds to this specific protein, shrinking
the tumors, at least temporarily. This treatment is
far less toxic than traditional chemotherapy[6], which
kills healthy cells along with the cancer cells. The new

WHILE YOU READ 3

After you read about
BRAF, use cause-and-
effect markers to put the
sequence in the correct
order: (a) binding of
drug to tumor protein;
(b) uncontrollable cell
division; (c) mutation of
the gene; (d) shrinking of
the tumor; (e) creation of
a defective protein.
Not all of the steps in the
sequence are introduced
by a signal.

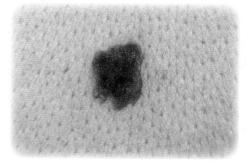

Melanoma

---

[3] *baseline:* the usual condition against which other conditions can be compared
[4] *metastasize:* spread (refers specifically to cancer cells)
[5] *tumor:* a mass of fast-growing cells that can cause illness
[6] *chemotherapy:* the treatment of disease with chemicals (refers specifically to cancer)

treatment is therefore preferable, provided that its long-term effectiveness can be demonstrated.

6   Genomic sequencing can also be a valuable tool in determining drug sensitivity and even dosage levels. In order to prevent strokes[7] or other problems associated with blood clots[8], many doctors prescribe blood thinners for their patients. One popular blood thinner, *warfarin*, has been prescribed for more than 50 years. However, doctors must be cautious when they prescribe it because its therapeutic **range** is quite narrow. If the dose is too low, the drug will be ineffective in preventing dangerous clots; if, on the other hand, the dose is too high, the patient may experience internal bleeding. Early clinical trials provided statistical information about effective dosage levels; however, subsequent trials have shown that genetics plays a major role in sensitivity to warfarin, specifically, that mutations of several genes are responsible for some of the variable sensitivity to the drug. Findings like these will allow doctors to personalize the dosage levels based on patients' genetic profiles.

IV. Genomics in Screening

7   **The promise of genomics extends beyond treatment to prevention of disease.** Scientists have already identified a number of genetic mutations responsible for certain cancers, some types of heart attacks, cystic fibrosis, and Huntington's disease. Based on this knowledge, they have developed screening procedures that can predict the likelihood that a person will develop the disease long before any symptoms are evident. In a few cases, the presence of the mutation makes it almost certain that the person will develop the disease, but in most cases, the test can only show that the odds are higher or lower than average. Further complicating the situation are the consequences of discovering this information. For some diseases, it is possible to decrease the likelihood that a person will get sick, and, if he or she does develop the disease, some form of treatment is available. For example, if patients' genomic sequence indicates that their odds of developing diabetes[9] are higher than average, they have several options that may delay or prevent the onset of the disease, including weight loss or a change in diet. In some unfortunate situations, however, no treatment is currently available, and the knowledge that the disease may develop is the only outcome of the screening procedure. However, since some of these mutations can be inherited, this knowledge could be useful in a patient's decision to start a family.

WHILE YOU READ 4

Which definition of *range* matches the meaning in this sentence? (a) The period of time or space in which something is possible (b) A set of related things

WHILE YOU READ 5

After you read the paragraph, look back at the bolded sentence. In this sentence, the author makes a claim. Highlight one sentence that provides support.

---

[7] *stroke:* a sudden change in blood flow that can lead to a loss of physical and mental ability
[8] *clot:* a lump of thick blood
[9] *diabetes:* a disease in which the body cannot control the level of sugar in the blood

8   This kind of information is a powerful tool, and it is likely that in the near future, it will be used to prevent and treat disease in thousands of patients. However, it also presents an ethical dilemma. How much information do people want about their future health, especially when this information only represents the probability that they will develop the disease? Consider the example of the gene APOE. People who have one copy of a particular variant of this gene are three times more likely to develop Alzheimer's, a devastating form of dementia[10]. However, for the two percent of the population that has two copies of the variant – one from each parent, the risk of Alzheimer's is 10 to 30 times higher than for those without the variant. This is not the kind of information that everyone wants. Dr. James Watson, one of the two scientists who discovered the struc- ture of DNA, and winner of the Nobel Prize, was one of the first people to have his genome sequenced. He made this genetic information publicly available for research purposes, with one exception: He asked not to be informed of the status of his APOE gene. As the field of genomics advances, the scientific community, together with the public, will have to grapple with ethical as well as medical challenges.

A DNA strand

---

[10] *dementia:* the gradual loss of mental abilities, especially with age

Main Idea Check

Here are the main ideas for five of the paragraphs in Reading 3. Match each paragraph to its main idea. Write the number of the paragraph on the blank line.

_____ A Sequencing a person's genome can help predict future health problems.

_____ B Sequencing the genomes of tumors holds promise for treatment of cancer and other diseases.

_____ C Diagnosis and treatment can be a guessing game.

_____ D Predicting disease presents ethical challenges.

_____ E Most health care today is based on the characteristics of groups, not individuals.

A Closer Look

Look back at Reading 3 to answer the following questions.

1 Why does the author characterize current practices in diagnosis and treatment as "imprecise"? Choose all that apply.

  a Doctors often need to do research before they can offer a diagnosis or recommend treatment.

  b Doctors often have to make diagnoses by methodically eliminating possible causes of illness.

  c Decisions about medication and dosage are based on large populations, not on the patient's experience.

  d Doctors usually understand only about 50 percent of the cases that they treat.

2 All genetic mutations are dangerous. **True or False?**

3 Why does the author include the example of the treatment of melanoma?

  a It illustrates the importance of sequencing not just a person's genome, but the genome of tumor cells.

  b It demonstrates how genomics can lead to treatments that are more effective for a longer time.

  c It shows that genomic sequencing is not always successful.

  d It demonstrates a technique that can prevent cancer tumors from metastasizing.

4 Why do drugs often vary in their effectiveness?

  a Sensitivity to drugs is different at different points in the day.

  b Doctors prescribe different dosage levels for different patients.

  c Genomic sequencing is sensitive to dosage levels.

  d There is a genetic component to drug sensitivity.

5 Why might patients choose to have genetic screening? Choose all that apply.

  a The result might affect their decision to have children.

  b The result might motivate them to seek treatment even before they get sick.

  c The result might motivate them to make changes in their lives.

  d The result might cause them to decide to change their genetic profile.

6 Dr. James Watson had his genome sequenced to find out whether he was likely to get Alzheimer's. **True or False?**

7 How might genomics change the way doctors practice medicine?
   a They will not have to order as many tests as they do now.
   b They will base their decisions on statistical evidence.
   c They will be able to provide more individualized care.
   d They will spend more time on treatment than on diagnosis.

Skill Review

In Skills and Strategies 5, you learned that you sometimes need to use a dictionary to choose the correct meaning for words with multiple meanings.

Ⓐ The following sentences are from Reading 3. Each of the words in bold has more than one meaning. Read the two definitions and then substitute each of them into the original sentence. Choose the definition that matches the meaning of the word in bold.

1 What if we could **concentrate** our efforts on prediction and prevention, rather than simply on diagnosis and treatment?
   a (give attention): to give a lot of attention to one thing
   b (come together): bring together in a large amount in one area

2 Current medical research is taking **promising** steps in these directions, propelled by the research findings of a new area of biomedical science called *genomics*.
   a (state certainly): saying with certainty that you will do something
   b (likely success): showing signs of future success

3 Other mutations, however, result in life-threatening conditions, such as cystic fibrosis, developmental **disorders**, and various types of cancer.
   a (confusion): a lack of organization
   b (illness): an illness of the body or mind

4 In other words, a person's genome will, in part, determine the **course** of his or her health care.
   a (direction): the path in which something goes, particularly a river or ship
   b (development): the gradual development of something, the way something happens
   c (class): a class at school

Ⓑ The words below appear in Reading 3. They all have more than one meaning. Use your dictionary to find the meaning of each word as it is used in the reading. Write the definition, including the part of speech, on the blank lines.

1 span (Par. 4) _____

2 trial (Pars. 5, 6) _____

3 screen (Par. 7) _____

Definitions

Find the words in Reading 3 that are similar to the definitions below.

1 the act of becoming involved in a difficult situation (*n*) Par. 1

2 to make someone want to do something (*v*) Par. 1

3 happening with certainty (*adv*) Par. 3

4 to establish the order of elements in something (*v*) Par. 4

5 later (*adj*) Par. 4

6 not important (*adj*) Par. 4

7 an illness (*n*) Par. 4

8 to stick to (*v*) Par. 5

9 having a healthy, healing effect (*adj*) Par. 6

10 related to the principles of right and wrong (*adj*) Par. 8

Words in Context

Complete the sentences with words from Reading 3 in the box below.

aspirations	devastating	odds	rules out	status
defective	inherits	onset	screen	trajectory

1 His use of steroids _____ the possibility of his participation in the Olympics.

2 There are specific symptoms that signal the _____ of the disease.

3 She called the admissions office to check on the _____ of her application.

4 Everyone at the company was surprised at the remarkable _____ of his career in just five years.

5 Since she was ten years old, she has had _____ to serve in the military.

6 He bought a new car last week, but the brakes were _____, so he decided to return it.

7 He is always late to every event, so the _____ are that he will not be on time for this one.

8 The officials at the airport _____ all luggage to make sure it is not dangerous.

9 The effect of the terrible news was _____ for all of us.

10 Every child _____ genetic material from both parents.

Critical Thinking

Reading 3 discusses the promise of genomics for screening and treating genetic diseases. It also discusses the possibility of health care that is tailored to individuals, based on their genomes.

A In a small group, discuss the dangers and problems that might arise as a result of genomic sequencing:

1 Finding out about life-threatening conditions could have a devastating emotional impact.

2 Automatic genomic screening of newborn babies takes away their right *not* to know about their genetic condition.

3 Genomic sequencing could lead to discrimination against people with genetic conditions:
  ● In the workplace
  ● In getting insurance
  ● In communities or specific social groups

4 With inexpensive sequencing, could someone steal and then use another person's DNA identity?

B With the rest of the class, try to work out solutions to some of these problems.

Research

You have read about the enormous potential of genomics for improving health, and you have discussed some of the possible problems associated with this new technology. Do some research on either the positive or possible negative outcomes of advances in genomics. In some cases, there may be both negative and positive aspects of a topic. Choose one topic for your research.

  ● DNA theft
  ● Screening for genetic disorders at birth
  ● Screening for Huntington's disease
  ● Screening for a BRCA mutation for breast cancer
  ● Accidental disclosure of genetic information
  ● Sequencing of tumor cell genomes
  ● Your choice of a genomics topic

Writing

Write a short report on your research. Write two paragraphs about your topic. The first paragraph should explain the topic. The second paragraph should explore its consequences for individuals or society.

Connecting to the Topic

Discuss the following questions with a partner.

1 What were the prospects for cancer patients in the twentieth century and before?

2 What do you know about advances in cancer treatment in the last 20 years?

3 Have you read or do you know of any stories of cancer survivors? Describe one of them briefly to your partner.

4 Do you think that the stories of cancer survivors can inspire patients who are suffering from cancer? Explain your answer.

Previewing and Predicting

Knowing what *type* of reading (for example, a textbook, a newspaper article, a story) you are about to read can help you decide what to expect when you begin to read. Reading the title and the first sentence of each paragraph, and looking at photographs can help you predict what kind of reading it will be.

A Read the title and the first sentence of each paragraph in Reading 4. Look at the graph. Then put a check (✓) next to kind of reading you think it will be.

_____ A A scientific study, that is, a report on research

___✓___ B A narrative, that is, a story about something that happened

_____ C An article about a recent event in the news

_____ D A section of a medical textbook

_____ E A business report about medical news

B Based on what you have read, do you think the outcome of the reading will be positive or negative?

C Compare your answers with a partner's.

While You Read

As you read, stop at the end of each sentence that contains words in **bold**. Then follow the instructions in the box in the margin.

◀)) A Case Study in Genomics

1   As a schoolboy, all Lucas Wartman ever wanted was to become a veterinarian[1] like his grandfather, but all that changed the summer he spent working in a hospital. There he witnessed firsthand the suffering caused by cancer. That experience left a deep impression on Wartman, eventually leading him to opt for a career in medicine that would allow him to devote himself to the study and treatment of cancer. Some ten years after that fateful summer, he enrolled in medical school, where he spent part of his time doing clinical research in oncology[2], focusing specifically on leukemia – a form of cancer that affects blood cells.

2   On the morning that Wartman was scheduled to interview for a residency[3] at Stanford University in California, he got a shock that changed his life forever. "I could not get out of bed for an interview that was the most important of my life," Wartman says, recalling that terrible day. Somehow he rallied and managed to complete the interview, but he still felt so tired that every step was an enormous effort. Puzzled and then alarmed when his health did not improve after his return to school, he went for tests to determine the cause for his fatigue. The tests revealed he was suffering from acute lymphoblastic leukemia, ironically, the very disease he had been investigating in his research.

3   Following the diagnosis, Dr. Wartman went through traditional chemotherapy, which sent his cancer into remission[4], stirring his hope that the cancer was gone for good. Secretly, Wartman was also scared, and with good reason, because the outlook for patients with the disease was overwhelmingly **negative**. For those patients who relapsed after remission, there was only a four to five percent survival rate for this particular form of leukemia. Five years went by without any recurrence of the cancer, fueling Wartman's confidence that his recovery would be permanent. He and his doctors believed he had conquered the disease, but then sadly, one day the symptoms recurred; the cancer had come back. Wartman searched for information on the survival rate for those who survived a second relapse, but to no avail. There was no record of survivors of a second relapse; patients simply did not survive. Nevertheless, Wartman didn't give up; he and his doctors decided to try again with a different treatment. He underwent a more aggressive chemotherapy program and received a bone-marrow transplant[5] from his brother, once again, sending the cancer into remission. Wartman and his team of doctors crossed their fingers, hoping that they had defeated the cancer this time, that there would be no

---

[1] *veterinarian:* a professional who is trained in the medical treatment of animals
[2] *oncology:* the medical specialty that focuses on cancer
[3] *residency:* the final stage in doctors' training when they begin to work in their own special area
[4] *remission:* a period when an illness improves and is less severe
[5] *bone-marrow transplant:* an operation in which cells from the inside of one person's bones is transferred to another person

second relapse. Again, they were wrong, and three years later, the symptoms returned.

4   Wartman began still another treatment program, but his condition was deteriorating rapidly. He knew that he was running out of time, but just as Wartman and his team were beginning to think there were no more options, Timothy Ley, Associate Director of the Genome Institute at Washington University, where Wartman worked, offered a radical suggestion in response to this crisis. Three years earlier, Ley had used a supercomputer to sequence the genome of another form of cancer; based on this experience, he thought he could sequence and analyze the genome of Wartman's tumor cells. Ley believed that genomic sequencing might provide information about which mutations were causing the **leukemia**.

5   At that time, genomic sequencing was being heralded as a life-saving medical **breakthrough**, but sequencing the genome of Wartman's tumor would be just the first step in a long journey. Once the genome of the tumor was mapped, this vast store of data would have to be analyzed, a process that could take months. Next, after researchers identified specific mutations in the genome, they would have to ascertain whether these mutations were important and if so, whether they were related to the disease. Many of the variations across the genome could turn out to be inconsequential or irrelevant. And finally, if they were successful in all of these efforts, the research team would need to match the mutation they had identified to a drug that could potentially counteract its effects.

6   In record time, Ley and his team sequenced and compared Wartman's normal and tumor genomes, as well as his RNA, a molecule closely related to DNA. The genome analysis yielded no clues, but the analysis of his RNA revealed that a single gene, called FLT3, was being overexpressed; that is, it was about 800 times more active than it normally should be, thus promoting the growth of the cancer cells. Members of the team were elated; they were confident that the FLT3 mutation was the cause of Wartman's leukemia.

7   Next came the hunt for appropriate treatment, a step that involved searching the drug-gene interaction database[6] to find a drug that might be effective against the overactive FLT3 gene. Their search revealed that one drug had been successful in blocking similar FLT3 activity in advanced kidney cancer. It had never been tried on a leukemia patient; Wartman would be the first. This drug, in conjunction with other treatments, caused Wartman's cancer to go into remission once again.

8   Wartman is cautious about saying this remission is permanent, but today, he is practicing medicine and living a full life. He and his doctors are certain that without this intervention, he would not have survived the second relapse. This story has a happy ending, but the implications of this pioneering treatment go far beyond Wartman's case. The research that led

WHILE YOU READ 2
Look back at paragraph 4. Highlight the signals of problem and solution.

WHILE YOU READ 3
Use your knowledge of vocabulary to guess the meaning of *breakthrough*. Does it mean (a) a type of therapy, or (b) a discovery that comes after a long period of effort?

---

[6] *drug-gene interaction database:* a computerized library of information that explains how specific genes respond to specific drugs

to his treatment suggests that cancers – leukemia, breast cancer, colon cancer, etc. – cannot be treated uniformly because each case may be different. Each cancer is as different from another cancer as one human being is different from another human being.

9   Dr. Wartman was lucky because he was working at a university where relevant research was being **conducted** and he had colleagues who were able and willing to assist him. This kind of procedure is both expensive and time-consuming, and therefore, not an option for everyone. However, this situation is gradually changing, with a dramatic drop in the cost of sequencing since the completion of the Human Genome Project. (See Figure 2.3.) Researchers predict it may soon be available for as little as U.S. $1,000. It is also getting quicker. In 2014, in a new and experimental procedure, doctors at the Laboratory of Genetics at the University of Wisconsin used DNA sequencing to quickly identify the bacteria that were causing a young patient's brain to swell up with fluid. This was the first time that researchers had sequenced not just a patient's DNA, but all the small pieces of other DNA found in the patient's body, including DNA from invasive bacteria. This analysis helped the Wisconsin research team identify the bacteria that were causing the patient's infection. In this case, speed was of the utmost importance because without this rapid analysis and subsequent diagnosis, the patient would almost certainly have died.

10   Of course, the procedures that helped Wartman and the Wisconsin patient were experimental and are still not available for most patients, but the hope is that soon this type of analysis will lead to diagnosis and treatment in the majority of cancer cases. Dr. Malachi Griffith, one of the Washington University scientists who worked on Wartman's case, believes that this will eventually become routine treatment. He says, hopefully, "We want to be able to take the tumor of every patient that comes into the clinic, sequence their genome, and produce a clinical report just like when a physician orders a blood test."

WHILE YOU READ ④

Which definition of *conducted* matches the meaning in this sentence?
(a) Carry out, organize
(b) Behave in a certain way

Figure 2.3 Cost of Sequencing a Genome

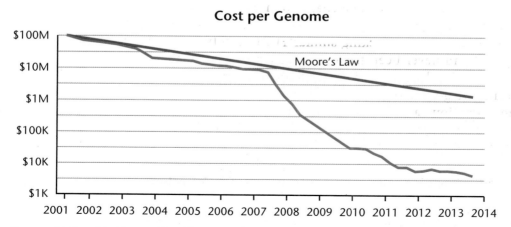

Source: *National Institutes of Health*

Main Idea Check

Here are the main ideas for five of the paragraphs in Reading 4. Match each paragraph to its main idea. Write the number of the paragraph on the blank line.

_____ A Genomic sequencing offered Wartman an alternative treatment.

_____ B A recent case demonstrates that sequencing can be a relatively quick process.

_____ C Sequencing the genome of Wartman's tumor would be the beginning of his long way to recovery.

_____ D The search for a potentially effective drug was successful.

_____ E Wartman tried several rounds of traditional cancer treatments.

A Closer Look

Look back at Reading 4 to answer the following questions.

1 What was the primary reason for Wartman's career choice?
   a He worked at a hospital, where he saw the devastating effects of cancer.
   b He admired his grandfather, who was a veterinarian.
   c He wanted to devote himself to medical school.
   d He was not sure what he wanted to do until he began to study oncology.

2 Why does the author describe Wartman's diagnosis as "ironic"?
   a Wartman got sick at the exact moment when he had a very important interview.
   b It is ironic that the news changed Wartman's life.
   c It took an unusually long period of time to establish Wartman's diagnosis.
   d Wartman never expected to get the disease that he was studying.

3 Only about five percent of those who survived a second relapse of this type of leukemia survived. **True or False?**

4 Indicate the correct order of the steps in Wartman's treatment. Write the correct number in each box.

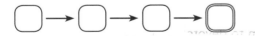

   A Researchers identified an overactive gene.
   B Researchers identified a drug that might work against the effects of the mutation.
   C Researchers sequenced Wartman's genome.
   D Researchers compared Wartman's genome to the tumor genome.

5 Most kinds of cancer require the same treatment. **True or False?**

6 How does Wartman's case illustrate the fundamental insight of genomics?
   a It demonstrates that we will need to build vast databases of genes and drugs in order to find effective treatments.
   b It suggests that the effectiveness of medical treatment may depend on a patient's genetic profile.
   c It shows that if doctors keep trying, they will eventually arrive at an effective treatment.
   d It suggests that we need to find a way to sequence cancer genomes more quickly and at a lower cost.

7 In 2014, the cost of genomic sequencing had dropped to about one percent of its original cost. **True or False?**

8 In what ways was the Wisconsin case an advance over Wartman's? Choose all that apply.
   a The sequencing was done more quickly.
   b The sequencing was done at a lower cost to the patient.
   c The sequencing included DNA that did not belong to the patient.
   d The procedure was experimental.

Skill Review

In Skills and Strategies 5, you learned that you sometimes need to use a dictionary to choose the correct meaning for words that have more than one meaning.

A **The following sentences are from Reading 4. Each of the words in bold has more than one meaning. Look up each word in a dictionary or online. Read each definition and then substitute each one into the original sentence. Choose the definition that matches the meaning of the word in bold and write it on the line below.**

1 That experience left a deep **impression** on Wartman, eventually leading him to opt for a career in medicine that would allow him to devote himself to the study and treatment of cancer.
   reaction, effect, influence

2 Following the diagnosis, Dr. Wartman went through traditional chemotherapy, which sent his cancer into remission, **stirring** his hope that the cancer was gone for good.
   causing a reaction

3 Once the genome of the tumor was mapped, this vast **store** of data would have to be analyzed, a process that could take months.

Supply, large amount.

4 Wartman is cautious about saying this remission is permanent, but today, he is **practicing** medicine and living a full life.

Performing a specialiced work.

B Some words have more than two meanings. Read the following two sentences from Reading 4. They contain the same word, but with a different meaning. Look up each word in a dictionary or online. Read each definition and then substitute each one into the original sentence. Choose the definition that matches the meaning of the word in bold and write it on the line below.

1 There was no **record** of survivors of a second relapse; patients simply did not survive.

2 In **record** time, Ley and his team sequenced and compared Wartman's normal and tumor genomes, as well as his RNA, a molecule closely related to DNA.

Vocabulary Development

Definitions

Find the words in Reading 4 that are similar to the definitions below.

1 related to medical treatment (*adj*) Par. 1 *clinical*

2 state of being extremely tired; exhaustion (*n*) Par. 2 *fatigue*

3 in a way that is the opposite of what is expected (*adv*) Par. 2 *ironically*

4 permanently (*adv*) Par. 3 *for good*

5 for the greatest part, overpoweringly (*adv*) Par. 3 *overwhelmingly*

6 the return of an illness or condition (*n*) Par. 3 *relapse*

7 unsuccessfully (*idiom*) Par. 3 *to no avail*

8 to experience something unpleasant or difficult (*v*) Par. 3 *undergo*

9 characterized by strong, forceful methods (*adj*) Par. 3 *aggressive*

10 to hope for the best (*idiom*) Par. 3 *cross one finger*

11 to reduce the effect of something by having the opposite effect (*v*) Par. 5 *counteract*

12 being the first to do something in a particular way (*adj*) Par. 8 *pionering*

13 always in the same way (*adv*) Par. 8 *uniformly*

14 tending to spread in an uncontrollable way (*adj*) Par. 9 *invasive*

15 greatest or most (*adj*) Par. 9 *utmost*

Synonyms

Complete the sentences with words from Reading 4 in the box below. These words replace the words or phrases in parentheses, which are similar in meaning.

alarmed	deteriorate	implications	rallied	recurrence
ascertained	elated	opted for	radical	yield

1 After careful consideration, he (chose) _opted for_ surgery instead of chemotherapy.

2 The new policy should ensure that the country sees no (return) _recurrence_ of the economic problems of the last decade.

3 He was (frightened) _alarmed_ by how thin his mother had become since he last saw her.

4 This decision will have serious (consequences) _implications_ for the future, so you should consider it very carefully.

5 Researchers hope that the study will (provide) _yield_ evidence that supports their theory.

6 After a few moments of rest, the team (recovered) _rallied_ and went on to win the game. (rally)

7 These ideas are too (extreme) _radical_. We need to move more slowly.

8 Health officials (discovered) _ascertaned_ that the outbreak of the infection began in a fast-food restaurant.

9 They were (overjoyed) _elated_ when they heard the news about the new baby.

10 Unfortunately, the patient's condition continued to (worsen) _deleriorate_ during the night.

Academic Word List

The following are Academic Word List words from Readings 3 and 4 of this unit. Use these words to complete the sentences. (For more on the Academic Word List, see page 299.)

ethical (adj)	inevitably (adv)	motivate (v)	status (n)	undergo (v)
implications (n)	intervention (n)	radical (adj)	subsequent (adj)	uniformly (adv)

1 Although the thieves tried to run away, they _inevitably_ will be caught eventually.

2 They hope to visit the Winter Palace on a _subsequent_ trip to Beijing. They did not have time when they went to China last year.

3 His doctor informed him that he would have to _undergo_ surgery in order to repair the damage to his heart.

4 Early _intervention_ by teachers and professionals can help troubled teenagers avoid criminal behavior.

5 Political candidates often give powerful speeches in an effort to _motivate_ people to vote for them.

6 The use of animals in scientific experiments raises _ethical_ questions for many people.

7 Her ideas are too new and _radical_. People are not ready to accept them.

8 The members of the committee were _uniformly_ opposed to the proposal.

9 The broader _implications_ of climate change are only now becoming apparent.

10 One of the responsibilities of this office is to check the immigration _status_ of all incoming students.

Critical Thinking

In Readings 3 and 4 you learned about advances in genomics and read a narrative about its personal impact on one patient.

A Work with a partner to discuss how genomics might have an effect on you personally or someone you know.

B Based on what you read in this unit and your own knowledge, answer the questions below with a partner. Review the readings if necessary.

1 Under what circumstances would you want your own genome sequenced?

2 Would you feel differently about genomic sequencing to find a cure and sequencing to screen for possible future diseases if you were sick?

3 If a family member found out about a dangerous genetic defect in his or her profile, would this encourage or discourage you from getting your own genome sequenced?

4 Would you agree to genomic screening for your baby at birth?

5 Would you recommend it for a sick family member or friend?

6 How expensive do you think genomic sequencing should be? Consider whether there could be negative consequences if it becomes very inexpensive.

7 What are your hopes for the future of genomics?

> **SYNTHESIZING**
>
> Critical thinking includes connecting new information to information you learned in previous readings.

Research

Continue your discussion of these questions as a whole class. Take notes on what your classmates are saying. Record how many people hold a particular view. You will use this information in your writing assignment. Consider the following questions as you listen to the discussion:

- What are the circumstances in which they are most likely to want or agree to the sequencing of their genome? What are their reasons?
- Do they feel differently about treatment versus screening?
- What worries them most about genomic sequencing? Why?
- What is the most divisive aspect of this issue? Why do you think this is the case?
- Did women respond differently than men? Are there any other clear differences in the responses across groups?

Follow up with individual classmates if you want more information about their views before writing.

Writing

Your assignment is to analyze and report the views of your classmates on the topic of genomics and genomic sequencing.

A Preparing to Write

1 Look over your notes from your class discussion.

2 Review Readings 3 and 4. Highlight any information to include in your report.

3 Organize your notes into an outline. I include the following sections:

- The circumstances under which your classmates were most likely to accept or even welcome sequencing for themselves or for members of their families. What were their reasons?

- The circumstances under which your classmates were most likely to reject sequencing for themselves or for members of their families. What were their reasons?

- The circumstances and issues that were the most divisive among your classmates on the subject of genomic sequencing

- Their general outlook for the future of this aspect or field of biomedical science

4 Consider any differences across groups: men vs. women, married vs. single people, etc.

B Writing

1 Write your report. Write one paragraph for each of the first three points in your outline.

2 Begin each paragraph with a general sentence that tells your reader what the paragraph will be about.

3 Include information about different groups to each paragraph if this is relevant.

4 You do not need to provide specific numbers, but try to give a profile of the class (e.g., *most students in the class. . ., all the women. . .,* etc.).

5 When you have finished, check your report for grammar and spelling errors.

Improving Your Reading Speed

Good readers read quickly and still understand most of what they read.

A Read the instructions and strategies for Improving Your Reading Speed in Appendix 3 on page 316.

B Choose one of the readings in this unit. Read it without stopping. Time how long it takes you to finish the text in minutes and seconds. Enter the time in the chart on page 317. Then calculate your reading speed in number of words per minute.

Using Graphic Organizers

In order to better understand and remember information in a text, it is important to take notes. You can make annotations in the text or mark it up by highlighting, underlining, or using your own system to emphasize important sections and key terms. Visual or graphic organizers are other tools you can use to comprehend and remember information. They allow you to actually see the text structure (see Skills and Strategies 4) and how the information is organized.

Examples & Explanations

Recent research has shown that humans carry millions of microorganisms and viruses in and on their bodies. Scientists refer to them as the human microbiome. In fact, the cells of the human body are outnumbered ten to one by the cells in the microbiome. The discovery of this massive microscopic community has prompted questions – as well as a robust research program – into the origins and functions of these microorganisms.

The first paragraph is an introduction. The last sentence tells the reader that the rest of the text will focus on the sources and functions of the microbiome.

Research into the microbiome is in its infancy, but preliminary research suggests that a baby's microbiome has several sources beginning at birth. ①During birth, the baby becomes covered with the microbes that live in the mother's body, a process that plants a sort of microbial garden in and on the newborn baby. ②Breast milk transfers more of the inhabitants of the mother's microbiome to the child, which is one reason that babies' microbiomes appear much like their mothers'. ③As children grow, their microbiomes expand and become more diverse as they are exposed to other microorganisms in the environment. These microorganisms are everywhere – on their toys, in their beds, and on the family dog. ④Children may also ingest microbes in the food that they eat. These preliminary ideas about the source of the human microbial population do not answer the even more pressing question: Why? What are all of those microorganisms doing all over our bodies?

The second paragraph focuses on the sources of microbes in the microbiome. You can illustrate this relationship using a graphic organizer. This same type of organizer can be used to display causes or reasons in a cause-and-effect text.

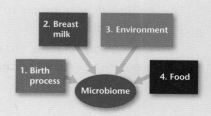

For decades, most people have considered microbes as pathogens, that is, causes of disease. ⑤Although it is true that many do cause disease, emerging research on the human microbiome has caused a 180-degree shift in this thinking ⑥as studies have begun to show that many microbes are beneficial, or even essential, for human health. The functions of microorganisms suggested by such studies fall into the following categories: (a) the training of immune cells, (b) defense against pathogens, and (c) the regulation of metabolism. Scientists suspect that when the microbiome, especially the part of it found in the human gut, falls out of balance, humans can become seriously ill. Researchers have even begun to trace the cause of some diseases of the modern era to disturbances in our microbiome.

The third paragraph discusses what these microorganisms do in the body. We learn that they can cause disease, but they also perform many beneficial functions that fall into three categories. You can use a graphic organizer to visualize this relationship.

Functions of Microbes	
cause disease	train immune system
	defend against infection
	regulate metabolism

Strategies

These strategies will help you create graphic organizers that represent important concepts in the text as you take notes.

- As you read, highlight or annotate main ideas and supporting details.
- Consider how the text is organized. Is it one of the text types described in Skills and Strategies 4? If so, consider using one of the organizers in this section in your notes.
- If it is a different text type, try to use or adapt one of these organizers for your specific purpose.
- Add important information, such as key words, to your graphic organizer. This makes important information, and how it is organized, more obvious.
- Use size or numbers to show the difference between more important and less important details.
- Keep your graphic organizer simple. If you include too much information, you will not be able to visualize the information as clearly.

Skill Practice 1

Read the following texts. As you read, notice that the student has highlighted the main idea and other important details. Check (✓) the graphic organizer that best represents the information in the text. Write in important details.

1 Modern pharmaceuticals have many origins. Some are created in laboratories; some have come from natural substances found in the environment, such as molds, plants, or even naturally occurring bacteria. The search for the newest drugs is taking place in an unlikely place – our own bodies. Recent research has revealed that some of the microorganisms in our microbiome are tiny drug producers.

   A scientist at the University of California, Dr. Michael Fischbach, has identified genes that make 3,000 different molecules that may be useful as medicine. Several genes work together to cause the proteins to create tiny amounts of these products. These genes are generally located together in a cluster. Fischbach and his colleagues wrote a computer program to identify these clusters in the human microbiome. Then they identified over 3,000 common gene clusters and chose one for development. Finally, they grew them in huge numbers in order to amass enough of their product to test. They discovered that this product has a structure that is very similar to the structure of an antibiotic, the type of drug taken to cure bacterial infections. Fischbach is now testing the effectiveness of this microbial "antibiotic."

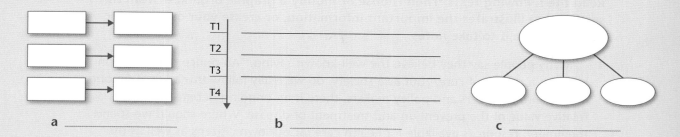

a _____ b _____ c _____

2 Recent research has convinced many of us of the value of our microbial communities. We understand that they are important for maintaining good health. However, the microbiome story turns out to be more complex. Our microbial companions are not selfless heroes acting on our behalf; instead, they are acting very much in their own interests.

   It seems that in order to advance their interests, these microbes can make us engage in behavior that may ultimately harm us, for example, by making poor food choices. These tiny organisms may be the ones that are really in control, especially when it comes to food. In cancer researcher Carlo Maley's words, these microbes have "the means, motives, and opportunity" to manipulate their hosts, in other words, us.

   Bacteria in the human gut manufacture tiny amounts of substances that can actually change the biochemistry of the human brain. It is possible that these changes encourage cravings for certain foods, such as a desire for sweet foods or chocolate. Scientists studying this phenomenon have hypothesized that this is because specific microbes thrive on these substances.

Neuroscientist John Cryan suggests another way in which microbes may influence our behavior and explains the reason for this microbial manipulation. It is still just a hypothesis, but he believes that microbes manufacture chemicals that may influence humans to be more social. His research has demonstrated that compared to mice with normal gut bacteria, lab mice without an active microbiome tend to avoid contact with other mice. That is not a favorable situation for bacteria. They thrive when their hosts are near one another in social groups since this allows them to move from one host to another. Therefore, it is in their interest for their human hosts to spend more time with one another. It seems that our microbiome may even make us friendlier! And, unlike their role in our food choices, that is probably a good thing.

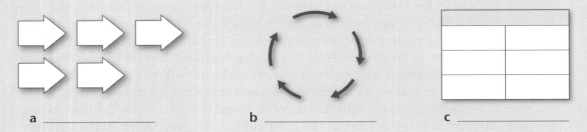

a _____   b _____   c _____

Skill Practice 2

Read the following texts. Then choose or modify a graphic organizer from this section that illustrates the important information, or create your own graphic organizer. Use it to take notes.

1   Many people say they believe the well-known saying, "An ounce of prevention is worth a pound of cure," but as a society, do we really follow this advice? Among health-care providers and policy makers, there is an ongoing debate about the relative value of the prevention and treatment of disease. Where should we spend the limited resources available for health care for our own citizens as well as the global population?

Whatever, we say we believe, it is clear that more money is currently being spent on treatment than prevention. In the United States, as in many other developed countries, spending on treatment is almost twenty times higher than spending on prevention programs. Many health-care professionals argue that prevention programs are much cheaper in the long run. They keep people healthy, which reduces overall health-care costs and also increases economic productivity. It is more expensive to care for people after they become seriously ill. An additional drawback of focusing primarily on treatment is that it may encourage the development of drug-resistant bacteria. Prevention, in contrast, generally does not require drugs and so does not entail this risk.

In spite of the clear benefits of prevention, the emphasis on treatment programs remains widespread. Several explanations have been advanced for this disparity. Perhaps most important is the distress factor. Patients who are in pain or even dying demand our immediate attention, whereas prevention programs seem comparatively less urgent. They lack the drama that attends treatment. It also harder to demonstrate success, that is, to show that positive outcomes are the result of prevention measures, at least to do so in ways that are persuasive to the public. Most evidence of their effectiveness is statistical in nature, in contrast to the concrete certainty of a cure. Finally, prevention programs are for healthy people, who may not always be willing to accept this kind of interference. Patients who need treatment have little choice in the matter.

2.   In 2014, the world was confronted with a major health-care crisis: a massive outbreak of the Ebola virus in West Africa. Ebola, a disease that originated in animals, particularly bats and monkeys, is often fatal in humans. The virus spreads through the population by human-to-human transmission. The 2014 epidemic was the worst in history, in part because the health-care systems in the affected countries were already fragile before the epidemic took hold. There was also a critical shortage of trained medical personnel and supplies. Many health-care workers are hesitant to work with Ebola patients because of the risk it poses to their own health.

At present, there is neither a cure nor a preventive vaccine for Ebola. However, there are measures that can be taken to deal with the situation to reduce the threat of infection. These include reducing the risk of animal-human transmission that can come from contact with infected bats or monkeys, reducing the risk of the person-to-person transmission by using gloves and other protective clothing, and separating the sick from the healthy.

The scientific community has also responded to this challenge by working as quickly as possible to find ways to treat the virus effectively. One remedy, which is based on the tobacco plant, was tested on two American patients, who did make complete recoveries. However, it is not clear whether the remedy or simply supportive care was the primary factor in their recovery. Other scientists are working on the possibility of a therapy that uses the blood plasma of patients who have recovered from the disease. Finally, some researchers are tackling the problem from the perspective of prevention; they are hoping to develop a vaccine. It is crucial to work on all fronts in order to prevent a recurrence of this type of epidemic in the future.

Connecting to the Topic

Discuss the following questions with a partner.

1 What are the origins of most of the drugs that we use to treat and cure diseases?

2 Do you know the background of a specific drug and how it was invented or discovered? Explain your answer.

3 Which do you think is more common in the creation of new drugs – the discovery of something that already exists, or invention, that is, the creation of something new? Explain your answer.

4 Who pays for the development of new drugs?

Previewing and Predicting

> Reading the title, section headings, and the first sentence of each section can help you predict what the reading will be about.

A Look at the illustration, read the section headings and the first sentence of each sentence in Reading 5, and think about the title of the reading. Then read the following topics. Write the number of the section (*I–III*) where you think that topic will be discussed.

SECTION	TOPIC
	Modern methods of drug discovery research
	A general description of the drug discovery process
	Drug design methods
	The steps in the discovery pipeline
	What happens after compounds are identified
	Drug discovery prior to the twenty-first century

B Compare your answers with a partner's.

While You Read

As you read, stop at the end of each sentence that contains words in **bold**. Then follow the instructions in the box in the margin.

Drug Discovery in the Twenty-First Century

by Dr. Brian Kay

I. What Is Drug Discovery?

1   Drugs improve the quality of life for millions of people. They enable patients to fight off bacterial and viral infections, they help diabetic patients respond to dangerous elevated glucose[1] levels, and they represent the first line of defense in treating cancer. It is difficult to imagine modern life without them. What most people don't appreciate, however, is that for every successful drug on the market, there are hundreds of failures. Many potential drugs never make it to the local pharmacy or hospital. This can happen for a variety of reasons: because they don't work in the way that researchers anticipated, they only work for some patients and not others, they turn out to be too toxic, or they have other serious side effects. The path to drug discovery is perilous, unpredictable, and extremely **expensive**.

2   A review of the history of drug discovery reveals the important role of chance. The story of the Scottish scientist Alexander Fleming may be a familiar one. In 1928, Fleming observed that a type of fungus, which had accidently contaminated a sample of bacteria, inhibited its growth. This casual observation, in the hands of a thoughtful, curious scientist, eventually led to the identification of penicillin, an immensely important antibiotic[2] that has had a profound and positive impact on society. Perhaps less familiar is the story of the Wisconsin farmer who, in 1933, noticed that his herd of cows experienced internal bleeding whenever they ate a specific type of sweet clover. This observation attracted the interests of biochemists at the University of Wisconsin, who analyzed the chemical compounds in the clover, ultimately leading to the identification of the anticoagulant[3], warfarin. Although warfarin was initially sold as a rat poison, medical researchers later found that it was very effective in preventing the formation of blood clots[4] in blood vessels, thereby preventing strokes. Today, warfarin is widely prescribed for the prevention of blood clots.

Alexander Fleming

> **WHILE YOU READ ❶**
>
> Look back at paragraph 1. This paragraph includes both problem/solution and cause/effect text organization. Underline the noun that signals problem/solution and the noun that signals cause/effect text organization.

II. The Twenty-First Century: Current Practices

3   Although serendipity can have a profound impact on developments in medicine, it is a rather haphazard and unsatisfying way to conduct

---

[1] *glucose:* a simple sugar
[2] *antibiotic:* a chemical that destroys harmful bacteria
[3] *anticoagulant:* a chemical that prevents blood from thickening and creating a clot
[4] *clot:* a thick lump of blood

research. So, instead of hoping to be lucky, the pharmaceutical industry takes a more direct, focused approach to discovering new drugs. Generally, it starts by identifying a vulnerable point within a pathogen's or cancer cell's development. This identification process, that is, the discovery of a gene and its protein product that plays a crucial role in growth or life of the cell or virus, generally involves the analysis of mutations. To discover the role of key genes in human cancer cells, scientists often analyze mutations in model organisms, such as yeast, fruit flies, worms, or mice, and then later demonstrate that the equivalent gene in human cancer cells has the same critical function.

4   Once experiments have demonstrated that a particular protein might be a worthwhile target, the next goal of such research is to identify a chemical that might inhibit the activity of that protein. This can **block** the growth of the virus, bacterial cell, or cancer cell. Teams of biologists and chemists are dedicated to drug discovery efforts at pharmaceutical companies. They work together to build a "drug discovery pipeline" to find and test a new drug. The first part of the pipeline generally consists of four different approaches: high-throughput screening of small molecule libraries; structure-based drug design; fragment-based lead discovery; and cell-based **screening**.

High-throughput screening of small molecule libraries

5   At pharmaceutical companies, there is a standard workflow for discovering small chemicals that inhibit targets. First, the protein for the target is produced in large amounts, and its function – whether to make a chemical reaction go faster or bind other molecules – is then measured by an appropriate assay. An assay is defined as a procedure for evaluating the presence or biochemical activity of a chemical. Then a chemical compound is added to the assay to determine if it will inhibit the protein's activity, and depending on the assay format, the intensity of color or emitted light will decrease.

6   Once a research team has established a reliable, reproducible assay, the next step is to screen "libraries" of chemical compounds to determine which compounds display the desired inhibitory activity. Pharmaceutical companies have libraries of approximately two million small chemicals, and every member of a library can be individually tested in an assay with the help of robots that fill tiny wells in small plastic trays. In a typical high-throughput screen, the percentage of wells with inhibitory activity is less than one percent.

Structure-based drug design

7   Another popular approach to discovery is to take a target protein and determine its three-dimensional structure. Once chemists and structural biologists know the shape of the protein, they look for an active site in the protein. These are pockets where proteins naturally bind small molecules, or peptides. Researchers then design small chemicals that will bind at these active sites, thereby interfering with the protein's activity. An analogy for this process would be using a magnifying glass to see inside a door lock,

WHILE YOU READ 2

Which definition of *block* matches the meaning in this sentence? (a) A solid hard piece of something (b) Prevent

WHILE YOU READ 3

Read the last sentence of paragraph 4. What text organization do you think will follow? _____ Underline the signal(s).

and then guessing the shape of a key in order to create a similar shape, which, when inserted into the lock, prevents the door from unlocking. The process of determining the appropriate shape of a chemical inhibitor, which in the past was based on intuition and experience, is now aided by powerful computer programs that are capable of searching large databases of compound structures and predicting those that might bind to the target's active site. Typically, chemists sift through the top 1,000 compounds, which, based on past experience, are judged to have attractive attributes, and then retest them in **follow-up** assays.

8   One of the most heralded successes of structure-based drug discovery occurred in 1995, with the announcement of inhibitors of the Human Immunodeficiency Virus (HIV) protease. This enzyme[5] is essential for the virus to copy itself and infect new cells. Once the DNA sequence of the virus was known, the gene for HIV protease could be isolated, the protein could be produced in large quantities, and the three-dimensional structure of the protein was determined. Scientists reasoned that if they could develop a small molecule that fit in the active site (Figure 2.4, left panel), it would inhibit the enzyme's activity. With several pharmaceutical companies working toward the same goal, several powerful drugs have been developed. The drug, Prezista, fits tightly into the active site of HIV protease (Figure 2.4, right panel), where it acts as a very effective inhibitor of the enzyme. Thus, Prezista blocks the production of the virus and allows the body to fight HIV more effectively. This important development has allowed many of those infected with AIDs to survive and lead productive lives.

Fragment-based lead discovery

9   A third approach, which is a variant of the structure-based design, is called fragment-based lead discovery. In the structure-based design approach, it can be very challenging to find a compound that fits exactly into the active site. In part, this is because the compounds in the library

WHILE YOU READ ❹
Use context and your knowledge of word parts to guess the meaning of *follow-up*. Does it mean (a) more important, (b) later, or (c) more demanding?

Figure 2.4 Model representing the three-dimensional structure of HIV protease (left panel) alone, and with the inhibitor, Prezista, in the protease's active site (right panel)

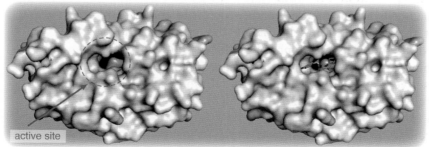

active site

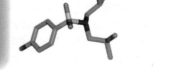

Enlarged view of Prezista

---

[5] *enzyme:* a substance produced by living cells to cause a chemical reaction

are large compared to the size of the site. In response to this challenge, fragment-based design starts with a library of smaller chemical fragments, which are tested to determine if any bind near or at the active site. Once one of these fragments has been identified as capable of binding to part of the site, the process is repeated with another set of chemical fragments, this time to find a second compound that can bind to a different site. If the two binding sites are near each other, chemists can synthesize a structural bridge between the two fragments. This new, larger compound binds better than either fragment alone and can block activity of the **target**.

10   A significant number of targets had eluded drug researchers because no compounds could be found to bind their active sites using traditional drug discovery approaches. Yet, fragment-based design has succeeded. The repeated screening process in this approach allows researchers to build their own compounds, ones that uniquely bind to active sites. Because of these successes, every major pharmaceutical company has now implemented this research strategy in their drug discovery pipeline.

Cell-based screening

11   The fourth method commonly used by pharmaceutical companies employs human cells*. In a sense, the living cell becomes a "test tube" in which the chemical compound's activity is assessed through changes in the visual appearance of cells, such as shape, size, or number. Alternatively, one can monitor changes in protein expression in cells, as visualized by expression of green fluorescent[6] proteins or binding of fluorescent antibodies. In this manner, the impact of chemical compounds on complex biological processes can be evaluated in a novel fashion.

12   Although cell-based assays are generally not high-throughput, that is, they cannot be done on as large of a scale as high-throughput screening methods, thousands to hundreds of thousands of compounds can still be tested on cells. In some cases, the assessment of a compound's activity is **captured** with a system that digitally photographs populations of cells incubated[7] with the compound, followed by automated image analysis. While cell-based screening requires more resources than high-throughput screening, the cell-based screening approach has several advantages. First, compounds can be tested in the context of a living cell, instead of proteins in a well, which is more representative of how a drug works in a person. Second, the use of human cells in this method readily identifies and eliminates compounds that are toxic and kill cells, before they move further into the pipeline. Third, to succeed in this phase of the testing process, compounds must be able to cross the cell membrane, a required attribute of most drugs. Thus, active compounds that have undergone cell-based screening have already cleared three major hurdles.

WHILE YOU READ 5

Look back at the second sentence of paragraph 9. What text organization do you think will follow? _____ Underline the signal(s) that indicate this type of organization.

WHILE YOU READ 6

Which definition of *captured* matches the meaning in this sentence?
(a) Recorded
(b) Taken as a prisoner

---

* These cells are taken from established cell lines that are grown in the laboratory, not from human beings.
[6] *fluorescent*: giving off light
[7] *incubate*: to keep something warm to allow it to grow

III. The Pipeline

13   Once promising chemical compounds are discovered through any of the above four methods, they are called *hits*. Chemists evaluate the chemical structures of the collection of hits according to several criteria, including novelty, similarity to known toxic compounds, and ease of synthesis. In follow-up analyses, chemists synthesize a set of related compounds, differing in very subtle ways, and then pick the best ones to pass onto biologists for testing. These prioritized compounds are called *drug leads*. In turn, biologists assess how long the compounds last in the body after administration, how quickly they are excreted or broken down, and what types of toxicity might occur in animal testing. Generally, all drugs are first tested in small animals, mice or rats, before they are tested in human volunteers. Many drug leads fail in one or more of these tests, but those that pass are then labeled as *drug candidates*. Before moving further down the pipeline, pharmacists determine a formula for the compound that remains stable in solution or pill form as well as the appropriate dosing regimen[8].

14   But this is not the end of the pipeline process. In the United States, for a drug candidate to transition into an actual drug used by the public, it must pass three rounds of patient testing, also known as clinical trials. Phase I tests a drug candidate in a small group of volunteers and determines a safe dosage, as well as identifies any side effects. Phase II then tests it on a larger group of people to see if it is effective in treating a particular illness. Finally, Phase III tests it on a large population of patients to confirm its effectiveness, monitors side effects, and compares it to commonly used treatments. Data are collected during Phase III in a double-blind manner, meaning that neither doctors nor patients know whether the drug or a placebo[9] is being administered. After thousands of patients have received treatment, a government agency carefully examines the resulting data. Only when a drug is demonstrated in clinical trials to be effective and safe does the government grant permission to a pharmaceutical company to sell it to the general public.

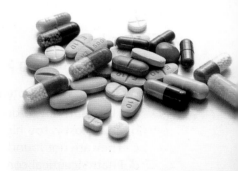

15   In many respects, the drug discovery process is a gamble for pharmaceutical companies. The chemical compounds must progress through many steps, in transitioning from hit to candidate to drug, and at any point, failure is a very real possibility. It has been estimated that for every successful drug, there were 1,000 compounds that failed to progress through the pipeline. Thus, there is considerable incentive to improve the drug discovery and evaluation process. If pharmaceutical companies can find a way to do this, the expectation is that the number of newly approved drugs will increase and will lead to an improvement in human **health**.

WHILE YOU READ ⑦

Look back at paragraph 15. Highlight the word that signals a cause.

---

[8] *regimen:* a set of rules, especially for health

[9] *placebo:* a substance that is not medicine, but is given to patients as medicine in order to test the effectiveness of a drug during a trial

Main Idea Check

For sections I–III of Reading 5, match the main ideas to the paragraphs in each section. Write the number of the paragraph on the blank line.

SECTION I: What Is Drug Discovery?

_____ A New drugs are often discovered by chance.

_____ B The drug discovery process is long and often unsuccessful.

SECTION II: The Twenty-First Century: Current Practices

_____ A In one approach, scientists try to determine the shape and structure of one compound that will fit into an active site.

_____ B In one approach, researchers use human cells to test the effectiveness of the compound.

_____ C After researchers determine a target, they need to identify a compound that can inhibit its activity.

SECTION III: The Pipeline

_____ A Chemists and biologists test and adjust promising compounds before the compounds enter the trial phase.

_____ B Before a drug can be sold, it must go through a series of trials on humans.

A Closer Look

Look back at Reading 5 to answer the following questions.

1 Why do so many potential drugs fail to make it to the market? Choose all that apply.
   a They turn out to do more harm than good.
   b Their cost is too high.
   c They are not found to be sufficiently effective.
   d Pharmaceutical companies decide not to pursue them.

2 Why was warfarin first used as a rat poison?
   a It was not yet proven safe to use on humans.
   b It caused internal bleeding in rats, leading to their death.
   c Scientists wanted to try it out on rats first.
   d Scientists were not sure what kinds of side effects it might cause.

3 Why does the author include the example of warfarin? Choose all that apply.
   a To show that drug discovery is a long and difficult process.
   b To show the role that chance plays in drug discovery.
   c To show that drugs do more than just benefit human health.
   d To show that a drug developed for one purpose may be later used for another.

4 Which of the following is a step in the first phase of the drug discovery process?

   a Scientists create mutations in organisms such as fruit flies, worms, or mice.
   b Scientists look for a chemical or compound that will increase a protein's activity.
   c Scientists identify a weak point in the development of a disease-causing cell.

5 High-throughput screening is an approach that allows scientists to test large numbers of compounds. **True or False?**

6 What developments have fueled the growth of structure-based drug design? Choose all that apply.

   a New assay formats
   b Knowledge of the three-dimensional structure of molecules
   c Computer programs that can handle large data sets
   d Massive libraries of chemicals and chemical compounds

7 What advantage does cell-based screening have over other drug discovery practices?

   a It reveals how the drug would work on humans.
   b It uses fewer resources than other types of screening.
   c It is not toxic.
   d It can be captured with digital photography.

8 What is the best way to describe the difference between a *drug lead* and a *drug candidate*?

   a Drug candidates, but not leads, have been tested on humans.
   b Drug leads, but not candidates, have been through the animal test phase.
   c Drug candidates, but not leads, have undergone toxicity tests.

9 Why do clinical trials use double-blind methods?

   a They do not rely on the use of placebos.
   b The government requires proof of safety and effectiveness.
   c They prevent participants from influencing the outcome.
   d They increase the incentive for pharmaceutical companies.

Skill Review

In Skills and Strategies 6, you learned that graphic organizers can help you comprehend and remember information. They can also help you visualize the organization of a text.

A 1 **Study the figure below. What text organization does it illustrate?**

a Cause and effect
b Steps in a process
c Problem-solution

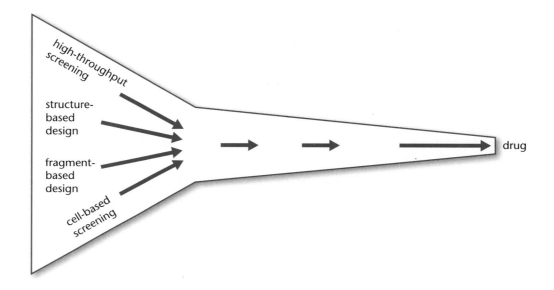

2 **Fill in the blanks in the figure.**

B **Review Section II of Reading 5 and look over any notes you have taken. Then answer the question.**

What is the text organization of this section?

_____

C **Now choose or modify the appropriate graphic organizer from this unit that illustrates the important information, or create your own graphic organizer. Use it to organize your notes.**

Definitions

Find the words in Reading 5 that are similar to the definitions below.

1 to be aware that something is valuable or important (*v*) Par. 1

2 poisonous (*adj*) Par. 1

3 dangerous (*adj*) Par. 1

4 to make something less pure (*v*) Par. 2

5 great; deep (*adj*) Par. 2

6 the fact of finding something interesting by accident (*n*) Par. 3

7 unplanned, lacking order (*adj*) Par. 3

8 equal to or having the same effect (*adj*) Par. 3

9 the ability to understand without using reason (*n*) Par. 7

10 as another option (*adv*) Par. 11

11 difficulty; obstacle (*n*) Par. 12

12 standards by which something can be evaluated (*n pl*) Par. 13

13 to combine two or more things to create something new (*v*) Par. 13

14 not likely to change; fixed (*adj*) Par. 13

15 something that encourages a person to do something (*n*) Par. 15

Words in Context

Complete the sentences with words from Reading 5 in the box below.

analogy	formula	immensely	prioritize	sift
compound	gamble	phase	side effects	ultimately

1 When he bought this company, most people considered it a / an _____, but it has turned out to be very successful.

2 A / An _____ can be a useful way to explain how something works; for example, a camera works like an eye.

3 Many products, such as Coca-Cola, have a secret _____.

4 The _____ of the new drug include headaches and weight gain.

5 This television program has become _____ popular in a short period of time.

6 The team of scientists began to _____ through the data to find a pattern.

7 Chemists discovered that this _____ is found in many plants and can cause a painful reaction.

8 It is important to _____ your tasks so that you work on the most important ones first.

9 The next _____ of the project will begin next year.

10 _____, the decision is yours, and you will have to decide what is best.

Same or Different

The following pairs of sentences contain vocabulary from all the readings of this unit. Write *S* on the blank lines if the two sentences have the same meaning. Write *D* if the meanings are different.

_____ 1 Although the new treatment appears **promising**, there are still many **hurdles** to clear before we can be certain of its effectiveness.

There are still many **obstacles** that must be **overcome** before we can **ascertain** that this treatment is **therapeutic**, but all the signs are positive.

_____ 2 In order to **eliminate** the threat of communicable diseases **for good**, we will need to invest in more **infrastructure**.

Recent **breakthroughs** in the treatment of communicable diseases indicate that the **outlook** for the future is very good.

_____ 3 Government workers were very concerned when they heard about an **outbreak** of cholera in a **remote** village in the mountains.

Officials were **alarmed** to hear that several people had **contracted** cholera in an **isolated** village in the mountains.

_____ 4 We have the **capability** to **detect** an epidemic in its earliest stages and to **minimize** its impact.

We know how to **facilitate** rapid **diagnosis** during the **onset** of an epidemic as well as design appropriate **interventions**.

_____ 5 The **trajectory** of the disease is quite predictable. It begins with **fatigue**, and then the patient's condition gradually worsens.

The **course** of the disease is similar in most patients. They begin to feel very tired, and then their condition slowly **deteriorates**.

_____ 6 **Ironically**, the **side effects** of the **aggressive** treatment were worse than the disease.

The **preliminary** results suggested that the **toxic** effects of the **radical** treatment were **inevitable**.

_____ 7 Chemists are able to **synthesize compounds** in the laboratory that remain **stable** in extreme conditions.

Scientists have **derived** a **formula** that **is compliant** with all of the required regulations.

_____ 8 The government works **in conjunction with** pharmaceutical companies to **track** how well new drugs are working.

Drug companies work with the government to **monitor** the effectiveness of their new products.

Disciplinary Vocabulary

The following words are from all the readings of this unit. Research shows that they frequently appear in academic texts related to biomedical science. Complete the sentences with these words.

chronic (*adj*)	concentrate (*v*)	disorders (*n*)	phase (*n*)	synthesize (*v*)
clinical (*adj*)	derive (*v*)	isolated (*adj*)	promote (*v*)	therapeutic (*adj*)
compound (*n*)	detect (*v*)	outcome (*n*)	sequence (*v*)	toxic (*adj*)

1 Is it possible to _____ DNA yet?

2 Some mushrooms contain _____ chemicals that can make people very sick.

3 We are just in the planning _____ of this project; building will begin late next year.

4 Many people buy products that they hope will _____ weight loss, but most of these products are not effective.

5 Dogs have a very powerful sense of smell, so they can _____ even very small amounts of chemical substances.

6 The government has approved a new drug that will help people who suffer from _____ pain.

7 The hospital has a new building that is for patients with heart and lung _____ .

8 Water is a / an _____ made of oxygen and hydrogen.

9 Until we know the _____ of the election, it will be difficult to make a decision about what to do next.

10 Emergency services had difficulty reaching several _____ villages after the earthquake.

11 Many medical professionals believe that exercise has a _____ effect, especially for reducing stress.

12 Many scientists make discoveries that later have unexpected _____ applications.

13 In 2000, scientists were able to _____ the entire human genome for the first time.

14 The people who will _____ the greatest benefit from the new program are families with young children.

15 If you _____ your energy on solving the problem, you'll find a solution.

Critical Thinking

In Reading 5, you learned about the long and complex process that leads to the development of new drugs. You learned about the many places along this pipeline where the process may end in disappointment.

EXPLORING OPINIONS

Critical readers form their own opinions about important topics in a text.

A Based on what you have read in this unit and your own knowledge, read the two statements below.

1 Pharmaceutical companies spend vast sums of money in the pursuit of new and effective drugs. Successful drugs can be very profitable. Most of the time, however, the search stops at a dead end, often only after the company has made a significant investment. Some policy makers maintain it is important for these companies to be able to recover their investment and make a profit.

2 Other policy makers have argued that many drugs should be on the list of things that are considered *public goods*. Public goods are provided without profit to all members of a society, usually by the government, but also by other organizations. Clean air and water, education, and national security are often considered examples of public goods.

B In a small group, answer the questions that follow. Review the reading if necessary.

1 Are pharmaceutical companies entitled to recover their investment in all of their research by charging high prices on their successful products?

2 What if, for example, a patient with cancer, or a community that is experiencing an epidemic, such as AIDS or Ebola, cannot afford to pay these prices?

3 What do you think would happen if the prices of drugs were lowered to make them more affordable to more people?

4 In general, who should pay the price of drug discovery?

5 Which statement do you agree with, 1 or 2?

Research

You have discussed the costs of drug discovery and the need for public access to drugs with your classmates. Now find out what experts are saying on the subject of the cost of new drugs. Research this issue to gather information about the perspective of (1) the pharmaceutical industry and (2) patients or doctors who say the cost of new drugs is too high.

Writing

Write two paragraphs. In the first paragraph, explain the perspective of the pharmaceutical industry. In the second paragraph, present the viewpoint of opponents who say the high cost of new drugs is unnecessary and unfair.

Exercise 1

Writers connect ideas between sentences in many different ways. The second sentence may:

   a contain a correction to a view that is reported in the first sentence

   b describe a cause of what is reported in the first sentence

   c provide a contrast to what is described in the first sentence

   d add a detail or details to support the more general information in the first sentence

How does the second sentence in each pair of sentences below connect to the first sentence? Write *a, b, c,* or *d* on the line depending on whether it is a correction, a cause, a contrast, or a detail.

_____ 1 "23 and me" is a company which, until recently, provided customers with tools and information to explore the secrets locked in their DNA. Customers provide the company with a saliva sample, and based on that sample, "23 and me" provides the customers with information about their ancestry as well as a complete genetic profile.

_____ 2 Since it was founded in 2006, the company had consistently argued that results of the DNA tests provide general information, a service that is not regulated by the government. Given that the information the company provides has clear health and medical implications, this claim seems unfounded at best.

_____ 3 In 2012, the company reversed itself, claiming that they provided a medical service that was worthy of patent protection. Undoubtedly, part of their motivation for this move was the possibility of the protection of their profits that a patent would confer.

_____ 4 In 2013, the government ordered "23 and me" to stop providing health information to customers based on their DNA profiles, so customers no longer have access to their "23 and me" medical files. However, the company is still permitted to provide its customers with detailed information on their ancestry, including what parts of the world their ancestors might come from and where their distant relatives might be found.

_____ 5 Although the company denies it, some reporters and industry experts maintain that the company's long-term goal is to amass a huge – and in all likelihood, very profitable – database of DNA profiles. The company could use the information in this database to sell customers health and medical products based on their DNA profiles.

Exercise 2

Make a clear paragraph by putting sentences A, B, and C into the best order after the numbered sentence. Write the letters in the correct order on the blank lines.

1 In the race to sequence the first human genome, the public and private sectors took different approaches. _____ _____ _____

| **A** These short sequences – between 100 and 1000 base pairs, could be then be reassembled as the complete sequence. | **B** In contrast, Craig Ventner, who headed the private venture, was convinced that sequencing short sections of the genome would be a faster and more effective method. | **C** Those in the private sector project, The Human Genome Project, wanted to methodically map every piece of the genome. |

2 Once the projects were complete and the race was over, the first individuals had an opportunity to have their genomes sequenced. _____ _____ _____

| **A** His genomic profile revealed that he was at risk for heart disease and had a higher than average chance of developing Alzheimer's later in life. | **B** One of the first in line for this opportunity was Craig Ventner. | **C** The profile also revealed that his body is able to process the caffeine in drinks like coffee and tea more quickly than most people. |

3 People decide to have their genomes sequenced for a variety of reasons. _____ _____ _____

| **A** Steve Jobs, the founder of Apple computer, suffered from pancreatic cancer, finally succumbing to the disease in 2011. | **B** This last-ditch effort was an attempt to guide his doctors in choosing a drug that could stop the spread of the disease that was ravaging his body. | **C** He had tried many different treatments, but before he died, he tried one final option – sequencing the genome of his cancer cells. |

4 Harvard Professor Henry Louis Gates had an entirely different agenda when he chose to have his genome sequenced. _____ _____ _____

| **A** The genomic profile was much more helpful, revealing that some of his ancestors lived in Africa, while others had descended from Irish royalty. | **B** He had always wondered who they were and where they came from, but written records had not been able tell him everything that he wanted to know. | **C** His motivation for deciding to do so was rooted in a search, not for medical answers, but for answers about his ancestors. |

5 Seong-Jin Kim was the first Korean to have his entire genome sequenced. _____ _____ _____

| **A** At the same time, he decided to have the genomes of other members of his family sequenced as well. | **B** He decided to include all of their genomes because he wanted to investigate a possible genetic component of gastric cancer in Korean families. | **C** He published the results of his investigations in hopes of convincing more Korean families to follow his example. |

3

BUSINESS

SKILLS AND STRATEGIES

- Making Inferences
- Identifying Language Chunks
- Summarizing

Making Inferences

Good writers do not always make their points explicitly; instead, they often convey facts and ideas indirectly. These facts and ideas are implied, requiring readers to make inferences, that is, to draw conclusions based on a combination of the information that the writer does provide, their own knowledge, and logic. You make inferences in daily life hundreds of times a day in order to make sense of the world. If you see a crying child next to a bicycle, and his knee is bleeding, you can infer that he fell down. You did not need to actually see him fall to understand what happened. Readers often need to make inferences like this to identify a writer's purpose, ideas, or point of view. Learning to make inferences will help you understand, analyze, and evaluate academic readings.

Examples & Explanations

①*Crowdsourcing* (derived from a combination of *crowd* and *outsourcing*) is a relatively new buzzword. ②According to the Cambridge Business English Dictionary, the term, coined in 2006 by Jeff Howe, means "the act of giving tasks to a large group of people or to the general public, for example, by asking for help on the Internet, rather than having tasks done within a company by employees." ③In the past, a company would often outsource less complicated projects, that is, assign them to smaller companies, for financial reasons.

The writer begins by explaining the origin and meaning of the term *crowdsourcing.* Then she provides some background to this topic. After you read sentence 3, ask yourself what you can infer based on just this sentence, especially the phrase *for financial reasons.* You can logically infer that: (i) it is cheaper to pay outside employees of smaller businesses than company employees, and (ii) the company does not think the smaller businesses can handle more complex tasks, so these are performed by company employees.

Author

* What is the authors
Purpose?
2. Persuade / Convince?
3. Entertain- laugh, provoke emotions.
4. Inform- Teach?

2. Does the author seem biased / unbiased?

For or Against or Neutral?

④Today, however, crowdsourcing has become a powerful and effective way for organizations to access a large and flexible virtual workforce while saving time and money at the same time.

⑤It also has the potential to inspire innovation because it encourages a wide range of people to contribute to a project, thereby eliciting exciting new ideas or improving upon existing practices.

Sometimes you can make inferences on just one or two key words. In sentence 4, the word *virtual* can help you infer that crowdsourcing typically takes place online. The sentence also contains the word *however,* which signals a contrast with past practice, as well as positive evaluations about crowdsourcing, such as *effective*, *flexible*, and *saving time and money*. What is the writer's purpose in including this information? Although she does not state directly that crowdsourcing has become a better alternative to previous practices, the writer does state that crowdsourcing saves money **and also** has other advantages. By connecting these two pieces of information in the text, you can infer that crowdsourcing may be a better option than giving jobs to a smaller company.

Often, you can infer a writer's point of view. Sentence 5 contains positive evaluative language, such as *inspire innovation* and *exciting new ideas*. These expressions should lead you to infer that the writer has a generally positive view of crowdsourcing.

However, do not infer beyond the evidence in the text. For example, you could not infer from the information in the paragraph that Jeff Howe is a friend of the writer.

Strategies

Use these strategies to help you make inferences:

- As you read, ask yourself why the writer has included this information. Can you infer something that is not stated in the text?
- Connect two or more pieces of information in the text to make an inference.
- Use logic and your own knowledge of the world to make inferences about the writer's intended meaning.
- Don't make assumptions. Be sure not to take your inferences too far beyond the information in the text.
- Look for positive or negative evaluative language to infer the writer's point of view.

Skill Practice 1

Read the following paragraph. As you read, think about the writer's intended meaning and point of view. Then read the sentences that follow the paragraph and choose the best inference.

One of the best known examples of crowdsourcing is the "Wiki," which is derived from a Hawaiian word for "quick" and is a web application that allows writers to compose a collaborative text. The most popular wiki is, of course, the Internet encyclopedia, *Wikipedia*. Founded in 2001, Wikipedia is now the sixth most-visited website in the world and supports roughly 264 languages. The main concept behind Wikipedia is sharing the knowledge of "the crowd." It enables people to enter, edit, or delete information on a simple, shared webpage. The goal of the site is to allow free, worldwide access to massive amounts of data and information. Contributors never receive compensation regardless of how much they write or how popular their articles become; instead, their reward is a sense of pride in knowing that they have contributed to global knowledge. Doubts about the accuracy of the information in Wikipedia have largely been dismissed by a series of studies demonstrating that the level of accuracy in the articles is similar to that of print encyclopedias or even academic journals.

1 One of the best known examples of crowdsourcing is the "Wiki," which is derived from a Hawaiian word for "quick". . . The most popular wiki is, of course, the Internet encyclopedia, *Wikipedia*.
   a The writer thinks that Wikipedia is the best wiki.
   b The writer believes that Wikipedia had its origins in Hawaii.
   c The writer assumes that most readers are familiar with Wikipedia.

2 The goal of the site is to allow free, worldwide access to massive amounts of data and information. Contributors never receive compensation regardless of how much they write or how popular their articles become.
   a Wikipedia is not a for-profit business.
   b Wikipedia writers do not work full time.
   c Most Wikipedia writers only write one or two articles.

3 Doubts about the accuracy of the information in Wikipedia have largely been dismissed by a series of studies demonstrating that the level of accuracy in the articles is similar to that of print encyclopedias or even academic journals.
   a Wikipedia articles are accurate because authors of academic journals are contributors.
   b Some readers have been skeptical about the accuracy of Wikipedia articles.
   c The level of accuracy in Wikipedia articles has increased.

Skill Practice 2

Read the following paragraphs and the inferences that follow. For each inference, underline the information in the paragraph on which it is based.

1   Nokia, the Finnish company long known for its innovative electronic devices, has launched "IdeasProject," which the company defines as "a global community devoted to open innovation." By enlisting active participants from more than 210 nations, Nokia is striving to refine and redefine its products by inviting consumers to collaborate with them. Unlike many companies that implement crowdsourcing projects, Nokia provides participants in IdeasProject ventures with clear, direct benefits. This kind of project can attract the attention of "tech-savvy" workers who may provide some of the most valuable ideas. For example, with the "HERE" maps project, a digital cartography crowdsourcing venture with more than 1,000 participants worldwide, Nokia wisely focused on today's generation of digital natives from 12 universities across the U.S. and Europe. For this project the company is relying on the idea that locals know their communities best. Both Nokia and the community will benefit from improved maps that result from this project.

   a Nokia's decision to launch a crowdsourcing project that would benefit its participants was unusual.
   b Few of the participants in the IdeasProject are old.

2   Crowdsourcing has moved beyond the business and technology sectors into all corners of knowledge production, even the production of news. In crowdsourced journalism, the people who have long been the consumers of news are suddenly in the driver's seat: blogging, posting videos, and contributing content to traditional news outlets. Crowdsourcing has been especially important in investigative news reporting because the public often has access to information that reporters do not. Professional journalists have begun to appeal to the public to contribute what they know to news stories. One major factor in the rise of these "citizen journalists" is the increase in the availability and the quality of the video cameras on mobile phones. People who are involved in newsworthy events can take videos and upload them before reporters even arrive on the scene. They can also provide concrete evidence of events that may

be denied by politicians, the police, or other authorities. The role of crowdsourcing and citizen journalists is likely to increase as more and more people have access to this technology.

a Citizen journalists' contributions are particularly important to "breaking" news stories, that is, those that are happening right now.
b Sometimes political leaders or other authorities lie about events.

Skill Practice 3

Read the paragraph and then make inferences to answer the questions that follow.

Paul Lewis, a reporter for the London-based newspaper *The Guardian*, has been one of the pioneers of crowdsourcing in journalism. Perhaps the most well-known example of his work occurred in 2009 during a large protest demonstration in London. A man named Ian Tomlinson was walking through the crowd of demonstrators on his way home from work, but he never arrived at home. Tragically, he was found dead on the ground. The police said he had a heart attack and hit his head when he fell. After examining Tomlinson's body, the medical examiner confirmed this as the cause of death. Lewis, who had covered the demonstration for *The Guardian*, decided to investigate. He sent out a request on Twitter for witnesses, information, photographs, and video footage, and dozens of people responded. He quickly found twenty reliable witnesses who were at the demonstration; some of them had taken photographs of the event, enabling Lewis to put together many details of what had happened. After six days, the crucial evidence arrived: a video recording of the demonstration taken by an American who had been on a business trip to London. He sent it to Lewis as soon as he saw the reporter's tweets. The video showed a policeman pushing Mr. Tomlinson, who then fell to the ground.

1 What can you infer about Paul Lewis' opinion of Mr. Tomlinson's death?

_____

_____

2 What can you infer about the police and medical examiner?

_____

_____

3 Why does the author call the videotape "the crucial evidence?"

_____

_____

Connecting to the Topic

Discuss the following questions with a partner.

1 Have you ever participated in or attended an event that was part of a "crowd" like a parade, a protest, or a community fundraiser?

2 Why do you think some people would be motivated to participate in a large group activity?

3 What are some other types of events that can be better accomplished by a group?

4 What are some possible benefits for a company of having tasks done by large groups of employees instead of one or two individuals?

Previewing and Predicting

You will understand a reading more easily if you can get an idea of its organization and content before you start reading. A quick way to do this is to read the first sentence or two in each paragraph. This can help you predict what the reading will be about.

A Read the first two sentences of each paragraph in Reading 1. Then choose the question below that you expect that paragraph to answer. Write the number of the paragraph next to that question. The first one has been done for you.

PARAGRAPH	TOPIC
6	What is an open source platform and why is it important?
	What is crowdfunding?
	Does crowdfunding have a successful record?
	How does the Internet facilitate crowdsourcing?
	What is one way more people can collaborate on a project for less money?
	How many factors play an important role in whether a crowdsourcing project will work or not?

B Compare your answers with a partner's.

While You Read

As you read, stop at the end of each sentence that contains words in **bold**. Then follow the instructions in the box in the margin.

◀) Crowdsourcing and Crowdfunding

I. A New Trend Begins

1   Two of the biggest buzzwords of the twenty-first-century business world contain the word *crowd: crowdsourcing* and *crowdfunding*. What is the common factor? There is a strong reliance on the knowledge and/or actions of a crowd to achieve a particular goal. In the same way that a brain hub allows scientists and inventors to thrive as a large unit, the "two heads are better than one" principle is the force behind the concept of crowdsourcing. Crowdsourcing efforts are complex and can be difficult to manage; however, at their best, they are an effective way of getting tasks completed quickly and **inexpensively**.

WHILE YOU READ 1

Highlight words or phrases in this paragraph that help you infer that the writer has a positive point of view of crowdsourcing.

2   It has never been easier to solicit a large group of individuals to do a job, thanks to the Internet. Jobs can be "microtasked" to willing workers in an online community – that is, the work can be broken up into small tasks, and those responsibilities can then be distributed, with payment, among the group of freelance[1] **workers**. Repetitive jobs are particularly good candidates for low-cost crowdsourcing. For example, to convert newspapers on microfilm[2] to digital images with low but effective resolution, the conversion rate is about 210 pages per hour, depending on the equipment used. At this rate, two freelance workers can each convert 1,000 pages a day for a company that needs to have 10,000 pages scanned, accomplishing this high-volume work in a short period of time. For other types of projects, such as tagging or putting captions on photographs, a company could hire 500 people to each write one caption or tag one photograph. Thus, with the power of the Internet, a task that would previously have taken a week or longer might be completed in a day or less.

WHILE YOU READ 2

Look back at this sentence. Highlight the definition of *microtasked*.

3   Jeff Howe coined the phrase "crowdsourcing" in his article "The Rise of Crowdsourcing" in *Wired* magazine. In this 2006 article, he provided an analysis of innovative corporate approaches to meeting **demand** with fewer resources. One of the cases Howe examined was the transformation by Larry Huston of his research and development team at Procter & Gamble[3]. Huston's innovative methods helped him not only meet the goals of the company's research and development department, but do so more productively within the projected budget. From 2000 to 2006, Huston engaged

WHILE YOU READ 3

Which definition of *demand* matches the meaning in this sentence?
(a) A very forceful request
(b) A need

---

[1] *freelance:* working independently, usually for various organizations rather than as an employee of a particular one

[2] *microfilm:* a roll of film that contains photographed information (newspapers, texts, etc.) in a reduced size and must be viewed using a special machine

[3] *Procter & Gamble:* a multinational consumer goods corporation that manufactures popular brands of beverages, foods, cleaning supplies, and personal hygiene products

1.5 million researchers to work and network outside of the confines of the corporate headquarters. By using this pool of virtual workers both to complete simple tasks and solve complex problems, the company was able to generate and complete many important initiatives. This new paradigm has enabled many companies to cut costs on outsourcing at the same time that they increase productivity.

Jeff Howe

II. Ensuring the Success of Crowdsourcing

4   There are two central ideas behind crowdsourcing: first, that the collective knowledge of a group may be greater than the knowledge of a single highly trained employee, and second, that any task normally performed by that one highly trained person can be outsourced to a group, many of whom can do adequate work at a much lower cost to the outsourcer. The Internet has played a pivotal role in the success of outsourcing, as companies broadcast crowdsourcing jobs to thousands of potential freelancers, not just locally but around the world, leveraging the skills of ten for the price of one.

5   As Jeff Howe began to study this approach, he identified four key factors in the success of a crowdsourcing project. The first was that although workers do not have to be professionals in a particular field, they at least have to be creative, enthusiastic, and experienced hobbyists[4]. In addition, Howe pointed to motivation as a key factor in a project's implementation. He realized that if the participants are committed to the project's goal because of their interests, it fuels their motivation, which in turn promotes the quality of their work. In the case of FamilySearch.org, a nonprofit genealogy[5] site, family history enthusiasts all over the world volunteered for large scanning, indexing, and transcribing projects simply because they were interested in and committed to the project. The result is that millions of records are now available to both amateur and professional genealogists worldwide. On July 20, 2014, a total of 66,511 contributors input 5.7 million records in a 24-hour period. Not only can motivated participants in projects like this accomplish massive tasks, they can also provide content that may not otherwise be available. Ancestry.com, the largest for-profit genealogy company in the world, has solicited countless numbers of volunteers to contribute their memories and documents to its World Archives Projects. These activities are particularly important for the non-profit sector. Finally, motivated participants care about the quality of

---

[4] *hobbyist:* a person who does something as a hobby
[5] *genealogy:* the study of the history of the past and present members of a family

their projects. Crowdsourcing such projects can often improve their accuracy by providing correction and verification of the **data**.

WHILE YOU READ ④

Which can you infer from this sentence?
(a) Freelance workers are more accurate than ordinary employees.
(b) A large number of people are more likely to catch mistakes than a few employees.

6   A third factor in the success of crowdsourcing is the use of an open-source platform. An open source means that it is freely available to anyone. If the mechanism for completing the production of the product is open source, production costs are generally lower, and it may also allow more individuals to participate. For example, the open-source platform known as Google SketchUp can be used to render 3D technical drawings and is a reasonable substitute for its commercial counterpart **AutoCad 3D**. Lastly, Howe found that employing groups of people with a wide variety of ideas and skills could deliver better quality results. As Howe puts it, "The most efficient networks are those that link to the broadest range of information, knowledge, and experience." Crowdsourcing has been a successful tool for nonprofit organizations, entrepreneurs, and start-up enterprises to develop content, solve problems, and complete large, and especially repetitive tasks.

WHILE YOU READ ⑤

Look back at this sentence. Based on this sentence you can infer (a) AutoCad 3D is expensive, or (b) AutoCad 3D is widely available.

III. Crowdfunding

7   In the same way that crowdsourcing can complete tasks quickly by distributing the tasks to a group, *crowdfunding* can help small businesses or individuals procure funds for specific **projects**. Crowdfunding is a type of crowdsourcing and has become a way for small start-ups or projects to acquire the capital that they need. The concept is simple: solicit financial support from a large group of people in the hope that each will contribute at least a small amount. The results can be astounding, with some companies having raised millions of dollars in online campaigns. A report by the research firm *Massolution* showed that money raised on global crowdfunding platforms grew from $2.7 billion in 2012 to $16.2 billion in 2014.

WHILE YOU READ ⑥

What evidence does the author provide to support this claim? Underline it.

8   Crowdfunding can be divided into two basic models – the first is a donation-based model whereby donors contribute to a particular project in return for certain benefits, in the form of an actual product or other type of reward, such as free tickets to an event that they helped support or a signed copy of a novel they helped publish. Crowdfunding experts believe that this model is effective because the benefits make donors feel appreciated. Online crowdfunding platforms like Kickstarter, Indiegogo, AngelList, or Crowdrise offer a way for businesses, artists, nonprofits or charities, and other causes to generate financial support, but there are costs associated with this approach. Most crowdfunding platforms charge a fee based on the amount they receive during the campaign. In addition, companies that raise money by using a crowdfunding platform have to consider the costs of advertising, publicity, and, of course, taxes, all of which can substantially reduce the total amount of funds received.

9   The second type of crowdfunding is *investment crowdfunding*. Using this model, entrepreneurs or businesses in need of capital offer stakes or sell shares in their ventures online. Investors then become stakeholders or shareholders, and instead of getting a gift, they may receive a financial return on their investment if the enterprise is successful. However, a return is not **guaranteed**.

10   Although the results of crowdfunding have been largely positive, its performance has not been uniform. Entertainment-based projects like video games and movies have tended to prosper while more practical projects have sometimes floundered. For example, crowdfunded 3D printers have not entered the market as quickly as advocates had hoped. At one point, there were 67 crowdfunded printers online with financial supporters contributing close to $7.2 million in support. Analysts showed that out of that number who had used Kickstarter or Indiegogo, only 32 percent of the successfully funded printer projects met their shipping deadlines. Financial backers are often emotionally invested in their crowdfunded projects, and when these projects are not successful, they may be disappointed, or in some cases, angry. Experts say that it is crucial for entrepreneurs to communicate openly with their backers, and for backers to understand the risks that they are undertaking. If all parties understand their roles, crowdsourcing can be a positive experience for everyone.

WHILE YOU READ 7

Identify the text organization of paragraphs 8 and 9: (a) contrast, (b) cause and effect, or (c) classification. Highlight the signals of this text type.

Main Idea Check

Match the main ideas below to five of the paragraphs in Reading 1. Write the number of the paragraph on the blank line.

_8_ A Some crowdfunding sites offer benefits instead of financial compensation to donors.

_10_ B Some crowdfunded projects have been successful, but others have not.

_5_ C To be successful a crowdsourcing project needs people who are enthusiastic, creative, and committed.

_7_ D Crowdfunding and crowdsourcing are based on similar principles.

_3_ E Proctor and Gamble's R&D department offers a good example of crowdsourcing.

A Closer Look

Look back at Reading 1 to answer the following questions.

1 What does the writer suggest about microtasking?

   a In the past, corporations only used internal employees to do small tasks.
   b The Internet has made it easier to break down large tasks into small parts.
   c When large corporations want to save money, they use only freelance staff.
   d Very few companies could do small jobs before the 1990s.

2 What does the writer imply about public participation in crowdsourcing projects?

   a Most people enjoy working in crowdsourcing projects without pay.
   b When companies do not offer payment, people are unlikely to join online projects.
   c If the crowdsourcing project is interesting, people are more willing to work without pay.
   d People will not participate in projects unless they feel good about their work.

3 What factors are important to the success of a crowdsourcing project? Choose all that apply.

   a The participants must be interested in the project.
   b The platform used must be open source.
   c The goal of the project must align with the interests of the workers.
   d The costs of the project must be cut.

4 Why is the popularity of crowdfunding sites on the rise?

   a Many large companies do not have adequate funding for projects.
   b Crowdfunding is a good way for corporations to pay their employees.
   c Crowdfunding sites are always successful.
   d Crowdfunding is a fast, cheap way for new businesses to raise money.

5 The primary goal of crowdfunding is to control cost. **True or False?**

6 What can happen to businesses that participate in *investment crowdfunding*? Choose all that apply.

  a They may get non-monetary rewards for their participation.
  b They may see financial returns on their investments.
  c They may become participants in the new company.
  d They may lose their investment.

7 What does the writer imply about crowdfunded 3D printer projects?

  a Investors will not have to wait long before they see positive results.
  b Financial backers of 3D printers may have been angry.
  c Crowdfunding often leads to shipping problems.
  d 3D printer manufacturers will continue to have shipping problems.

Skill Review

In Skills and Strategies 7, you learned that academic writers do not always state claims directly. They can also make implications.

A Look over Reading 1 again. Read each of the statements below and decide if it is a directly stated claim (*D*) or an implication (*I*).

STATEMENT	DIRECT OR IMPLIED?
Using a large number of people for a project does not always have a positive result. (Par.1)	
Scans do not have to be high quality in order to be readable. (Par.2)	
Crowdsourcing has benefited genealogists around the world. (Par.5)	
Small businesses and entrepreneurs may acquire start-up funds through crowdfunding. (Par.7)	
The value of the benefits that backers receive in the donation-based model is not equal to the funds they provide. (Par.8)	
People who use crowdfunding sites to raise money pay fees on the total amount received. (Par.8)	
Projects like renovating a house or building may not be as successful with crowdfunding as producing a video game or movie. (Par.10)	

B Compare your answers with a partner's.

Definitions

Find the words in Reading 1 that are similar to the definitions below.

1 the condition of depending on someone or something (*n*) Par. 1 *Reliance, reliant.*
2 to ask for something in a persuasive way (*v*) Par. 2 *Solicit, solicitation.*
3 to change the character or appearance of something (*v*) Par. 2 *Convert*
4 the smallest degree of detail visible in an image (*n*) Par. 2 *Resolution*
5 new attempts to achieve a goal or solve a problem (*n pl*) Par. 3 *Initiative*
6 important because other things depend on it (*adj*) Par. 4 *Pivotal, pivot*
7 to spread or use resources in a way to gain advantage (*v*) Par. 4 *leverage*
8 businesspeople who take risks and start something new (*n pl*) Par. 6 *Entrepreneur.*
9 to obtain something with great effort (*v*) Par. 7 *Procure.*
10 to struggle awkwardly (*v*) Par. 10 *Flounder.*

Synonyms

Complete the sentences with words from Reading 1 in the box below. These words replace the words or phrases in parentheses, which are similar in meaning.

advocate	confines	paradigm	sector	transcribe
capital	enterprises	productivity	thrived	venture

1 The toy and game industry targets a market (division) __Sector__ consisting of both adults and children.
2 With crowdfunding, a start-up company can raise (investment money) __Capital__ quickly and effectively.
3 At first, the start-up company (prospered) __thrived__ but then began to lose money.
4 The increase in (output) __Productivity__ may be connected to outsourcing.
5 Steve Jobs was a / an (supporter) __advocate__ of user-friendly computers.
6 Crowdfunding may seem like a risky (undertaking) __venture__, but it can be a successful way to raise investment funds.
7 Volunteers participated in projects that required them to (change speech to text) __transcribe__ official records.
8 GM created a new business (model) __Paradigm__, which other companies quickly followed.
9 The impact of crowdsourcing on various new (businesses) __enterprises__ is very positive.
10 The directors of many start-up companies prefer to work outside of the (limits) __confines__ of traditional business models.

Critical Thinking

Reading 1 contains a lot of information on crowdsourcing and crowdfunding. In addition to stating claims and facts, the writer also makes suggestions and implies ideas and opinions about the topics.

ANALYZING INFORMATION

Critical thinking involves thinking carefully about important topics that the writer has not completely explained.

Discuss the following questions with a partner.

1 In which sectors of the business world, other than nonprofit or IT, could companies use crowdsourcing to their benefit?

2 What do you think are some major drawbacks to crowdfunding?

3 What do you think might be the most challenging aspects of crowdsourced projects? Why?

4 What qualities might make a successful crowdfunded project?

Research

Choose a project mentioned in Reading 1, or one of your choice, that has been crowdsourced or crowdfunded. Find answers to the questions below.

- What can you infer about the success or failure of the project?
- Do you believe that the project has potential for future growth?
- Which genres do you think are the most successful? (IT, genealogy, newspapers/ media, art/design, gaming/entertainment, etc.)

Writing

Write a brief analysis of the project that you have researched. What can you infer about the success or failure of the project? Do you believe this project will continue in the near future or be terminated due to change in trends or popularity?

Connecting to the Topic

Discuss the following questions with a partner.

1 How do you think most people feel when jobs are transferred overseas?
2 What types of companies do you think are the most likely to hire workers in other countries?
3 Do you think companies can save money by moving jobs overseas? Why?
4 What problems might occur from hiring employees in other countries?

Previewing and Predicting

Reading the title and subheadings can help you predict what a reading will be about.

A In Reading 1 you were introduced to the term *outsourcing*. Read the title of Reading 2. What do you think *Outsourcing: Managing Labor Needs* will mainly be about?

B Read the section headings (*I–III*) and look at Figure 3.3. Then read the questions below. Write the number of the section in which you are likely to find the answer to each question.

SECTION	QUESTION	
	What are businesses doing today to meet their labor needs?	
	In what year did one of the largest manufacturing companies begin to use outsourcing as a way to cut costs?	
	What types of jobs can be transferred overseas?	
	Where are most overseas jobs located?	
	Why did GM decide to stop outsourcing some jobs?	
	Are businesses still outsourcing?	

B Compare your answers with a partner's.

While You Read

As you read, stop at the end of each sentence that contains words in **bold**. Then follow the instructions in the box in the margin.

Outsourcing: Managing Labor Needs

I. Motivation and Impact

1   *Outsourcing* is prevalent in almost every business sector as a way for companies to delegate tasks to independent contractors and external suppliers – people who do not work for the company directly. They may outsource tasks to another company or crowdsource them to individuals. For a corporation, outsourcing can be a cost-effective strategy because it reduces overhead[1]. Cost savings are often the greatest if a task is outsourced to workers in other countries where labor costs are lower, a practice sometimes called *offshoring*. Corporations often outsource some of their support functions to overseas contractors, such as accounting, telecommunications, or information technology (IT). One frequent choice for offshoring is customer service, with many U.S.-based businesses establishing call centers overseas, particularly in India and the Philippines, where English skills tend to be high. Businesses may even outsource some of their core functions; manufacturers often outsource jobs like building computer components or assembling parts of a car to overseas **firms**.

2   There are valid economic reasons for outsourcing and offshoring. However, these practices are not just about reducing overhead costs; they can also improve a company's efficiency. The increasingly global nature of work has made outsourcing easier by giving companies access to an enormous pool of independent contractors and freelancers all over the world. Employing these independent contractors instead of full-time workers means not having to pay full-time benefits or office costs. Companies can also take advantage of the flexibility of this type of workforce, hiring people only when they are needed for specific tasks. Yet equally important is the opportunity to secure talented, skilled individuals who can complete tasks quickly, efficiently, and at a high level of **quality**.

3   For these and other reasons, outsourcing has increased steadily since the 1980s. Statistics show that more than 2.6 million jobs had been outsourced from the U.S. as of 2013, mostly to India and China. (See Figure 3.1.) Among U.S-based companies, 43 percent of all IT jobs were outsourced by 2013, while 12 percent of call centers (customer service and telecommunication) were located in countries quite far from the customers they serve. In addition, 38 percent of all research and development tasks and 26 percent of product distribution jobs were performed by workers outside of North America, and 53 percent of all manufacturing jobs had moved offshore. The United States has experienced particularly high levels

WHILE YOU READ 1
Highlight the main idea of paragraph 1.

WHILE YOU READ 2
Look back at paragraph 2. Highlight transition words that introduce contrasting claims.

---

[1] *overhead:* the regular and necessary costs involved in running a business, such as rent, salaries, electricity, etc.

Figure 3.1 Percentage of U.S. Jobs Outsourced by Sector(2013)

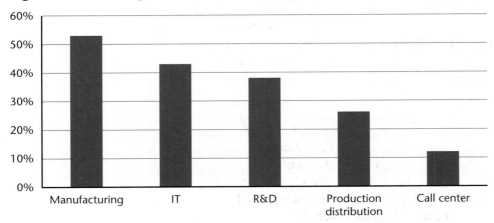

of outsourcing, but the practice is common in other developed countries as well.

4   It may have many benefits, but there is an undeniable downside to outsourcing. Outsourcing, and especially offshoring, provokes a negative response from the public because, although it means cost reductions for the corporation, it typically also means downsizing the domestic labor force. It has had a huge impact on U.S. cities that depended on manufacturing. A good example is Flint, Michigan, which was once a manufacturing hub, primarily serving the automotive industry. General Motors (GM) – a leading U.S. car manufacturing company – employed 30,000 people at one Flint plant alone, but after a steady loss of jobs to offshoring, the plant closed down for good in 2010. Around this time, the unemployment rate in the city peaked at 28 percent. Outsourcing and the resulting job losses at home can lead to a backlash against companies that pursue this strategy, damaging their public image. Before undertaking such a move, therefore, companies need to weigh the potential financial gains with the negative public perception it can **bring**.

5   This perception affects not just the workers who lose their jobs; it has an impact on consumers as well. They see products that are manufactured overseas as a threat to their jobs and the country's economic security. Perhaps that is why slogans[2] such as "buy national" have become more pervasive since the 1980s. According to a 2009 study, consumers who believed that they should only purchase merchandise produced in their home country shared a negative attitude toward outsourcing. Analysts agree that Americans, in particular, resist outsourcing efforts and feel protective of domestic jobs. American consumers may refuse to purchase products manufactured overseas and instead demonstrate their patriotism by "buying American." This attitude is a factor in policies of **protectionism** – laws and regulations that restrict business between countries, limit imports,

WHILE YOU READ 3

What can you infer from paragraph 4?
a) There was a negative reaction against GM.
b) GM stopped offshoring.

WHILE YOU READ 4

Use punctuation signals to find the definition of *protectionism*. Highlight the definition.

[2] *slogan:* a short phrase that is easy to remember and makes people notice something

and impose or increase tariffs[3] on merchandise manufactured in other countries. Some economists see such policies as a hindrance to overall economic growth; nevertheless, emotional attachments to domestic companies often remain strong. The fact that a company with a name like Texas Instruments, a leading producer of semiconductors[4], now outsources much of its manufacturing to Asia can be particularly hard for some Americans to accept.

II. A Case Study – General Motors

6   In the 1980s, General Motors closed ten American factories and moved its production to Mexico. However, this outsourcing strategy was not limited to its manufacturing divisions. By 1996, most of GM's technology work was being done by Electronic Data Systems (EDS), a GM subsidiary. Company leaders decided it made more financial sense to outsource its IT services by converting EDS into a separate business entity. EDS then became the company's supplier for all of its IT needs. From GM's perspective, this was a smart move because the company's leaders wanted to concentrate their efforts on the core business – the automotive industry. It was not cost-effective for GM to spend **countless** hours and millions of dollars on IT services; in fact, its IT costs were pushing the company into the red[5]. The primary benefit of outsourcing IT services was the speed of execution: by focusing on its core business, EDS, like GM, could get the job done more quickly and efficiently. The strategy allowed GM to reduce its IT budget by over $1 billion. As a global company, it was better for GM to take advantage of independent operating businesses like EDS, all carefully linked in a standardized process. Following this strategy, GM was able to streamline its infrastructure, optimize its operations, and cut costs.

7   Fifteen years later, however, GM began to reverse its outsourcing practices. As cars became more computerized, the company needed employees with different kinds of specialized skills. Specifically, the company needed to become more innovative in supporting the digitalization of the company's operations, especially in IT. Relying on old-technology mainframe computing, GM experienced manufacturing slow-downs in its operations all over the globe. GM's directors realized that they needed to develop a twenty-first-century IT infrastructure. So after more than a decade of outsourcing 90 percent of its IT services, GM began to build up an in-house IT staff. GM aimed to keep the costs low while increasing productivity by moving the operations of 23 data centers back to the United States. Always looking for greater productivity and efficiency, GM's goal was to have innovation centers, where tasks that once took 12 to 18 months would now take only three to six months. This new "in-sourcing," or "on-shoring," strategy reversed a pervasive trend in the automotive and IT industries.

WHILE YOU READ 5

Use context and your knowledge of word parts to guess the meaning of *countless*. Is it (a) an unknown number, or (b) a large number?

---

[3] *tariff:* government charges on goods entering or leaving a country
[4] *semiconductor:* a substance, such as silicon, that allows electricity to flow through it, used in making electronic devices
[5] *in the red:* operating at a loss, not making a profit

III. Recent Strategies

8   Since 2012, a few other firms have pursued a similar strategy. In the same way that GM was a role model for outsourcing, its move toward in-sourcing may once again be setting an example for global business practices. GM believes that bringing jobs back to a more consolidated hub will help them gain more value and efficiency from their employees and make their products more competitive. The Chief Information Officer asserts that although the company still employs more than 50,000 workers around the globe, it expects to bring nearly 10,000 jobs back to the United States over the next **decade**.

9   Another sector in which a reversal of the offshoring trend is evident is customer service. At one point, 30 percent of call centers for high-tech firms were located overseas, but in recent years that number has fallen by more than half. One reason for this trend relates to the nature of the calls themselves. In the past, when customers had simple requests, such as resetting a password, they needed to speak to a person. Today, many of these simple requests have been automated. This leaves the more complex questions and problems for the call centers. Resolving these kinds of problems requires excellent language and communication skills, which leads to the second reason that many call centers are returning to locations closer to home. Many callers experience communication difficulties when they contact overseas call centers, leaving them feeling frustrated and their problems often unresolved. For companies concerned about customer service, this is a problem; thus, after a decade of offshoring this part of their business, many companies have abandoned this **strategy**.

10   Alongside this in-sourcing trend, many entrepreneurs and businesses continue to outsource in order to access the highest qualified and most cost-effective labor, particularly in brain hubs like Los Angeles or New York. Even if a company decides not to look outside the country, there are plenty of domestic workers to whom they can outsource tasks, especially if they crowdsource them. Workers in brain hubs, and in urban areas in general, tend to earn higher salaries than those who live outside of cities. Crowdsourcing allows companies to tap into a large, but non-local workforce. This is an ideal solution for many companies – outsourcing within the country instead of offshoring helps maintain a skilled low-cost domestic workforce and, at the same time, satisfies those consumers who want to support the "buy national" trend.

11   In the end, experts predict that outsourcing will maintain a firm foothold in the corporate world, especially in the form of crowdsourcing. The growth and accessibility of independent contractors has permanently changed the face of the workforce and the way companies do business. The global outsourcing trend is likely to continue throughout the twenty-first century.

WHILE YOU READ 6
From this paragraph, you can infer that in-shoring has erased the effect of offshoring. (a) True (b) False

WHILE YOU READ 7
Underline the writer's claim in this paragraph. Highlight the support for the claim.

Main Idea Check

Match the main ideas below to five of the paragraphs in Reading 2. Write the number of the paragraph on the blank line.

___2___ A Outsourcing is beneficial to companies because it reduces costs and improves efficiency.

___6___ B General Motors saw positive results when it outsourced its information technology business.

___5___ C Negative perceptions of outsourcing affect consumer behavior and economic policies.

___7___ D General Motors has had to change its outsourcing policies and bring jobs back to the United States to increase productivity.

___1___ E Outsourcing occurs in many aspects of business.

A Closer Look

Look back at Reading 2 to answer the following questions.

1 The only reason for offshoring is to cut costs. **True or ~~False~~?**

2 How do some Americans react to the outsourcing of jobs and business? Choose all that apply.

~~a~~ They support higher taxes on imported goods.
~~b~~ They buy only products that were made in the United States.
c Americans refuse to purchase local products in other countries.
d They move overseas to find employment.

3 Based on Figure 3.3, what can be inferred about the American automotive industry or machine production jobs? Choose all that apply.

a Companies like GM have more than half of their staff at their headquarters.
b Though more than half of all manufacturers have outsourced their work, there are still roughly 1.2 million manufacturing workers located in the United States.
c There are not enough jobs for workers in the manufacturing industry in the United States.
d More jobs in manufacturing were outsourced than jobs in any other industry in the United States.

4 A majority of research and development tasks for American companies are offshored. **True or ~~False~~?**

5 What can be inferred about why GM transferred its car manufacturing to Mexico?

   a GM was trying to grow its technology business.

   b GM's headquarters wanted to keep car production separate from their other business.

   c GM was attempting to reduce costs.

   d GM wanted to make a move that would challenge other companies in the automobile industry.

6 Put each event into a period on the timeline that best represents the history of GM's outsourcing practices.

1980s ⟶ 1990s ⟶ 2000s ⟶ 2010s

B	D	C	A.

   a Some companies follow GM's lead and begin in-sourcing.

   b GM offshores most of the manufacturing of its cars.

   c GM consolidates most of its IT work in data centers in the United States.

   d GM's cars become more computerized.

7 Why have many companies stopped offshoring their customer service centers?

   a Many customer service requests are too complex for workers at overseas centers.

   b Overseas call centers did not save money for the companies that used them.

   c Labor costs in the countries where the centers are located have gone up.

   d Customers and call center employees sometimes have communication problems.

8 What does the writer imply about the relationship between crowdsourcing and outsourcing?

   a Crowdsourcing is more complicated to maintain than outsourcing.

   b A company that practices crowdsourcing or outsourcing will lose its value.

   c The practice of using independent contractors is likely to decrease.

   d Crowdsourcing may help maintain the outsourcing trend because it is efficient and cost-effective.

Skill Review

In Skills and Strategies 7, you learned that writers do not always state information directly. Sometimes a writer implies ideas or states facts from which the reader must make inferences.

A Review paragraphs 6–11 in Reading 2. Read the inference statements below based on information in these paragraphs. Then find a sentence from the paragraph in parentheses that supports the inference. The first one has been done for you.

1 **Inference:** Many Americans lost their jobs when GM moved its automotive production to Mexico. (Par.6)

   Evidence: *In the 1980s, General Motors (GM) closed 10 American factories and moved its production to Mexico.*

2 **Inference:** GM's IT infrastructure was leading in inefficiency. (Par. 7)
   Evidence: _____
   _____

3 **Inference:** The insourcing process at GM is gradual. (Par. 8)
   Evidence: _____
   _____

4 **Inference:** Some of the employees at overseas call centers have limited English skills. (Par. 9)
   Evidence: _____
   _____

5 **Inference:** Though some companies are now bringing outsourced jobs back to headquarters, outsourcing remains a widespread practice. (Par. 10)
   Evidence: _____
   _____

B Compare your answers with a partner's. Discuss how the evidence supports the inference.

Vocabulary Development

Definitions

Find the words in Reading 2 that are similar to the definitions below.

1 existing commonly or happening frequently (adj) Par. 1 *Prevelant*

2 to bring together the parts of something (v) Par. 1 *Assemble*

3 based on truth or reason (adj) Par. 2 *Valid*

4 to cause a particular feeling or reaction (v) Par. 4 *Provoke*

5 to reduce the number of employees as part of a larger change in a company (v) Par. 4 *downsize*

6 a strong, negative response (n) Par. 4 *backlash*

7 a situation without risk or danger (n) Par. 5 *Security*

8 a feeling of love for one's country (n) Par. 5 *Patriotism*

9 something that limits a person's or thing's growth or development (n) Par. 5 *hindrance*

10 a company that is owned by another company (n) Par. 6 *Subsidiary*

(11) central or most important (adj) Par. 6 *Core*

12 made the same as others of its type (adj) Par. 6 *Standardied*

13 to cause something to go in the other direction (v) Par. 7 *reverse*

14 to make something happen by using computers or machines (v) Par. 9 *automated*

(15) annoyed; disappointed and discouraged (adj) Par. 9 *frustrated*

Words in Context

Complete the sentences with words from Reading 2 in the box below.

Secure your position.

consolidated	entities	foothold	regulations	streamline
delegate	execution	merchandise	secure	unresolved

1 We need to ___*Secure*___ a contract before any work on the project can begin.

2 It is important for a new company to establish a strong ___*foothold*___ in the market before trying to expand its business.

3 ___*Merchandise*___ is usually less expensive if it is purchased close to where it is produced.

4 The Chief Executive Officer intends to ___*Streamline*___ the company's business operations.

5 There have already been numerous delays in the production schedule, and problems with the supplier remain ___*Unresolved*___

6 The business community often complains that there are too many government ___*regulations*___

7 The law requires that the company's divisions be taxed as separate _entities_.

8 Good managers do not try to control everything; they _delegate_ responsibility for different projects.

9 Careful planning ensured the successful _execution_ of the project.

10 The plan to move the sales and manufacturing operations to one _consolidated_ division will save the company millions of dollars in operating costs.

combine

Academic Word List

The following are Academic Word List words from Readings 1 and 2 of this unit. Use these words to complete the sentences. (For more on the Academic Word List, see page 299.)

advocates (n)	converted (v)	initiatives (n)	sector (n)	subsidiary (n)
assembled (v)	core (adj)	paradigm (n)	security (n)	valid (adj)

1 For many consumers, patriotism is a / an _core_ issue when they decide on purchases.

2 The corporation sold its _subsidiary_, which was a smaller electronics company, and made a good profit.

3 In the 1990s, outsourcing became the dominant _paradigm_ for managing labor demand.

4 Local politicians are usually strong _advocates_ of any program that promises jobs to their community.

5 In almost every business _sector_, examples of outsourcing can be found.

6 During times of economic uncertainty, many workers worry about the _security_ of their jobs.

7 The manager presented a / an _valid_ argument for why he needed to hire additional employees.

8 In the early days of computers, many hobbyists _assembled_ the machines themselves.

9 Most businesses _converted_ to the metric system decades ago.

10 The start-up company launched several new _initiatives_ to raise capital.

Critical Thinking

In Reading 1, you learned about the impact of
crowdsourcing on jobs in the twenty-first century.
Reading 2 discussed the effects of outsourcing on both
businesses and consumers. Think about the similarities and
differences between these two business practices.

> **ANALYZING INFORMATION**
>
> Critical thinking involves thinking carefully about important topics that the writer has not completely explained.

Discuss the following questions with a partner.

1 How does outsourcing benefit domestic or foreign
freelance employees?

2 What might be some downsides of a global manufacturing model – for example,
manufacturing car parts in one country, assembling vehicles in another, and then
marketing and selling them worldwide?

3 How beneficial do you think outsourcing or crowdsourcing can be for small start-up
companies? What types of problems do you think they might encounter?

Research

**Many of the world's largest companies, such as Toyota, the Gap, Nike, and
Samsung, offshore their manufacturing and/or assembly processes. Select one of
these or another large company that was not discussed in the reading. Find answers
to the following questions.**

- Where are its products or product components made? Why did the company choose
  to manufacture its products there?
- Where are its products assembled? Why did the company choose to assemble its
  products there?
- Has the company experienced any negative reactions to outsourcing?
- What are its latest labor trends? Is it expanding outsourcing, doing more insourcing,
  using crowdsourcing, etc.?

Writing

**Write a short case study on the company you researched. Follow the steps below to
write three paragraphs.**

- Give a brief history and background of the company.
- Present the findings from your research. Include information like how many
  employees work overseas and in which countries, what jobs are being transferred
  offshore, what problems the company has encountered, and if outsourcing has been
  a success or failure.
- Describe the company's experience with outsourcing and make predictions about
  its future.

Improving Your Reading Speed

Good readers read quickly and still understand most of what they read.

A Read the instructions and strategies for Improving Your Reading Speed in Appendix 3 on page 316.

B Choose one of the readings in this unit. Read it without stopping. Time how long it takes you to finish the text in minutes and seconds. Enter the time in the chart on page 318. Then calculate your reading speed in number of words per minute.

Identifying Language Chunks

Two or more words that frequently appear together as phrases are called *language chunks*. Not only are these combinations of words frequent, the words in them are also closely bound to one other. In other words, the words in a chunk occur together more frequently than would be expected by chance. For example, the phrase *a big man* is relatively frequent, but the words in the phrase are not closely bound to one other. In contrast, the phrase *a big deal* is frequent, but the words are tightly bound to one other. *A big deal* is a chunk; *a big man* is not. The word combinations in language chunks are both frequent and closely bound to one another. Readers who recognize these combinations of words can better understand academic texts and read more quickly. Knowledge of language chunks is also very useful for writing.

Examples & Explanations

Executives at multinational corporations speak in a common language – the language of business. It has specialized terms like **operating expenses** and **best practices.**

Some of the most frequent chunks are in the form adjective + noun. These words frequently occur together, but they are not completely fixed. You could use other word combinations, for example, *operating costs* or *superior practices.*

Sharing knowledge of specialized vocabulary makes it easy for business people to communicate efficiently. Is there anything wrong with having this form of communication? One issue is that **most of the time,** ordinary people do not understand what business people are discussing. So a good **rule of thumb** is to use specialized vocabulary only when you are talking to someone you are sure will understand.

Many chunks are noun phrases with the pattern noun + *of (the)* + noun. In some cases, such as *most of the time*, it is easy to understand what these expressions mean. In other cases, such as *rule of thumb*, the meaning (=an approximation based on experience) is harder to figure out. The second type is usually fixed, so you cannot substitute other words.

To **make an impression** – a good one – during a business presentation, it is better to avoid technical terms and overused expressions. If you use a lot of technical language, you **take a risk** that your audience will get lost.

Verbs also often appear in chunks. Verbs such as *be, do, have, make,* or *take* often form chunks with nouns, such as *make room* or *do business*. Sometimes an adjective comes before the noun, as with *take a serious risk.*

Business terms vary somewhat depending on the type of business. In general, however, most business people use **more or less** the same phrases. **Now and then**, someone will invent a new phrase, like **bait and switch** – which means to advertise one thing but then sell something different – and soon everyone is using it.

People in business are **under pressure** to stay **ahead of the curve** of technology. Using popular phrases and expressions can help them maintain the image that they are **on the cutting edge** of their business. **In the end**, however, it is their performance, not their words that is important.

Two nouns, verbs, adjectives, or adverbs linked together by *and* or *or* are called "binomials." In this paragraph you can find the binomials *more or less* and *now and then*. The order of the words in a binomial is fixed and cannot be reversed.

Some chunks appear as prepositional phrases, for example, *under pressure* and *in the end*. Some are so frequent that they have acquired special meanings. *Ahead of the curve* and *on the cutting edge* are common chunks found in business and technology texts. They are used to refer to a person or company that is innovative or the first to do something.

Language Chunks

Here is a list of some common language chunks. Typical business chunks are marked with an asterisk (*).

ADJECTIVE + NOUN	NOUN + NOUN	BINOMIALS
bottom line*	business plan*	black and white
cutting edge*	call center*	brick and mortar*
dominant role	cash flow*	by and large
global market*	customer service*	here and there
high level (of)	interest rate*	more or less
limited capacity	language barrier	now and then
native speaker	parent company*	pros and cons
wide range (of)		trial and error

NOUN PHRASES	VERB PHRASES	PREPOSITIONAL PHRASES
comfort of home	to bridge the gap	ahead of the curve*
degree of success	to conduct business*	behind the scenes
point of sale*	to make a deal*	in the cloud
rule of thumb	to make a move	on the horizon
window of opportunity	to solve a problem	on the rise
	to take a pay cut*	on the same page
	to take a risk	out of pocket*

Strategies

These strategies will help you notice and learn language chunks:

- Look for patterns as you read. When you see a group of words more than once, try to learn these words together.
- When you learn a new noun (*range, barrier*), notice adjectives or verbs that go with it (*wide/narrow range; create/overcome a barrier*).
- When you see the verb *be, do, have, make,* or *take,* pay attention to the noun that follows as these combinations often form verb phrase chunks.
- Notice chunks that follow the patterns "noun + noun" or "noun + *of (the)* + noun."
- If you cannot figure out the meaning of a phrase from the context, look up one of the words in a learner dictionary. If the phrase is a common chunk, these dictionaries often contain example sentences that may include it.

Skill Practice 1

Read the following paragraph. Then find and highlight five examples of noun + noun chunks.

Outsourcing business to different countries presents its own set of challenges. When various important divisions of a company are spread all over the globe, problems with communication can arise. One of the main sources of miscommunication that occurs is obvious: language. Language barriers can have an impact on many facets of business operations: customer service, communication (email or phone), and feedback between employees and supervisors. On top of that, if the leaders of the parent company use only English, business phrases that are not common in the employee's native language may be difficult to interpret. Some phrases are not translatable, or are culturally specific – like the many idioms used in business that are associated with American sports. If a task is a "slam dunk," it means you are certain to succeed in it. However, those two words might not translate easily for someone whose native language is not English and who is not a sports fan. Although outsourcing has many advantages, there are, indeed, situations in which language issues among employees can lead to problems.

Skill Practice 2

Read the following paragraph. Then highlight the following language chunks: adjective + noun (2); noun + noun (2); noun phrase (1); verb phrase (2); binomial (3); prepositional phrase (1).

Businesses are no longer limited to just brick-and-mortar spaces. This means that any business that hopes to make a profit must look beyond its physical location to find ways to expand its business. An online store allows a company to buy and sell anywhere in the world. Amazon.com, for example, has an online presence that manages supply and demand by offering a wide range of consumer products. It is especially attractive for customers who prefer to shop from the comfort of home. Shoppers can take their time and buy whatever they want, whenever they want. Amazon already plays a dominant role in commerce in the United States and its business operations are on the rise overseas.

Skill Practice 3

Complete the passages with the language chunks in the box below.

at your best	cash flow	making a fortune	spend the night	tossing and turning
business plan	draw attention	sooner or later	take a deep breath	waste time

Breaking into the business world is no easy task. Business school graduates dream of _____ but first they have to land a job. The first step in the job search
          a
process is the interview, an event that can create a great deal of anxiety among new graduates. The best way to succeed in an interview is to be well prepared but relaxed. The night before, try to get seven to eight hours of sleep. If you _____
                                                                  b
_____ , you will not be _____ during your interview. In the
          c   d
morning, before you start your interview, _____ and relax. During the
                                                        e
interview, be sure to _____ to your accomplishments, but don't
                              f
_____ on irrelevant details. You may get questions you don't expect, such
          g
as how to evaluate a _____ or how to improve _____. If you
                              h   i
don't get a job after the first interview, be patient. _____ , you will find a
                                                                        j
job that matches your skills and your aspirations.

Connecting to the Topic

Discuss the following questions with a partner.

1 Are North American and British English the same? What differences are there? Can there be language barriers among people who speak the same language?

2 What language do most businesspeople use when they travel internationally?

3 What kinds of problems do you think could arise if people in international business do not speak the same language?

4 What can multinational companies do to improve communication problems around the globe?

Previewing and Predicting

> Reading the title, section headings, and first sentence of each paragraph is a quick way to predict what a reading will be about.

A **Read the first sentences of paragraphs 2–7 in Reading 3 and think about the title and section headings. Then read the following topics. Write the number of the paragraph where you think each topic will be discussed.**

PARAGRAPH	TOPIC
	How English became the major language used for international communication
	Multilingualism in the international business community
	An explanation of the term "Global English"
	Problems with a simplified invented language
	The use of English in multinational corporations
	The status of English in the 20th and 21st centuries

B **Compare your answers with a partner's.**

While You Read

As you read, stop at the end of each sentence that contains words in **bold**. Then follow the instructions in the box in the margin.

The Language of Twenty-First-Century Business

I. The First *Lingua Franca* of Business

1   The term *lingua franca* has its roots in Europe, the Mediterranean, and the Middle East. During the Middle Ages, this language, based on Italian, with elements of Arabic, French, Greek, and Spanish, was used as a means of communication by people whose own native languages were not mutually intelligible. Lingua franca was often used by European merchants to communicate with other merchants in the Near East. Today the term lingua franca is used to describe any language of wider communication used by people who do not share a language. For example, beginning in the seventeenth century, French became the dominant language of business, culture, and diplomacy in Europe. Arabic serves as a lingua franca in the Islamic world today, as does Swahili in parts of eastern **Africa.**

WHILE YOU READ 1

Look back at paragraph 1 and highlight two adjective + noun chunks.

2   The dissemination of the English language accompanied the expansion of the British Empire. Later, as the populations and influence of its former colonies, especially the United States, grew, the use of English spread exponentially. English slowly replaced French as the language of diplomacy and law, and eventually also pushed aside German as the dominant language of scientific publications. In the late 1880s, a Polish eye doctor and linguist, Ludovic Zamenhof, invented a language called *Esperanto,* which he hoped would be a politically and culturally neutral lingua franca. He and many supporters believed that it would replace English as the primary language for international communication. In fact, however, the language was based exclusively on European languages, and never came close to becoming a significant lingua franca. Instead, English continued to develop as a vehicle of communication for people of diverse backgrounds, especially for international business.

II. The Rise of Global English

3   By 1950, English had become widely accepted as the language of international business. Today, as an official language in more than 60 countries, and with as many as 1.8 billion speakers worldwide, English retains its dominant role in diplomacy, business, and science. How long this dominance will last has been the subject of debate. British linguist David Graddol has suggested that English might soon be replaced by emerging international and regional languages such as Arabic, Hindi, or Chinese in its role in international business; yet others disagree that English will **relinquish** its top spot any time soon. Countries all over the world have invested heavily in the teaching of English as a foreign language, many with a great degree of success. Most experts believe that English is now

WHILE YOU READ 2

Use context and contrast signals to decide the meaning of *relinquish*.
(a) decide on
(b) give up
(c) continue

the most widely spoken language in the world, yet, only about 12 percent of the world's population claims English as a first language. In fact, non-native speakers of English vastly outnumber its native speakers, prompting the use of the term Global or World English to reflect the global context of its use.

4   Global or World English is the English spoken in countries where it is not an official language. It is believed that there are nearly 1 billion speakers of English as a second or foreign language. With this number of speakers, the varieties of native and non-native English around the world are growing more diverse. The English spoken by a call center employee from India, for example, may be difficult for a customer in New Zealand to understand. An American engineer from Alabama may struggle to converse with a colleague from Glasgow, Scotland. Though the language of communication is English, this does not always mean the speakers are intelligible to one another.

Figure 3.2 English-speaking Populations Worldwide

Percentage of English speakers by country:
■ 80–100%   ■ 60–80%   ■ 40–60%   ■ 20–40%   □ 0–20%

5   A number of multinational corporations have imposed English as their main language of communication. This type of company may have divisions located in Brazil, China, France, Germany, Italy, Japan, Mexico, and the U.S, and the employees from these various locations need to be able to communicate effectively. For example, when global manufacturing corporations, like the German-based company Bitzer, have to send their mechanical engineers overseas to troubleshoot problems, the language of communication is often English. But the English spoken among the supervisors, engineers, production teams, and sales forces is not always the same. When communication breaks down, productivity and efficiency suffer, which translates into potential losses for international **corporations**.

WHILE YOU READ ❸

Look back at paragraph 5. What can you infer?
(a) Miscommunication can cause mistakes.
(b) Miscommunication can cause conflict.

III. "Globish": Attempting to Break through Barriers

6   Language diversity is pervasive and perhaps inevitable in international business, but it can become an impediment to conducting business effectively. When Jean-Paul Nerrière worked for IBM[1] in Paris in the 1980s, he came to the realization that he and his colleagues spoke a different kind of English than their American counterparts. Nerrière's co-workers were a diverse group, from about 40 different countries. They spoke a minimal, utilitarian variety of English, using the 1500 to 2000 words that were necessary to get a point across. Miscommunications started soon after their American colleagues introduced themselves. Inspired to solve the problem, Nerrière devised a formal subset of English consisting of about 1500 words and some basic grammar rules. He called it "Globish" – a combination of "global" and "English."

WHILE YOU READ 4

Look back at paragraph 6. Highlight two verb phrase chunks.

7   But questions soon arose in the international business community as to whether Globish, with its minimum vocabulary and simplistic grammar, could really bridge the gap between employees with different language backgrounds. Critics pointed to its limited capacity to express more complex thoughts and concepts. There are no jokes, no slang[2] or idioms, no eloquence. There is nothing to foster personal connections between its speakers. Nevertheless, Globish has been useful when there is no other means of communication and for some, it can be a useful first step in acquiring a higher level of proficiency in **English**.

WHILE YOU READ 5

Look back at paragraph 7. What is the author's claim? Highlight three pieces of evidence that support this claim.

IV. Loss and Translation: The Impact of Technology on the Language of Business

8   As much of the world rushes to acquire English proficiency, others are looking to the future and asking if these efforts are really necessary. With innovative technologies, such as translation programs and mobile apps already on the horizon, learning any second language may soon be a thing of the past. Businesses have jumped on the bandwagon[3] of instant online translation programs for written texts, such as Babylon, Google Translate, or Bing Translator. Part of the problem with these automatic translation programs and sites has been that they cannot deal with the nuances of language and particularly idiomatic expressions. In general, a human translator is needed to modify the output of these translators in order for the product to be acceptable. Every year brings improvement in accuracy of automated translators, however, and we may soon be able to use them in a wider range of contexts.

9   Until this technology is perfected and widely used, the business world will still need to reach speakers of many languages. Since the goal of most companies is to expand their customer base and increase sales, many global

---

[1] *IBM:* International Business Machines, a computer and technology company
[2] *slang:* informal language
[3] *jump on the bandwagon:* to join an activity that has become popular

businesses maintain an international online presence by having websites in several languages. On Bitzer's website, for example, a user can navigate through the homepage in one of six different languages. To date, for the website development as well as communication among international employees, the best way for the business sector to overcome language barriers has been through professional translation services, in other words, humans with knowledge of more than one language. Professional translators ensure that websites, marketing materials, and employee documents have been written or translated with a high degree of accuracy.

10   The biggest challenge in bridging the gap between two languages, however, is not in the translation of written texts, but in the real-time translation of speech. The new speech translation device "Sigmo" is beginning to tackle this problem. Sigmo is the size of a small Post-it note and allows almost real-time translating of 25 languages. The user simply presses one button and speaks, and the device sends the words to the cloud[4] for translation via a Bluetooth[5] connection to the user's phone. Seconds later, the spoken translation emerges in another language. A second button reverses the process, so the user can understand what a speaker of another language is saying. In a similar effort, in 2014, Skype and Microsoft collaborated on software that offers real-time translation for Skype conversations in English, Italian, Mandarin Chinese, and Spanish as well as instant translation of text messages in 45 languages. Innovations like Skype Translator and Sigmo are still at an initial stage and will undoubtedly require improvements, but these speech-to-speech systems may prove a first step in eliminating the need to learn English or any other second language. English may be the last lingua **franca.**

WHILE YOU READ 6

Look back at paragraph 10. What form of text organization does it use: (a) classification, (b) cause and effect, or (c) problem-solution? Highlight signals that support your choice.

---

[4] *the cloud:* a computer network where data can be processed and stored
[5] *Bluetooth:* a system that allows the exchange of information between electronic devices

Main Idea Check

Match the main ideas below to five of the paragraphs in Reading 3. Write the number of the paragraph on the blank line.

_____ A There are many different varieties of English, and speakers sometimes have difficulty understanding one another.

_____ B In order to overcome barriers in the international business world, a reduced version of English was invented.

_____ C Technology may soon provide the means to overcome language barriers.

_____ D Translating spoken language is more difficult than translating written language.

_____ E English is the most widely spoken language in the world, but linguists do not agree about its future.

A Closer Look

Look back at Reading 3 to answer the following questions.

1 What is true about _lingua franca_? Choose all that apply.
   a It was used for business communication.
   b It was based on Arabic and French.
   c It was used by people who did not share a native language.
   d It was created by a physician and scholar.

2 David Graddol would agree with which of the following statements? Choose all that apply.
   a Chinese will be the next lingua franca.
   b Soon there will be more native speakers of English than non-native speakers.
   c The languages of large and economically important countries often become lingua francas.
   d The dominance of English is temporary.

3 Out of the world's population, fewer people have English as their native language than the total number of non-native English speakers worldwide. **True or False?**

4 What can you infer about communication between an engineer from the United States who speaks a different level of English than a supervisor from another country?
   a They both will have to use a translation device.
   b They will need to communicate through an interpreter.
   c Miscommunications are likely to happen.
   d Every job level requires a different kind of vocabulary.

5 Why was Globish developed? Choose all that apply.
   a Some people need fewer than 2000 words to communicate sufficiently.
   b Not all people who speak English can understand each another.
   c Its inventor could not communicate in English.
   d Different varieties of English have different ways of saying "hello."

6 Which conclusions can you infer based on information in paragraph 7? Choose all that apply.

   a Globish was a failure and is not used today.

   b Globish is not an ideal solution to problems of international communication.

   c Native speakers have more than 2000 words in their overall vocabulary.

   d Most non-native speakers of English learned Globish as their first step in language learning.

7 Electronic translation programs are not yet used very widely. **True or False?**

8 According to paragraph 9, what is still the best way to bridge the language gaps that might exist in a multinational corporation?

   a Employers should make employees study one of six different languages.

   b Companies have to provide translation devices to their employees who travel.

   c Companies need to hire people who are fluent in both languages and who also know business and technical terms.

   d Employees should have access to a website that is translated into their own language.

Skill Review

In Skills and Strategies 8, you learned that words frequently occur together in chunks. These include combinations of adjective + noun and noun + of + noun. Noticing these chunks will help you read more quickly and with a better understanding.

A Quickly scan paragraph 3 of Reading 3 to find these chunks. Then list the chunks in the table below.

B Quickly scan the rest of Reading 3 to find other chunks that contain the following words and highlight them. Then fill in the blanks below to complete each chunk. The words are listed in the order that they appear in the reading.

ADJECTIVE + NOUN	NOUN + *OF* + NOUN
1	1
2	2
3	
4	
5	

1 call _____

2 bridge the _____

3 _____ capacity

4 _____ horizon

5 thing of the _____

6 _____ base

7 degree of _____

8 initial _____

C Compare your answers with a partner's.

Definitions

Find the words in Reading 3 that are similar to the definitions below.

1 not favoring any side or group (*adj*) Par. 2

2 only (*adv*) Par. 2

3 discussion; difference of opinion (*n*) Par. 3

4 to be more numerous than (*v*) Par. 3

5 to talk with someone (*v*) Par. 4

6 to establish as a rule to be obeyed; to force the acceptance of something (*v*) Par. 5

7 to try to find a solution (*v*) Par. 5

8 designed to be useful rather than decorative (*adj*) Par. 6

9 to encourage (*v*) Par. 7

10 qualities of something that are not easily noticed but may be important (*n pl*) Par. 8

Words in Context

Complete the sentences with words or phrases from Reading 3 in the box below.

counterpart	eloquence	inevitable	mutually	supervisor
devised	expansion	intelligible	simplistic	vastly

1 U.S. President John F. Kennedy was an excellent public speaker, known for his
_____ and ability to inspire his listeners.

2 Most of the workers are unhappy with their new _____ because he does
not let them take breaks very often.

3 The speaker had such a strong accent that most of what he said was not

_____ .

4 Engineers _____ a way to move supplies more quickly to the
manufacturing facility.

5 The end of the videotape market was _____ as soon as DVDs appeared.

6 The graphics on the website are too _____ and do not fully illustrate the
complexity and power of the new software.

7 The engineer who was visiting from headquarters in Germany was unable to
understand her _____ in the Japanese office.

8 Overseas _____ of a company often brings new job opportunities
for employees.

9 The merger of the two companies was _____ beneficial.

10 The management styles of the two companies were _____ different,
which led to some initial conflict.

Critical Thinking

In Reading 3, you learned about how the language of business has changed and evolved over the centuries, from innovations like "Globish" to the use of translation devices, which can help solve communication problems in international business.

> **AGREEING AND DISAGREEING**
>
> When a writer explores different opinions on a topic, critical readers ask themselves what their own opinions are – which opinions they agree with or disagree with.

A Discuss the following questions with a partner.

1 What are some of the problems with Globish?

2 Of the possible solutions for bridging the language gap mentioned in the reading, for example, using Globish or translation devices, which do you think is best? Why?

3 What do you think are other possible solutions to bridging the language gap in international business?

B Read the following statements about the languages mentioned in Reading 3. Put a check (✓) in the box that expresses your opinion. Then discuss your opinions with a partner.

	AGREE	STRONGLY AGREE	DISAGREE	STRONGLY DISAGREE
English should remain the dominant language of business.				
Globish instruction should be offered to employees of all international companies.				
Esperanto should again be promoted as a global language.				
Arabic, Chinese, or Hindi will eventually replace English in international business.				
English will be the last lingua franca.				

Research

Research a multinational corporation that might find it difficult to use English as its primary language of communication. Find answers to the following questions.

- What are the company's main communication-related challenges?
- Where has miscommunication had the greatest impact?
- Why might using English be a problem for the company? Find arguments for and against using English to improve communication.
- What are the risks of using or not using English in the future?
- What are other possible solutions for the company to avoid miscommunications?

Writing

Write a report on your research. Use the questions listed above to form the outline for your report. Include some frequently used language chunks in business or another field on which you are reporting.

Connecting to the Topic

Discuss the following questions with a partner.

1 What kinds of devices, products, or services were used for entertainment 50 years ago?

2 What companies or industries have gone out of business because of new innovations?

3 Do you think books, DVDs, or other items will seem outdated in next 50 years? Why?

Previewing and Predicting

Reading the first sentence of each paragraph is a quick way to predict what a text will be about.

A Read the title of Reading 4 and the first sentence of paragraphs 2–11. Then put a check (✓) next to the topics you think will be included in the reading.

_____ A How disruptive innovation has transformed society

_____ B Which companies have succeeded due to new innovations

_____ C The negative impact of disruption on some businesses

_____ D The origin of encyclopedias

_____ E Generational differences of Internet users

_____ F What happened when people stopped buying encyclopedias

_____ G How *Encyclopaedia Britannica* found success

_____ H The ways in which social media can disrupt business

_____ I The use of Twitter by nonprofit organizations

_____ J How nonprofit organizations use social media for outreach

B Compare your answers with a partner's.

While You Read

As you read, stop at the end of each sentence that contains words in **bold**. Then follow the instructions in the box in the margin.

Disruptive Innovation and the Challenges of Social Media

I. Disruptive Innovation

1   After the automobile was invented, horses and cars shared the road for years. Then Henry Ford revolutionized manufacturing with his assembly line[1] process and made cars affordable to the American middle class. After that, the transportation industry changed completely. Today upstart companies like Uber and Lyft[2] are threatening to do the same to the taxi business. Changes in technology have long impacted the way companies do business on many levels. Occasionally, innovations appear unexpectedly and completely change a market, often replacing long established products or practices. This is known as *disruptive innovation*. Although the word "disruptive" has a negative connotation and disruptive innovation can indeed be bad news for established companies that are forced to change or close, the process is actually a generally positive force for both businesses and **consumers.**

2   In *The Innovator's Dilemma*, Clayton M. Christensen offers his theory of disruptive innovation, which analyzes the impact of technological development in society. When the book appeared in 1997, the growth of the Internet and related technology was quickly transforming daily life, from how people listened to music to how they stored their documents and data. Christensen's premise was that while traditional companies are focusing on their established, often high-priced products, a disruptive innovation can enter the market and transform it by introducing a simpler, more accessible, and more affordable product to a larger customer base. According to Christensen, disruptive innovation usually begins in a less popular, less profitable sector of the market. Over time, a product or idea alters the way that sector is perceived. A prime example is the personal computer. When Apple introduced its first personal computer, the market was dominated by large, very expensive mainframe **computers.** The first Apple computers were marketed to school age children, so few big companies paid much attention. They viewed these new computers as little more than toys. True, they were not powerful, but unlike mainframe computers, ordinary people could afford to buy them. Slowly, as the quality of personal computers

> **WHILE YOU READ** ①
> Highlight the definition of *disruptive innovation* in paragraph 1.

> **WHILE YOU READ** ②
> Review the last two sentences. Highlight three different adjective + noun chunks.

---

[1] *assembly line:* an arrangement in a factory in which each machine or worker has a particular job to complete before the next job is started by another machine or worker
[2] *Uber and Lyft:* ride-sharing services in which passengers use an app to arrange for a driver to pick them up

improved, they began to take over parts of the market formerly occupied by mainframes. Disruption of the market had begun.

3   Christensen's primary focus was on how and why such disruptions cause businesses to fail. He found that failure was not always due to poor decisions by business executives. In fact, they often made seemingly sound business decisions that focused on the long-term success of their products. However, perhaps because they were concentrating on sustaining their own innovations, they often missed the big picture, ignoring or under-estimating the innovations happening around them, as in the case of the personal computer.

4   The power and frequency of disruptive innovation has never been as evident as in the past few decades. Two recent examples– the impact of technology on publishing and the impact of social media on business practices – provide dramatic evidence of this trend.

II. The Demise of Print Reference Books

5   Have you ever thumbed through a volume of a huge encyclopedia set looking for information? If so, then you know how cumbersome print encyclopedias could be. Yet until digital encyclopedias became available, people either had to buy them or go to a library to access the informa-tion in them. Despite their size and expense, in the twentieth century it was common to find a set of *Encyclopaedia Britannica* or *World Book Encyclopedia* in private homes, especially in North America. In the United States, many so-called "baby boomers," members of the generation born just after World War II, grew up with print encyclopedias. These reference books were considered an important part of middle class homes and chil-dren's education.

6   This attitude meant that print encyclopedias did not disappear immedi-ately with the rise of the Internet, but their eventual demise was inevitable. The last print edition of *Encyclopaedia Britannica* was published in 2010. Two years later, after having printed seven million sets of encyclopedias over 244 years, the company shut down its print operations. What led to the disappearance of most print encyclopedias? It was a combination of new technology and a new business model. In the early 1990s, digital multimedia encyclopedias like Microsoft's *Encarta* began to erode the market share of print encyclopedias. Wikipedia accelerated this trend after it appeared in 2001. This crowdsourced product quickly became the most popular source for information for several reasons. It was free and acces-sible to anyone with an Internet connection, it could be instantly updated, and it had a much larger capacity than a print encyclopedia. Compared to the print version of *Encyclopaedia Britannica*, which contained roughly 40,000 articles, the English version of Wikipedia boasts nearly five million articles and is constantly **growing**.

7   The story of *Encyclopaedia Britannica*, however, is not one of failure at the hands of disruptive innovation. At the same time that it shut down its

WHILE YOU READ 3

Look back at paragraph 6. How is this paragraph mainly organized?
a) cause-effect
b) comparison-contrast
c) problem-solution

printing presses, the company also embraced a new business model. Today they offer online subscriptions to their encyclopedias as well as DVD versions. Although their products cost money, the company's president claims that they are superior to free online reference tools. Not only has the publisher managed to transition from print to digital, it has begun to see an increase in profits over the past several years.

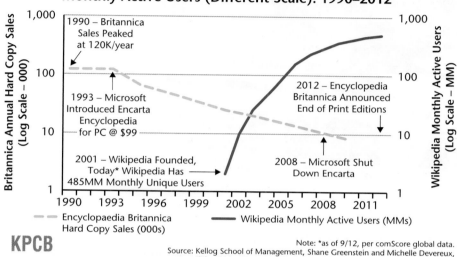

Encyclopedia Britannica Hard Copy Sales vs. Wikipedia Monthly Active Users (Different Scale). 1990–2012

1990 – Britannica Sales Peaked at 120K/year

1993 – Microsoft Introduced Encarta Encyclopedia for PC @ $99

2001 – Wikipedia Founded, Today* Wikipedia Has 485MM Monthly Unique Users

2012 – Encyclopedia Britannica Announced End of Print Editions

2008 – Microsoft Shut Down Encarta

- - - Encyclopaedia Britannica Hard Copy Sales (000s)

——— Wikipedia Monthly Active Users (MMs)

KPCB

Note: *as of 9/12, per comScore global data.
Source: Kellog School of Management, Shane Greenstein and Michelle Devereux, "The Crisis at Encyclopedia Britannica."

III. The Challenge and Opportunity of Social Media

8   Social networking websites like Facebook, Twitter, and LinkedIn have business platforms that are based on disruptive innovation. The concept of disruption is integral to their operations. More than 10 years ago, Facebook founder Mark Zuckerberg and a few colleagues **exploited** technology to change the way people communicate. Facebook allowed its users to personalize and customize its product, and the company then incorporated those preferences into the continuing development of its platform. In time, Facebook became not only an online place for personal communication and sharing photographs, but also a way for forward-thinking businesses to attract new customers and increase profits. As online marketing activities became more common in the business world, nonprofit organizations, such as museums and charities, also began looking at how they might utilize social media.

9   Nonprofit institutions depend on public and private support for finances and staffing. They typically engage potential donors directly – by phone, email, or invitation to events – to encourage them to give money to or volunteer for their organizations. With the rise of social media, however, their efforts to reach donors are changing. For these organizations, social media presents both an opportunity and a challenge in their relationship with their donors. People are used to networking and doing business on

WHILE YOU READ ④
Which definition of *exploited* matches the meaning in this sentence?
(a) used unfairly
(b) used well

social media, but many nonprofits do not yet feel comfortable soliciting money and services directly via social media.

10   In response to this dilemma, nonprofit organizations, along with for-profit companies, are using social media sites to reach out to donors in more subtle ways. For instance, they encourage people to "like" their organizations or to "share" special events in their status updates on Facebook. In this way they can increase their online presence, drive users to their own websites, and generally build awareness of their causes at little or no cost. In this example of technology disrupting established practices, the donor outreach model is transformed. In the end, if all goes well, they recruit more donors and volunteers, attendance at fundraising events rises, and donor commitment **increases**.

> **WHILE YOU READ 5**
>
> Look back at paragraph 10. How is this paragraph organized?
> a) cause-effect
> b) comparison-contrast
> c) problem-solution

IV. The Next Big Thing

11   It is probably not an exaggeration to say that the face of today's business is a product of disruptive innovation. Mapmakers and cartography companies like Rand-McNally have accepted the need to embrace collaborative map-making apps in order to avoid becoming obsolete. Streaming music sites have made record stores a thing of the past. Most major bookstore chains, which once had a global customer base, have closed their doors completely. A few, like U.S.-based Barnes and Noble, have managed to survive by moving their physical stores to college campuses and maintaining an online presence. Sadly, most independent bookstores have disappeared, victims of the disruptive forces of technology: electronic books, digital media, and devices like digital readers, smartphones, and **tablets**.

> **WHILE YOU READ 6**
>
> Look back at this sentence. Highlight any words that help you infer the writer's attitude toward the disappearance of independent bookstores.

12   What comes next for business? Will the next generation of cars come from 3D printers? Probably not. Will digital currency replace real money? Perhaps. The question is not only who will anticipate the effects of disruptive technology but also who will deal with them most successfully. After all, ten years ago there were dozens of social networking sites around the world, most of which have since been crushed by the dominant player in the market, Facebook. What is certain is that there will be a new disruptive innovation, and it will likely begin slowly, in an unnoticed corner of a market, until it displaces the current leading technology or business model and becomes the next big thing.

Main Idea Check

Match the main ideas below to five of the paragraphs in Reading 4. Write the number of the paragraph on the blank line.

_____ A Businesses are sometimes unsuccessful because they focus too much on improving their own products and not enough on potential outside threats.

_____ B Digital reference tools eventually meant the end of print encyclopedias.

_____ C Social media companies have embraced disruptive innovation and are influencing the way businesses function.

_____ D The theory of disruptive innovation may explain why popular technology falls out of use.

_____ E Digital products have pushed aside print ones, forcing many traditional companies to close their doors.

A Closer Look

Look back at Reading 4 to answer the following questions.

1 Why does the term *disruptive innovation* have a negative connotation?
   a "Disruptive" and "innovation" do not make sense when the words are combined.
   b Disruption implies that older products no longer have a place in our society.
   c In general, disruption causes problems.
   d It indicates that consumers will have bad experiences.

2 What conclusions did Clayton Christensen reach in his study of disruptive innovation? Choose all that apply.
   a Some companies miss opportunities because they only focus on existing products.
   b New, innovative products are not necessarily expensive.
   c Companies should not spend money on research and development.
   d The computer industry changed dramatically because mainframes became obsolete.

3 What can you infer about baby boomers? Choose all that apply.
   a Some prefer to get their news from newspapers rather than online sources.
   b They rarely use the Internet.
   c They extended the life of print encyclopedias.
   d They tend to be richer and more powerful than members of other generations.

4 How did the print version of *Encyclopaedia Britannica* differ from Wikipedia? Choose all that apply.
   a It was cheaper.
   b It was heavier.
   c It was more extensive.
   d It was harder to update.

5 What can you infer about nonprofit organizations?
  a Most of their donors do not use social media.
  b They get most of their funding from government grants.
  c They don't spend a lot of money building their websites.
  d They have generally reacted more slowly than businesses to disruptive innovation.

6 Nonprofit organizations can benefit from using social media. **True or False?**

7 Which of the following does the writer think might next be affected by disruptive innovation?
  a Music stores
  b Banking
  c Education
  d Automotive industry

8 What is true about disruptive innovation?
  a It has both advantages and disadvantages.
  b It does not happen frequently.
  c It is mostly seen in social media technology.
  d It is so powerful that it will force out all the old technology.

Skill Review

In Skills and Strategies 8, you learned about language chunks. These include prepositional phrases and combinations of adjective + noun, noun + noun, and noun + *of (the)* + noun. Noticing these chunks will help you read more quickly and with a better understanding.

A **Quickly scan Reading 4 to find language chunks that contain the following words and highlight them. Then fill in the blanks below to complete each chunk. The words are listed in the order that they appear in the reading.**

1 _____ connotation

2 prime _____

3 _____ executives

4 the _____ picture

5 middle _____

6 _____ share

7 at the _____ of

8 _____ updates

9 in the _____

10 a thing of the _____

B Complete the following sentences using collocations from the list above.

1 U.S automakers have slowly regained some of the _____ that they had lost.

2 If corporations try too hard to maintain an existing product, they may fail to see the _____ .

3 Many energy entrepreneurs believe that our dependence on oil and gas will soon be _____ .

4 The excited graduates went on social media sites to change their _____ .

5 For people who don't like change, even the word "technology" has a _____ .

6 Most advertisers hope to capture the attention of _____ consumers because they have considerable purchasing power.

7 Top _____ earn up to 300 times as much as the employees who work in their companies.

8 Many businesses suffered _____ overseas companies with lower labor costs.

9 _____ , what company shareholders want to see is profits.

10 Assistive technology is a _____ of how innovative products can help people improve their lives.

C Compare your answers with a partner's.

Definitions

Find the words in Reading 4 that are similar to the definitions below.

1 a feeling or idea suggested by a word, in addition to its basic meaning (*n*) Par. 1

2 an idea or theory on which an action is based (*n*) Par. 2

3 to turn pages of a book or magazine quickly and only read parts of it (*phrasal v*) Par. 5

4 difficult to do or manage; taking a lot of time and effort (*adj*) Par. 5

5 the end of an operation or existence of something (*n*) Par. 6

6 to accept with enthusiasm (*v*) Par. 7

7 necessary and important as part of the whole (*adj*) Par. 8

8 to change something to make it more useful or suitable for a particular person (*v*) Par. 8

9 organizations that give money or other assistance to people in need (*n pl*) Par. 8

10 to make use of something (*v*) Par. 8

11 not obvious (*adj*) Par. 10

12 to persuade to join (*v*) Par. 10

13 no longer used or needed, usually because something newer has replaced it (*adj*) Par. 11

14 money (*n*) Par. 12

15 to force something out of its usual place (*v*) Par. 12

Word Families

A The words in **bold** in the chart are from Reading 4. The words next to them are from the same word family. Study and learn these words.

ADJECTIVE	NOUN	VERB
-----	acceleration	**accelerate**
disruptive	**disruption**	disrupt
-----	erosion	**erode**
preferable	**preference**	prefer
-----	**underestimate**	underestimation

B Choose the correct form of the words from the chart to complete the following sentences.

1 Most people have a / an _____ for either PC or Mac computers.

2 Storms and bad weather can _____ Internet service, phone lines, and even television reception.

3 You should not _____ how much time it takes to bring a product to market.

4 There has been a recent _____ in the demand for rare metals, which are a crucial element in computer chips.

5 As the popularity of Facebook has increased, membership in many older social networks has continued to _____ .

6 Most people _____ to buy products they already know. They are suspicious of new ones.

7 Natural disasters and political events can cause a / an _____ in the energy market.

8 The company has tried to _____ the production schedule to meet growing demand.

9 After the poor sales report, there was a / an _____ in support for the company's director.

10 Early negative predictions led to a / an _____ of the demand for the new app.

Academic Word List

The following are Academic Word List words from Readings 3 and 4 of this unit. Use these words to complete the sentences. (For more on the Academic Word List, see page 299.)

| converse (v) | debate (n) | expansion (n) | inevitable (adj) | mutually (adv) |
| currency (n) | displaced (v) | imposed (v) | integral (adj) | utilized (v) |

1 Many companies have _____ the talents of freelance workers.

2 The government has _____ higher standards for workplace safety.

3 Innovative devices _____ the older model, which is now outdated.

4 Publishers have accepted the _____ decline of print books and entered the electronic book market.

5 New translation devices may allow travelers to _____ in another language without using a dictionary.

6 Collaboration is a / an _____ part of the company's management philosophy.

7 The _____ of the company was due to the purchase of two new subsidiary companies.

8 There has been considerable _____ about the cost and efficiency of alternative energy sources.

9 The two business professionals _____ agreed to the terms of the contract.

10 There is a profitable market in the trading of foreign _____.

Critical Thinking

Reading 4 points out that disruptive innovation often appears while the leading companies are focused on sustaining innovation in a particular market.

> **CLARIFYING CONCEPTS**
>
> Critical thinking includes exploring a concept in a text by restating it and applying it to a different context.

A Discuss the following questions with a partner.

1 What are some examples of sustaining innovations? How have they sustained rather than disrupted their industry or market?

2 What are some examples of disruptive innovations that are not mentioned in Reading 4? How did they disrupt an industry or market?

B Read the following examples of innovations. Put a *D* if you think they are disruptive and an *S* if you think they are sustaining. Discuss your choices with your partner.

INNOVATION	DISRUPTIVE OR SUSTAINING?
Internet crowdfunding platforms	
DVDs	
MOOCs	
3D printing	
3D video gaming	
Electronic currency	
Wearable technology	

Research

Research a leading company or organization associated with one of the innovations in the chart above. Find answers to the following questions.

- What is their innovative product or service?
- Who or what was the industry leader before its appearance?
- What are the advantages and disadvantages of the product or service?
- How has the industry changed since its appearance?

Writing

Write a report on your research. Include your answers to the questions above in your report. Conclude with some of your own predictions based on your research.

Improving Your Reading Speed

Good readers read quickly and still understand most of what they read.

A Read the instructions and strategies for Improving Your Reading Speed in Appendix 3 on page 316.

B Choose one of the readings in this unit. Read it without stopping. Time how long it takes you to finish the text in minutes and seconds. Enter the time in the chart on page 318. Then calculate your reading speed in number of words per minute.

Summarizing

Summarizing is a way of expressing the essential ideas and major points of a reading in your own words. To summarize, you need to read critically and identify main ideas, and then report them clearly and concisely. As you read, take notes and identify major ideas and facts that are important to mention in the summary.

Examples & Explanations

①ª Text:

In art, business, science, or technology, the "borrowing" of ideas has always been an issue. For example, experts point to Leonardo da Vinci's fifteenth-century rendering of *Vitruvian Man,* which was based on earlier sketches of human proportion that have since been lost, as a form of "copying" from the original. As the name suggests, da Vinci's sketch of human proportion was based on the work of the ancient Greek architect, Vitruvius. A more subtle form of "appropriation" is the subsequent reproduction of the *Mona Lisa* by Marcel Duchamp in 1919 – where the artist gave Mona Lisa a mustache and beard. A number of art historians assert that Duchamp altered the original image to make a provocative statement about Leonardo's genius on the 400th anniversary of his death.

①ᵇ Summary of the text:

According to the writer, copying is part of human history and may happen in any field. He **mentions** several examples from art history as evidence. These include the ways that Leonardo da Vinci improved upon Vitruvius's descriptions of human proportion and Marcel Duchamp altered the *Mona Lisa* as a statement on the original artist's genius.

The writer of the summary (1b) takes the main idea and key points from the longer, more complex passage above (1a) and consolidates them into a concise paragraph (3 sentences). She uses the signal phrase *according to* and the reporting verb *mentions* to introduce what was stated in the original text.

②Summary of an interview:

When Steve Jobs used Pablo Picasso's famous statement, "Real artists steal," he was mainly **referring to** his visit to Xerox PARC in 1979. Jobs got the "germ of the idea" from what he was shown there. In the documentary *Triumph of the Nerds* (1996), Jobs **revealed** that while he was at Xerox, he was shown three things. He **stated** that he was "blinded by the first thing that they showed," which was Graphical User Interface, or GUI. As Jobs **mentioned**, GUI changed how people use computers – instead of using codes, Apple employed "icons."

③Summary of a text:

According to the writer, most of the major computer and electronic device businesses have experienced patent disputes at one time or another. **Based on** information from sources at Apple Inc., the company has **admitted** to being in legal disputes with Samsung over smartphone designs. Microsoft also filed a lawsuit against Samsung; it **claimed** that there were issues connected to the use of Windows programs and Android operating systems.

Summary 2 is an example of a summary of a segment from a documentary film called *Triumph of the Nerds*. The writer takes the main ideas from an interview with Steve Jobs and describes the major points that Jobs raised in the film. The writer includes the sequencing marker *when* as well as the reporting verbs *refer to*, *reveal*, *state*, and *mention* in the summary.

In summary 3, the writer has taken information from a longer passage and consolidated the key points into a short paragraph. Words and phrases like *according to*, *based on*, *admitted*, and *claimed* are used to report what was stated in the original text.

The Language of Summarizing

Here is a list of words and phrases that are commonly used for summarizing.

SUMMARY WORDS AND PHRASES			
Signal Phrases	**Reporting Verbs**		**Sequence Markers**
according to	to admit	to maintain	first
based on	to argue	to mention	next
in the article	to assert	to note	then
in the author's/writer's opinion	to claim	to remark	before
it is important to	to describe	to report	after
the author/writer	to discuss	to reveal	when
the key/main point	to explain	to state	finally
the main idea	to indicate	to suggest	last
to sum up			

Strategies

These strategies will help you summarize.

- Identify the main ideas and key points in the reading.
- Look for reporting verbs used by the writer that can help you identify ideas the writer has summarized, paraphrased, or quoted from experts or other sources.
- Avoid including minor details from the reading in your summary.
- Use signal phrases and reporting verbs to introduce key points.
- Use sequence markers, and organize your summary in the same order as the reading.
- Keep your summary concise. It should be proportional to the length of the original text.

Skill Practice 1

Choose the correct verb from the box below to complete the sentences in the summary.

admitted	described	exposed	to sum up
argued	explained	remarked	

In his 2011 article in *The New Yorker*, "Creation Myth: Xerox PARC, Apple, and the truth about innovation," Malcolm Gladwell _exposed_ the truth behind the
a
"creation myth" of Apple's mouse and the use of Graphical User Interface (GUI). In the article, Gladwell _described_ an important event from 1979, when young
b
innovator Steve Jobs was able to make a deal with Xerox to visit their center. According to Gladwell, Jobs offered Xerox one hundred thousand shares in his new company if it would "open its kimono," or show him its technology. The day after his visit to Xerox PARC, Jobs met with his designer, Dean Hovey, and _argued_ for Apple's need
c
to create a "mouse." Hovey _remarked_ that he had no idea what a mouse was
d
and also _explained_ how he used to design something that was completely
e
different from the mouse Steve Jobs had seen at Xerox. Later, Xerox _admitted_
f
that they had made a mistake and missed an opportunity to become one of the largest technology companies in the world. _To sum up_, Malcolm Gladwell concisely
g
captured the essence of what happened between Xerox PARC and Apple. Steve Jobs was a visionary who took an idea and improved upon it, and the rest, as they say, is history.

4   The piece at issue in the Rogers case was on display at the Whitney. Entitled *String of Puppies* (1988), it is a life-sized wooden sculpture of eight German Shepherd puppies held by a man and woman seated on a bench. The original was a black and white photograph by a photographer named Art Rogers. Koons bought a notecard with an authorized reproduction of the photograph and had artisans turn it into a sculpture made according to his precise instructions. That resulted in the puppies becoming blue, and there were now daisies on the heads of the people holding them. In the process, Rogers's charming but forgettable image became a part of the history of American art. The photographer had a very American reaction: he sued the prominent artist who copied his photograph – and he won.

Jeff Koons poses with one of his sculptures at the 2014 Whitney Museum retrospective.

5   Things started turning around for Koons in 2006, when he won in an appeal of a copyright-infringement case concerning his painting *Niagara*. The painting was part of a series called *Easyfun-Ethereal*, commissioned by the Guggenheim Museum in Berlin and first exhibited there in the autumn of 2000.

6   In the case of Blanch v. Koons, the plaintiff[2], a photographer named Andrea Blanch, had taken a picture of a woman's lower legs and feet in a pair of Gucci sandals, originally for a story in *Allure* magazine. Koons admitted scanning Blanch's image into a computer, after which the background was removed. Koons then had assistants paint the legs and feet with few alterations. Now, along with three other pairs of legs and feet, they dangled from the top of a large canvas over a landscape filled with dessert treats. The photographer sued Koons for unauthorized copying, but she lost; the court held that Koons had made enough changes – that is, that he had sufficiently "transformed" the work by its use in a different way and with many other elements – so that its presentation and meaning were altered. By its adaptation by Koons, the image had become a commentary on pop culture, to no unlawful detriment to **Blanch**.

III. What You Need to Show Fair Use

7   What does it mean when cute but uninspired pictures of puppies or a view of luxury footwear become the subjects of expensive lawsuits? It is all about the protection of artistic "expression" by copyright law. For an artist to obtain copyright protection for what he or she has made, the artist must have done something that is minimally creative. When that is accomplished, the artist has the exclusive right to make copies of his or her work. The doctrine of fair use appears at Section 107 of the Copyright Act. Very generally speaking, under the fair use doctrine, a copy is not infringing if it is significantly different in key ways from the work it references. There are four statutory factors used in determining if fair use may be found. The key point, however, is that the second work should in some way transform the first work. That can happen if the second work has a different expressive purpose or character. A finding of fair use can depend in part on the nature of the first work. For that reason, for works in genres that depend highly on uniqueness, such as literary fiction, it is easier to overcome a defense of fair use offered by someone with a later but similar work. Fair use can also depend on how much of the first work was used and how the second work affects the potential market for the first **work**.

IV. The Golden Age You Never Knew

8   You never know a golden age while you are living in it – a fact that the defenders of copyrights in the visual media discovered when content went digital and copying became easy enough for just about anyone to do.

WHILE YOU READ ③

Look back at this paragraph. Highlight the sentence that contains the key point about this court case.

WHILE YOU READ ④

Look back at paragraph 7. Highlight the phrase that signals an important point about fair use. Then underline the point.

---

[2] *plaintiff:* a person who accuses someone else of doing something illegal in a court of law

It is important to remember that judges are human, and they are not well-disposed toward ruling as unlawful the things that their own children and grandchildren do without even thinking about whether they are lawful or not – such as electronically copying photographs made by others. That is very likely a factor in the reasoning behind cases such as Cariou v. Prince that have loosened the criteria for the finding of fair use and so potentially altered the market for "appropriation art," and the photographs that are copied by appropriation **artists**.

9   To backtrack a bit: for about six years, the photographer Patrick Cariou lived among Rastafarians in Jamaica. In the year 2000, his photographs from that experience were published in a book under the title *Yes Rasta*. Richard Prince, a prominent appropriation artist, used thirty photographs from this book as the basis of a series of canvases called *Canal Zone*. For his works, Prince scanned Cariou's photographs and then altered and combined them to varying degrees with photographs by others; Prince sometimes added dollops of **paint**.

10   In 2008, Cariou commenced a lawsuit in federal court in New York City against Prince, Prince's gallery, Gagosian, and the gallery's owner, Larry Gagosian, for the *Yes Rasta* "appropriation." In 2011, a federal judge granted summary judgment (that is, a judgment prior to trial on the facts as submitted) to Cariou on his claims of copyright infringement. The court thereby completely rejected the fair use defense. The remedy was severe: the defendants[3] were ordered to surrender all the Prince artworks and exhibition catalogues to Cariou. They were also required to notify purchasers of the Prince works already sold that those works could not be displayed—because to do so would be a further infringing act. Millions of dollars of art by a famous artist could be destroyed, and pieces already sold appeared to have been rendered **unmarketable**.

11   Then in 2013, a federal appellate court[4] reversed the decision and remanded the case, meaning that it ruled differently and sent the case back to the lower court to be handled in a manner consistent with the appellate court's decision. Although there had been no trial, the appellate court concluded that twenty-five of the thirty Prince works were not infringing under the doctrine of fair use. It left to the lower court to proceed toward trial, if need be, on the question of fair use for the remaining five. The Cariou case thereby took fair use in art law to a new place: as the one dissenting judge on the three-judge panel said: "Indeed, while I admit freely that I am not an art critic or expert, I fail to see how the majority in its appellate role can "confidently" draw a distinction between the twenty-five works that it has identified as constituting fair use and the five works that do not readily lend themselves to a fair use determination…. Certainly we are not merely to use our personal art views to make the new

WHILE YOU READ **5**

Look back at paragraph 8. Highlight the phrase that signals a claim made by the writer.

WHILE YOU READ **6**

Which is a key fact in paragraph 9?
a) Cariou lived in Jamaica
b) Prince appropriated Cariou's photographs

WHILE YOU READ **7**

Reread paragraph 10. Highlight a verb that means *to give up*.

---

[3] *defendant:* a person who is accused of doing something illegal in a court of law
[4] *federal appellate court:* court in any of eleven areas in the United States in which lawyers can argue that a decision made in a lower court should be changed; also known as a *court of appeals*

legal application to the facts of this case…. It would be extremely uncomfortable for me to do so in my appellate capacity, let alone my limited art **experience**."

12 Although the sudden twist of fate in the Cariou case shocked photographers and their lawyers, it was really making law out of what had been happening for years in the art market. Five years earlier, at the 2008 edition of The Armory Show in New York (to take an example almost at random), so many works used pop-culture motifs owned by others that it presented a common theme. Cosima von Bonin, representing the growing school of such borrowers, stuck mass-produced plush toys on a clothesline and called the work *Marathon* (2007), exhibited at the booth of the Friedrich Petzel **Gallery**. Not long into the show, it sold for $120,000. It is anyone's guess if there are copyright registrations covering some or all of the toys used in the von Bonin work, but von Bonin surely purchased the toys rather than making copies of them. Under what is known as the "first-sale doctrine," she could lawfully suspend them from a line and charge a lot of money – without interfering with anyone else's rights. What she could not have done was make copies of anything protected by copyright that she bought for inclusion in the work.

WHILE YOU READ 8

Reread paragraph 11. What can you infer about the writer's attitude toward the court decision?
a) He agrees completely with the decision.
b) He questions the decision.

WHILE YOU READ 9

Find and highlight an example of a pop culture motif in this sentence.

Marathon (2007) by Cosima von Bonin

13 There are different problems when a work protected by copyright gets copied by appropriation artists. That was even more in evidence at an exhibition at the International Center of Photography (ICP), also in

d Analysts claim that there will be many problems for artists as well as product designs with the disruptive innovation of 3D printing. The writer indicates that design templates could be copied and sold by anyone because the copyrights are not protected.

B Read the following paragraph. Then write a summary for it. Include signal phrases, reporting verbs, and sequence markers.

Internet-based "stock photography or illustration" companies, like Getty Images, Corbis, and Shutterstock, offer some options to those who want to use photographs legally. The royalty-free (no-fee) option for photographs from their stock allows unrestricted use without any fee. The photographer (owner) still holds the copyright, but gives everyone the ability to use the photo. However, this solution would not work for individuals or companies that want exclusive rights to an image. Another option is a rights-managed agreement whereby a client can use a photograph, illustration, or video for a certain length of time as per a contract, for a certain fee. These options offer users some relief from the question of copyright infringement or the legal question that might arise from using photographs without permission. People need to remember that just because an image is on the Internet does not mean that it is free.

_____

_____

Vocabulary Development

Definitions

Find the words in Reading 5 that are similar to the definitions below.

1 the beginning of an event (n) Par. 1 _Advent_

2 the reduction of the size or importance of something (n) Par. 1 _diminution_

3 a loud complaint or demand (n) Par. 1 _clamor_

4 an exhibit which shows the development of an artist's work over a period of time (n) Par. 2 _museum_

5 legally protected from unlawful use, pertaining to the control of published material or an object (adj) Par. 2 _copyright-protected_

6 an illegal action that limits someone's rights or freedoms (n) Par. 3 _infringement_

7 people who do skilled work with their hands (n pl) Par. 4 _Artisan_

8 harm or damage (n) Par. 6 _detriment_

9 the state of great comfort or elegant living (n) Par. 7 _luxury_

10 friendly and helpful (adj) Par. 8 _well-disposed_

11 to begin something (v) Par. 10 _commenced_

12 to send an accused person or case away from court while awaiting trial (v) Par. 11 _remanded_

13 to be equal to (v) Par. 11 _consistent_

14 prevention of something from working or developing successfully (n) Par. 15

15 the process of making new laws or old laws less strict as necessary, often due to changing social conditions (n) Par. 16 _liberalization_

Words in Context

Complete the passages with words or phrases from Reading 5 in the box below.

around the clock	dangled	motifs	sue	unauthorized
broadening	dissenting	recognizably	twist of fate	uninspired

colgaba   _motivos_   _demandar_   _Amplicación_   _expresión opinión_

1 The photograph _dangled_ from the picture hanger on the wall for several minutes before it crashed to the floor.

2 Hospitals may have difficulty maintaining _around the clock_ care for patients if they are forced to cut back on staff.

3 The artist incorporated some of the _motifs_ he had seen on African carvings into his work.

4 When one artist's work or ideas are _unauthorized_ used in another artist's work, there may be legal issues.

5 In a strange _twist of fate_, the copyright infringement case was overturned, and the owner won back her rights.

6 If an artist feels _uninspired_, it is possible that motivation may come from another artist's work.

7 The company was _broadening_ its small customer base by testing out a new way to use an old product.

8 A famous musician tried to stop the publication of his _recognizably_ biography.

9 The _dissenting_ voice at the meeting was one director who argued against changing the design of the product.

10 RCA Corporation tried to _sue_ television pioneer Philo Farnsworth for royalties – money owed to him for his camera tube design.

Same or Different

The following pairs of sentences contain vocabulary from all the readings of this unit. Write *S* on the blank lines if the two sentences have the same meaning. Write *D* if the meanings are different.

_S_ 1 Appropriation artists should try to avoid **infringement** on another artist's copyright.

Artists who use the work of others should not imitate **copyright-protected** pieces too closely.

_S_ 2 When a company **downsizes**, it is usually a sign of economic depression.

When a business **consolidates**, an overall **diminution** in **productivity** is **inevitable**.

_S_ 3 Although Steve Jobs' behavior at times made his personal relations difficult, Apple, the **enterprise** he founded, **thrived**.

Steve Jobs was a successful **entrepreneur** despite the fact that his personality was sometimes a **detriment** to his career.

_D_ 4 Raising funds for a start-up is often a **cumbersome** task.

It can be a challenge to **secure capital** for a new business **initiative**.

_S_ 5 Businesses are more likely to **recruit** freelance workers with special skills than those with more general skills.

Freelancers who can **customize** their work to meet the needs of a client may **solicit** jobs more easily than those who cannot.

_D_ 6 The decision to **automate** operations was crucial in **reversing** the company's decline.

Streamlining the company's business was a **pivotal** step in their **expansion**.

_D_ 7 Although CD players seemed to make record players **obsolete**, many music enthusiasts have shown a **preference** for the sound of vinyl records.

When CD players finally gained a **foothold** in the market, many consumers decided to get rid of their old record collections.

_D_ 8 The **advent** of internet shopping **accelerated** the **demise** of many traditional stores.

As online shopping became more **prevalent**, stores in malls soon **floundered** and many closed.

Disciplinary Vocabulary

The following words are from all the readings in this unit. Research shows that they frequently appear in academic texts related to business. Complete the sentences with these words.

barrier (*n*)	consumers (*n*)	implementation (*n*)	outsourcing (*n*)	shareholders (*n*)
capital (*n*)	effective (*adj*)	initiatives (*n*)	productivity (*n*)	stakeholders (*n*)
compensation (*n*)	entrepreneurs (*n*)	innovations (*n*)	sector (*n*)	ventures (*n*)

[handwritten: Accionistas, paules interesadx, Emprendimiento, empresarios]

1 Many companies believe they save money by _outsourcing_ jobs to freelance workers overseas.

2 When a business closes, it affects all of the _stakeholders_: management, employees, investors, and the community where it is located.

3 The government decided to delay _initiatives_ of new employments laws in order to give companies more time to prepare.

4 The legal aspect of appropriation can be a / an _implementation_ to an artist's creativity.

5 The part of the economy that is made up of companies is known as the business _Shareholders_.

6 In today's world there are still fewer female _entrepreneurs_ than male, but the government has been encouraging women in start-up business companies by offering loans and grants.

7 Advertisers of luxury goods target _____ with the greatest purchasing power.

8 The government has proposed a new policy that will make it easier to raise the _capital_ needed to start new businesses.

9 Using freelancers might be more _effective_ when a project needs to be done quickly.

10 Manufacturing companies expect high _compensation_ in their factories as well as high standards.

11 Several companies announced _consumers_ that will make their operations greener and more sustainable.

12 Many experts believe that new ideas and _productivity_ are the key factors that drive economic development.

13 There were protests at the annual meeting of the company's _sector_ last week.

14 When a company has to downsize, most employees receive financial _compensation_.

15 Silicon Valley, California, is the home of many technology start-up _ventures_.

Critical Thinking

In Reading 5, you learned about the appropriation of art, fair use, and its legal implications.

A Look back at the reading. Choose one of the following cases or examples and evaluate it. Decide why you agree or disagree with the final decision in the case.

1 Blanch v. Koons

2 Cariou v. Prince

3 Cosima von Bonin Appropriation

4 Glenn Ligon Appropriation

B Discuss your opinions with a partner.

> **AGREEING AND DISAGREEING**
>
> When a writer explores different opinions on a topic, critical thinkers ask themselves what their own opinions are – which opinions they agree with or disagree with.

Research

Research a company, invention, or idea that has been involved in patent, intellectual property, copyright, or appropriation disputes. Choose from the list below or find one by searching the Internet.

- Modern Dog Design v. Target Corporation
- Kellogg C. v. National Biscuit Co.
- Mattel v. MGA Entertainment Co.
- Michael Baigent and Richard Leigh v. The Random House Group Limited
- A&M Records, Inc. v. Napster Inc.
- Nancy Stouffer v. JK Rowling (Harry Potter)
- Apple v. HTC

Find the answers to the following questions:

1 What was the case about?

2 What were the main arguments of the plaintiff and the defendant?

3 What was the outcome of the case? Who won, and why?

Writing

Write two to three paragraphs to report on the results of your research. Begin by describing the two sides of the case. Integrate the answers that you found to the questions above. Summarize the problems and arguments. Give a short summary of the outcomes of the case and include why the judge or jury found in favor of the plaintiff or defendant in the case.

Exercise 1

Writers may connect ideas between sentences in many different ways. The second sentence may:

   a   describe the **result** or outcome of what is reported in the first sentence

   b   provide a **solution** to a problem described in the first sentence

   c   add a **detail** or details to support the more general information in the first sentence

How does the second sentence in each pair of sentences below connect to the first sentence? Write *a*, *b*, or *c* on the line depending on whether it is a result, a solution, or a supporting detail.

_____ 1   In the *Da Vinci Code* case, the authors of the novel *Holy Blood, Holy Grail* believed that Dan Brown had infringed upon their copyright by presenting his ideas about historical events in the same way that they had done. Dan Brown's case was dismissed, and he was not found guilty of infringement.

_____ 2   In 1999, Amazon Inc. filed a patent and began to use an easier and quicker way to make purchases called "1-click," on its website. Amazon sued Barnes & Noble company for copyright infringement that same year for their "Express Lane" option, which was almost identical to Amazon's 1-click system.

_____ 3   In recent years Google has faced threats of enormous fines by the European Union (EU) due to the company's perceived practices of limiting competition and violating personal privacy. Instead of fighting the EU in court, Google has generally agreed to change their policies and avoided paying fines and losing business.

_____ 4   In the case of *Star Wars* v. *Battlestar Galactica* – a popular 1977 film versus a subsequent television series – the main problem was that the writer and producers of *Star Wars* believed that the writers of the *Battlestar Galactica* series had stolen about 34 ideas from *Star Wars*. Despite the fact that the *Battlestar Galactica* creator Glen Larson met the producer of *Star Wars* in person to ensure that there were no problems, Larson was still sued.

_____ 5   Microsoft and Apple were in court for years over the issue of "Graphical User Interface" – the component that allows a user to click on icons and drag files instead of typing in codes. Part of the main problem was that Microsoft developers had helped Apple create its software.

Exercise 2

Make a clear paragraph by putting sentences A, B, and C into the best order after the numbered sentence. Write the letters in the correct order on the blank lines.

1 Copyright infringement has often been an issue in the music business. ____ ____ ____

| **A** Harrison's first successful single in his solo career sounded too much like a song called "He's So Fine" that was recorded nearly 10 years earlier. | **B** George Harrison, former member of the 1960s group The Beatles, was sued because of copyright infringement. | **C** Harrison had to pay nearly $600,000 in fines by order of the court due to "subconscious plagiarism," or copying a melody too closely without realizing it. |

2 "Sampling" in music is taking a small sample of a recording from a song and reusing it. ____ ____ ____

| **A** As a result, many recording artists encountered legal trouble from "sampling" that seriously impacted their creativity. | **B** The main problem was that some of the samples were from songs that were highly recognizable to the listener. | **C** Hip-hop music was one of the first genres of music to officially "sample" from other artists' work. |

3 Historically, patents have served to protect the person who originates an idea or the inventor of a product. ____ ____ ____

| **A** When an inventor filed a patent, it was the first step in protecting their intellectual property from "theft." | **B** However, once an inventor becomes a patent holder, he or she can sell the patent. | **C** If a company purchased a patent, they then have the rights to use the inventor's creation. |

4 A trademark is different from a copyright because it defines the brand of the company. ____ ____ ____

| **A** The logos for Google and Goojje look so much alike that people might assume they are both owned by Google. | **B** The issue is that designers see so many designs, they might unintentionally copy something they have already seen. | **C** The brand is generally recognizable to the customer because of a certain logo that the company has created to distinguish its product. |

5 The Los Angeles Dodgers, an American baseball team that moved from New York to Los Angeles in 1957, were originally named the Brooklyn Dodgers. ____ ____ ____

A The L.A. Dodgers filed a complaint with the U.S. Patents office claiming that they own the logo and that customers might believe the burgers are owned and produced by the Dodgers.

B Though the team "The Brooklyn Dodgers" no longer exists, the team's logo is very distinctive.

C A Brooklyn restaurant uses the same "font" and name: "The Brooklyn Burger."

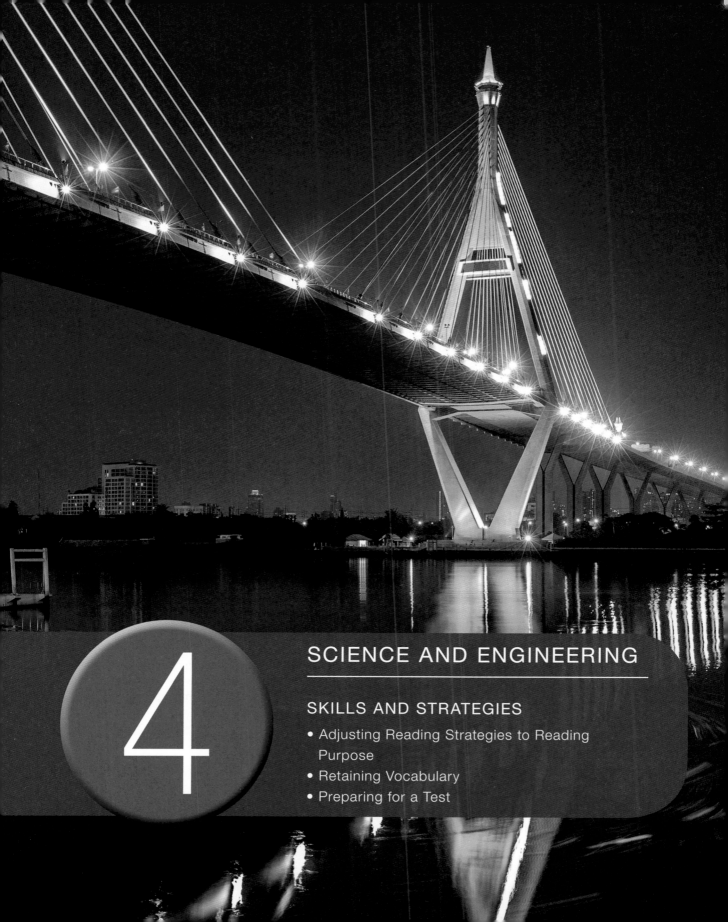

SCIENCE AND ENGINEERING

4

SKILLS AND STRATEGIES

- Adjusting Reading Strategies to Reading Purpose
- Retaining Vocabulary
- Preparing for a Test

Adjusting Reading Strategies to Reading Purpose

We read for a variety of purposes. We read to find specific information, to understand the general idea of a text, to learn; and in academic contexts, we also read to evaluate information and use it in other tasks. Although the underlying reading process in all of these is the same, good readers use different strategies to match their reading purpose.

Examples & Explanations

The New Plastic

Polystyrene, sometimes called Styrofoam, is a very useful man-made material in that it is very light, very stable, and relatively inexpensive. For these reasons, it is used in a lot of packaging. It will keep fragile equipment or other products safe during shipment. It can also keep hot things hot and cold things cold, making it an ideal medium for serving coffee and ice cream at fast-food restaurants. You have probably drunk coffee from white polystyrene cups many times, but what happens when you throw that cup away? Actually, nothing happens. Polystyrene takes hundreds of years to break down, suggesting that it is not a very environmentally friendly product.

One company wants to replace polystyrene packaging with a new product. This company can supply packaging material in any shape and will grow it to order – from mushrooms. The roots of mushrooms form a dense network structure called mycelium, which the company combines with agricultural waste products, like rice bran or corn husks, and then places the mixture in a mold that has the right shape for packaging. Within a few days, the mushrooms

You can vary your reading strategy for this text based on the reading purpose.

Purpose 1: If you need to find a specific piece of information, you don't need to read every word. You can **scan** the text quickly to find it. For example:
• What is another word for polystyrene?
• What is mycelium?

Purpose 2: If you just want to get a general idea of the reading, you could **skim** the text. When you skim, you read:
• the title
• headings
• the first and, sometimes, last sentence of each paragraph
After you skim this text, you will know it is about a new, environmentally friendly packaging material that is made from mushrooms.

break down the waste material, forming a lightweight solid mass inside the mold. Workers take this material out of the mold and heat it to kill all of the living organisms. The product is now ready to use.

This process provides packaging in the right shape to protect fragile items like a computer or dishes during shipping, but with an important difference. You can throw it in your garden, and it will disappear in about a month. Mushroom-based material is now being tested as a building material and even for surfboards. One company official calls the mycelium product "the new plastic."

Purpose 3: Sometimes you will need to read more carefully in order to learn the material in the text or use it as a source for another task, or in order to think critically about the information that is presented. When you need to read carefully, follow these steps:

- Before you begin reading, skim the text to get an idea what it will be about.
- Ask yourself what you already know about the topic. For example, you might think, "I know about Styrofoam coffee cups."
- Read slowly and pause periodically to check your comprehension, and predict what might come next. When you reach the end of the first paragraph, you might ask yourself, "Is there an alternative?"
- If you come to a place you don't understand, go back to where your difficulty began and reread. Or, scan ahead and see if later information clears up your confusion. When you reach the end of the second paragraph, you might think, "Wait, I am not sure how that works." Then you might decide to reread the previous sentences.

Strategies

These strategies will adjust your reading strategy to match your reading purpose.

- Choose the strategy that is appropriate for your reading purpose.
- Adjust your reading speed. Read more slowly at the beginning of each paragraph and when you want to learn and remember information.
- If you are reading an academic text for a class, use careful reading strategies to increase your capacity to learn and remember the material in the text. Stop when you come to a part you don't understand and resolve the misunderstanding before you continue.
- If you will have to respond to the reading, you may need to read it more critically. You will not only have to remember the content of the reading, but you will also have to interpret the ideas and form your own opinions of them.

Skill Practice 1

Scan the text below to find the answers to the following questions.

1 When was the Mohs hardness scale established? _____

2 Does the rank of 1 mean hard or soft? _____

3 What is the ranking of quartz on the scale? _____

4 How are abrasives used in industry? _____

The Mohs Hardness Scale

1   The Mohs hardness scale characterizes the relative hardness of minerals, defined as resistance to scratching. Other hardness scales are somewhat different from the Mohs scale in that they rely instead on the ability to create an indentation, or depression, into the mineral. On the Mohs scale, as on all hardness scales, hardness is determined by the strength of the bonds between atoms in a crystal.

2   The scratching method of determining hardness goes back at least as far as ancient Greece. The Mohs scale, developed in 1822 by Frederich Mohs and familiar to most rock collectors, ranges from one to ten, with one as softest and ten as hardest. It is easy to use and requires no special tools or equipment beyond the minerals themselves. The scale uses ten minerals as standards, with talc, a very soft material used to make baby powder, at one on the scale, and diamonds, the hardest natural material in the world, standing at ten. The common mineral quartz is a seven on the scale. The hardness of the mineral to be tested is determined by finding the hardest material it can scratch and/or the softest material that can scratch it. The scale provides an approximate measure that is adequate for amateurs who collect rocks and minerals as a hobby, who want to determine the identity of unknown minerals.

3   However, the scale is not precise enough for scientists or even for industry, where hardness is a valuable property. Abrasives, which are made of hard materials, are used to cut and polish softer materials and are widely used in a variety of industries. Industrial diamonds, for example, play a significant role in the manufacturing of metal products and in oil drilling.

4   In nature, it is easy to see the long-term effect of a mineral's hardness since differences in hardness are responsible for the appearance of many rock formations. Rocks usually contain more than one type of mineral, and as rain, wind, or the ocean wears them away, the harder minerals remain as the softer minerals erode and are washed away.

Skill Practice 2

Now read the text from Skill Practice 1 with a different purpose. Skim it quickly to get a general idea of its content. Then answer the questions below. Write *T* (True) or *F* (False) on the blank lines.

_____ 1 Scratch tests for hardness are new.

_____ 2 Hardness is determined by the strength of atomic bonds.

_____ 3 The Mohs scale requires special equipment.

_____ 4 The Mohs scale is useful for scientists.

Skill Practice 3

Ⓐ Read the following text. Your purpose is to study the material carefully and critically. Critical reading means you need to understand everything in the text and be able to evaluate the information in it. As you read, slow down when you come to parts you don't understand and reread if necessary. Take notes on the claims that the author makes and whether there is evidence for these claims.

Rare Earth Materials

1   Rare earth elements are metals and metal oxides with similar characteristics, the most important of which are their powerful magnetic properties. In spite of their name, they are actually not especially rare and, in fact, are relatively plentiful in the earth's crust. Rare earth metals and materials that contain them are crucial elements in the electronic devices that we use every day, including computer memory chips, rechargeable batteries, and cell phones. They are also used in larger devices such as wind turbines and electric and hybrid cars.

2   The demand for rare earth magnets has increased dramatically in recent years, with the explosion of computer and cell phone use, and the batteries that many of these devices require. Rare earth magnets are especially desirable because even relatively small magnets are able to produce incredibly strong magnetic fields. These smaller magnets also make it possible to manufacture lighter but stronger products, which are critical in electronics and communication equipment, especially the sophisticated equipment that is used by the military. One can quickly conclude that these earth elements play an essential role in the defense industry. Military experts assert that without these materials, defense industries and military forces would face major obstacles in their operations. Access to a continuous supply of these materials is a matter of national security.

3   Rare earth elements are extremely important, but they are also quite expensive. They are mined and produced almost exclusively in one place – China. China became the world's leading producer of rare earth oxides in the early 1990s and has led the market ever since, producing about 95 percent of the global supply of rare earth materials in 2010. Experts believe that about 50 percent of the world's reserves

of these materials are in China. Eventually, however, even these reserves will be exhausted. Thus, they also suggest that we should begin recycling electronic products today to conserve our resources of rare earth metals for tomorrow.

B For each of the claims below, decide if the author provides support for the claim. If there is support, provide it in the blank that follows the claim. If there is no or insufficient support, write *none* in the blank.

CLAIM	SUPPORT FROM THE READING
Rare metals are not rare.	
Rare earth materials are in increasing demand.	
Rare earth magnets are superior to traditional magnets.	
Without rare earth materials, military forces will be in trouble.	
China leads the market in the production of rare earth materials.	
Recycling is our best course for the future.	

C Answer the questions below. Then discuss your answers with a partner.

1 Is the text written for an audience from the United States or China? Support your answer by underlining evidence in the text.

2 How would you describe the writer's attitude toward Chinese dominance of the world's rare earth metal market? Support your answer by underlining evidence in the text.

Connecting to the Topic

Discuss the following questions with a partner.

1 What is your definition of *strong,* as this term relates to materials (e.g., wood, metal, etc.)?

2 What do you think the world's strongest material is?

3 Are all metals strong? Is glass? Is brick? Is concrete? Explain your answers.

4 In building and manufacturing, what qualities might be important in addition to strength?

Previewing and Predicting

> Looking at illustrations and graphic material can help you predict what a reading will be about.

Ⓐ Read the title of Reading 1, and look at the photographs, illustration, and table. Then answer the questions below.

1 Which material has the lowest tensile strength? _____

2 Which materials have the highest tensile strength? _____

3 What structures were advances in the pursuit of strength? _____

Ⓑ Compare your answers with a partner's.

While You Read

As you read, stop at the end of each sentence that contains words in **bold**. Then follow the instructions in the box in the margin.

The Pursuit of Strength

1   Building a bridge across a river, protecting the head and body of soldiers, keeping homes warm and dry, or designing the most advanced cell
phone all pose unique challenges. In construction and manufacturing, the
choice of appropriate materials is a vital matter with potential life-or-death
consequences. The development, selection, and evaluation of new materials are part of the field called materials science. The roots of the field date
back to prehistory, when early humans <u>first discovered the properties of
different types of stone and used this knowledge to create the first tools.
Later, as</u> they discovered <u>iron</u> and learned to make <u>bronze</u>, they began to
exploit more fully the properties of natural materials and modify them to
suit their needs. These endeavors of our ancestors are, to a large degree,
reflected in contemporary materials science **practices**.

I. Properties of Materials

2   Modern materials science engineers approach their task with a specific,
desired application in mind, then they consider the properties that are
required for that application, and finally, they identify a material with the
properties that most closely approximate those requirements. Materials
exhibit an array of inherent properties – electrical, thermal[1], optical[2], and
mechanical – that describe how they behave. For example, a particular
material may or may not conduct heat or electricity, it may be transparent
or opaque, or it may reflect light. When the public thinks of the properties
of materials, however, it is their mechanical properties that most frequently
come to mind. These include the following mechanical properties.

- Toughness describes the capacity of the material to absorb energy
  without breaking or cracking, ranging from tough to brittle.
- Hardness describes resistance to scratching, ranging from hard
  to soft.
- Stiffness is a measure of how much force is required to change the
  material's shape. Materials range from stiff to flexible.
- Elasticity and plasticity are measures that come into play when a
  force is applied to the material. Elasticity refers to the ability of the
  material to return to its original shape, and plasticity, its ability to
  retain a new shape, once the force is removed.

II. What Is Strength?

3   Each of these properties can be useful, given a specific purpose; nevertheless, the property that builders and engineers have historically pursued
most vigorously is strength. Although the idea of strength may at first

WHILE YOU READ 1

Which definition of
exploit matches the
meaning in this sentence?
(a) To use well for your
own benefit (b) To use
unfairly for your own
benefit

WHILE YOU READ 2

Look back over
paragraph 1. What is
your purpose in reading
this text? (a) Finding
specific information
(b) Understanding the
general idea (c) Learning
about content

---

[1] *thermal:* related to heat
[2] *optical:* connected with light or how things are seen

Figure 4.1 Typical Tensile Strength of Materials

MATERIAL	POUNDS/INCH²	METRIC MEASURE (MN/m²)
Iron	20,00–40,000	140–280
Copper	20,000	140
Wood (spruce)	15,000	100
Glass	5,000–25,000	30–170
Cotton	50,000	350
Concrete	600	4
Rope	12,000	80
Brick	800	5

Source: Gordon (1968)

appear straightforward, the concept is actually complex. For non-experts, toughness and hardness may appear to be elements of strength, whereas for engineers, there are two very different, but equally important, types of strength, and both are distinct from toughness and hardness. The first is tensile strength, which is the measure of how far a material can be pulled before it breaks. (See Figure 4.1.) Compression strength, in contrast, is the measure of how much a material can be compressed before it either collapses (e.g., a metal can) or splinters and breaks apart (e.g., a glass).

4 Strong materials have always been vital to successful construction, with most early construction relying on gravity and materials with compression strength, like stone and brick. If stones are properly fitted together, gravity will compress the structure and hold everything in place, even without an internal support structure like modern steel beams. This principle successfully guided the construction of the great cathedrals[3] of medieval[4] Europe. Windows and doors, however, presented problems for medieval architects in these stone buildings because they broke the path of compression. The arch represented a huge step forward in early construction because it solved this problem by distributing the force of compression. (See Figure 4.2.) To construct larger and more complex structures, builders subsequently turned to materials with greater tensile strength, such as metals. A modern suspension bridge, for example, combines the compression strength of concrete with the tensile strength of steel. (See Figure 4.3.) As crucial components of building and civil engineering practices, these two kinds of strength remain central **pillars** of modern construction.

III. Steel and Beyond

5 Modern steel is hard and tough, but most of all, it is exceptionally strong; its tensile strength can exceed 225,000 psi (pounds per square inch) or, 1500 MN/m², (meganewtons per square millimeter). Steel is composed

WHILE YOU READ ❸
Use context clues to determine the meaning of *pillars*. Highlight clues and choose the correct meaning.
(a) Concepts (b) Forms of support (c) Sources of development

Figure 4.2 An arch

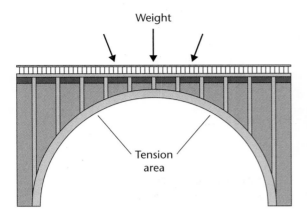

Weight

Tension area

Figure 4.3 A suspension bridge

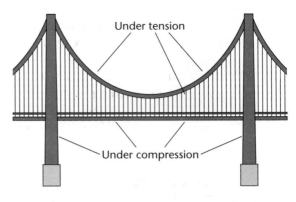

Under tension

Under compression

primarily of iron, and includes small but crucial quantities of carbon and other elements. It is the addition of carbon that alters the structure of iron and confers steel's unparalleled strength. The formula for making steel was discovered independently long ago in several civilizations, with the first evidence of steel tools dating back almost 4,000 years to Anatolia, now a part of Turkey. However, it was only in the middle of the nineteenth century that a series of inventions made it possible to manufacture the cheap, high-quality steel that dominates modern construction and **met-allurgy**. Today, there are many different types of steel that serve a variety of purposes, including the construction of roads, bridges, and other infrastructure, as well as the manufacture of cars and machinery. Steel is so central to contemporary life that it is difficult to imagine our lives without it; indeed, the use of steel is often considered a measure of a country's economic development.

WHILE YOU READ 4

Use your knowledge of word roots and context to figure out the meaning of *metallurgy*. Is it (a) the scientific study of metals or (b) the discovery of new metal elements?

6   Yet, as with any material, the use of steel involves tradeoffs. Although the strength of steel makes it an ideal choice for many purposes, it has drawbacks, the most significant of which is its weight. It is so heavy that is it impractical for many purposes, for example, the construction of aircraft. In addition, although it is strong, an exceptionally powerful force, like a bullet, can rupture it. For a long time, there were few alternatives to steel; however, some candidates have emerged in the past hundred years. First, starting at the end of the nineteenth century, advances in metallurgy led to the wider availability of aluminum, a far lighter metal than steel, and some years later, titanium – both metals that are now widely used in the construction of aircraft.

7   The twentieth century saw the rapid development of synthetic materials. Metals are natural materials that are processed to attain specific desirable properties, whereas synthetic materials are created entirely in the

---

[3] *cathedral:* a very large church
[4] *medieval:* related to the period between about 500 and 1500 CE, primarily referring to Europe

Critical Thinking

In Reading 1, you learned about some of the basic physical properties of materials.

CLARIFYING CONCEPTS

Critical thinking includes exploring a concept in a text by restating it and applying it to a different context.

A In your own words, describe the following properties and give an example of something that displays this property. Then compare your list with a partner's.

1 Strength

2 Hardness

3 Toughness

4 Stiffness

B Discuss the following questions with a partner.

1 Why do you think that strength has been the property that engineers have pursued the most vigorously?

2 If strength is the most valuable property, what do you think the second would be? Explain your answer.

Research

Research a material or product with extraordinary properties. Choose from the list below or identify one yourself:

- Carbine
- Carbon nanotubes
- Wurtzite boron nitride
- Lonsdaleite

- Bucky paper
- Dyneema
- Palladium microalloy
- Ultra-stable glass

Find answers to these questions:

- What makes it special?
- How was it discovered or created?
- What are its current applications, if any?

- Is it widely available?
- What are the drawbacks of using it, if any?

Writing

Write a report on what you found in your research. Begin by describing the material or product. Then discuss its uses and limitations.

Connecting to the Topic

Discuss the following questions with a partner.

1 What do you think are some of the strongest materials found in nature, in other words, materials that are not man-made?

2 How do you think the physical properties of steel compare with those of natural materials, such as bamboo or seashells?

3 What could be some of the challenges to using these natural materials on a large scale?

4 Why would scientists sometimes turn to nature's materials and design for inspiration?

Previewing and Predicting

Reading the title and section headings and looking at illustrations and photographs can help you predict what a reading will be about.

A **Read the title and section headings in Reading 2, and look at the photographs. What do you think this reading will be about? Put a check (✓) next to the topic or topics that you think will be included in the reading.**

_____ A An analysis of the material in sea shells

_____ B Ocean animals that are in danger

_____ C Research on spider web silk

_____ D The beauty of spider webs

_____ E Strong materials found in nature

B **Compare your answers with a partner's.**

While You Read

As you read, stop at the end of each sentence that contains words in **bold**. Then follow the instructions in the box in the margin.

◀)) Biomimetics

1   For centuries, engineers and scientists have been borrowing design ideas from **nature**. The structure of the lily pad is said to have been the inspiration for the design of London's Crystal Palace, a towering monument of iron and glass, built in 1851. The design for the Eiffel Tower, too, was based on a structure found in nature – the human thighbone[1]. More recently, the inspiration from biology has progressed to a smaller scale, with investigations into the molecular structure of living materials that are responsible for their unique properties. Scientists are attempting to unlock nature's secrets in order to imitate them and perhaps, even enhance them.

WHILE YOU READ ❶

Underline the sentences that support this claim.

I. Nature's Template

2   As part of the field of *biomimetics*, which refers to any man-made products based on designs, structures, or processes that are adapted or derived from nature, these investigations seek to improve the materials we use in manufacturing and in consumer products. Joanna McKittrick, a professor of Mechanical and Aerospace Engineering at the University of California, San Diego, offers her own view of biomimetics: "Mother Nature gives us templates. We are trying to understand them better so we can implement them in new materials" (Jacobs School, 2013). Biomimetics has heavily influenced the field of materials science. Here the search is on for materials with desirable combinations of properties that cannot be found in traditional materials, like metals and ceramics.

3   Long aware of the brilliance of natural design and the valuable properties of natural substances, materials scientists are now probing the plant and animal world in pursuit of substances that are stronger, lighter, and tougher than those available today. Some of these natural materials, such as metal and wood, have been available in abundance, while others are difficult to secure in large quantity. The first task of biomimetics, therefore, is the discovery of new materials with these desirable properties. The second, and equally important, task is working with nature to make new products available on a large scale. Based on what they have discovered in nature's designs, scientists and engineers are developing more efficient and **cost-effective** ways to reproduce these new materials and products in their laboratories.

II. Lightweight and High Tensile Strength

4   Due to its strength and versatility, steel has been the mainstay of modern industrial manufacturing for more than a hundred years, yet some of nature's humblest creatures make material that is considerably stronger. In tensile strength, spider silk rivals both steel and Kevlar. However, it has

WHILE YOU READ ❷

Use context and your knowledge of word parts to guess the meaning of *cost-effective*. Does it mean (a) inexpensive, (b) high profit compared to cost, or (c) inexpensive to produce in large quantities?

---

[1] *thighbone:* one of the bones of the upper leg

additional properties that these other materials do not possess. Able to stretch five times its original length without breaking, it remains flexible in cold temperatures, it is biodegradable, and above all, due to its low density, it is remarkably light. A pound of spider silk could extend the entire length of the **equator**.

5   Unfortunately, there is a major obstacle to commercial production of natural spider silk: its production requires an extraordinary investment of labor. As part of an artistic project, 70 people spent 4 years collecting silk from a million spiders to create an 11-by-4-foot (3.5 × 1.2 meter) textile[2], which now hangs in the Museum of Natural History in New York. Clearly, spider silk production is not a very practical enterprise. Any hope for doing so on an industrial scale cannot rely on spiders. Nevertheless, materials engineers are determined to figure out a cost-effective way to mass-produce it by cutting the spiders out of the process. Currently underway are two projects to tackle this problem, both using genetic engineering to produce spider silk without spiders. Scientists at the Japanese startup company Spiber have deciphered the genetic code responsible for the production of a key protein in spider silk, fibroin. They have used this information to genetically engineer bacteria to produce silk fibers in the laboratory. Just one gram of the protein can yield more than five miles (eight kilometers) of genetically engineered thread. In another spider-silk project, Randy Lewis, a molecular biologist at the University of Wyoming, in the United States, is also using genetic engineering, but taking a somewhat different approach. He has inserted the gene for spider silk protein production into female goats. As a result of this genetic alteration, the goats produce milk that contains the silk protein, fibroin. After a complex extraction process, a single liter of goat's milk yields just a few drops of the purified protein, which can be used in the manufacture of silk threads. Neither project has produced any silk for commercial purposes yet, but the scientists hope they will achieve that goal in the very near **future**.

Item made of spider silk

WHILE YOU READ ③

What can you infer about the properties of spider silk? (a) They are man-made. (b) They are similar to the properties of steel. (c) They are desirable.

WHILE YOU READ ④

What is the text structure of paragraph 5? Highlight some of the words that signal this structure.

III. High-compression Strength and Toughness

6   Materials with high-compression strength, such as ceramics and glass, are often quite brittle. Chalk, a common example of calcium carbonate, is among the world's most abundant substances. It exhibits surprisingly high

---

[2] *textile:* cloth

compression strength, maintaining its form even under heavy pressure. Yet, it is so brittle that even a small child can snap a piece of chalk in half. When a blow introduces a crack into its structure, the chalk cannot absorb the energy. The crack is propagated throughout the structure, and it eventually breaks the chalk apart.

7   The abalone, a sea snail that has existed for millions of years, has solved this problem at the microscopic level, with a shell that exhibits both compression strength and considerable toughness. The calcium carbonate in the shell consists of multiple layers of hexagonal plates which fit together like bricks in a wall. (See Figure 4.5.) On their own, these plates are brittle, much like chalk, and would offer little protection for the abalone. However, between these plates, the abalone inserts a protein that it is constantly producing. This layer of protein toughens the shell and allows it to absorb energy without cracking or breaking as chalk does. In fact, the shell is so strong that sea mammals trying to smash the shells against rocks in order to pry out the tasty snail are often unsuccessful. Using the insights they have gained from the abalone shell, materials scientists are working to create stronger ceramics and other new materials.

8   Always eager to develop and test innovative ideas, the scientists in charge of these biomimetic projects believe they have much to learn from Mother Nature, who is undoubtedly the greatest innovator of all. In nature's laboratory, there is both fierce competition and great danger, and as a result, all successful designs have gone through rigorous and thorough testing – thousands or even millions of years of life on Earth.

Figure 4.5 An abalone shell

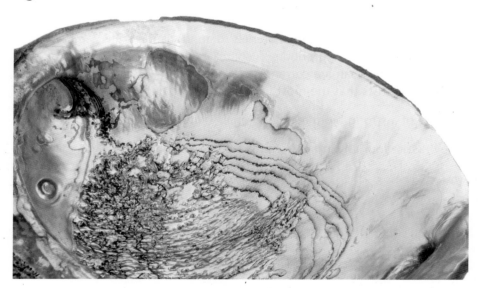

Main Idea Check

Match the main ideas below to five of the paragraphs in Reading 2. Write the number of the paragraph on the blank line.

_____ A The unique composition of the abalone shell makes it exceptionally tough.

_____ B The goal of biomimetics is to find and modify natural materials for new uses.

_____ C Nature offers the toughest testing ground.

_____ D There are several projects in progress working to produce spider silk in the laboratory.

_____ E One of the most common natural substances has important properties similar to the man-made materials, ceramics and glass.

A Closer Look

Look back at Reading 2 to answer the following questions.

1 How does the biomimetics approach differ from that of materials science in general?
   a The biomimetics approach includes materials that have desirable properties like ceramics and metals.
   b A biomimetic search for ideal materials includes those that are found in abundance in nature.
   c The biomimetics approach is generally more cost-effective than that of traditional materials science.
   d A biomimetic search for material with ideal properties is not limited to those currently available.

2 What is the major challenge for those working in biomimetics?
   a Bringing the production of biomimetic materials to an industrial scale
   b Finding a market for biomimetic products
   c Finding stronger materials than are currently available
   d Convincing other scientists that the most important materials are in nature

3 Kevlar is an example of a strong biomimetic material. **True or False?**

4 In the chart below, write four advantages and one drawback of spider silk.

ADVANTAGES	DRAWBACK

5 What do the two spider silk projects have in common? Choose all that apply.
  a They both use genetic engineering.
  b They have both succeeded in commercial production of spider silk.
  c They have both isolated a key protein.
  d They both create fibroin in a laboratory.

6 Calcium carbonate exhibits high tensile strength. **True or False?**

7 What is the effect of the protein layer in the abalone shell?
  a It provides nutrients for the animal.
  b It increases the compression strength of the material.
  c It seals the plates together.
  d It prevents the spread of cracks.

8 In what way is nature's laboratory rigorous?
  a Nature has been going on for longer than modern science.
  b Organisms with bad design will quickly die.
  c Nature has found ways to make good products.
  d All designs found in nature are successful.

Skill Review

In Skills and Strategies 10, you learned that readers adjust their reading strategies based on their reading purpose. A critical response requires careful reading, including interpretation and attention to how authors convey their own point of view.

Work with a partner or small group. Read the questions below and then review Reading 2.

Ⓐ What might some possible uses of commercial spider silk be?

Ⓑ Consider the author's point of view.

1 Does the author offer an optimistic or pessimistic perspective on the value and the future of biomimetics? Find evidence in the text for your response.

2 Is the treatment balanced? If yes, find evidence in the text for your response. If no, describe what the author might have included to present a more balanced view of the topic.

Definitions

Find the words in Reading 2 that are similar to the definitions below.

1 something that is used as a model for something else (*n*) Par. 2

2 a high level of intelligence or skill (*n*) Par. 3

3 to search into or examine (*v*) Par. 3

4 to produce a copy of something (*v*) Par. 3

5 the most important part of something (*n*) Par. 4

6 to be as good as (*v*) Par. 4

7 able to bend without breaking (*adj*) Par. 4

8 intended to make money (*adj*) Par. 5

9 work that involves effort (*n*) Par. 5

10 to discover the meaning of something that is difficult to understand (*v*) Par. 5

11 a set of symbols that gives information about something (*n*) Par. 5

12 the process of removing something or taking something out (*n*) Par. 5

13 to break something quickly with a sharp noise (*v*) Par. 6

14 to spread (*v*) Par. 6

15 to be made or formed of other things (*phrasal v*) Par. 7

Words in Context

A Use context clues to match the first part of each sentence to its correct second part and to understand the meaning of the words in bold.

_____ 1 The window was painted shut, so

_____ 2 By using the camera both during daylight and at night,

_____ 3 Carbon dioxide has many of the properties of a gas,

_____ 4 When they arrived at the convention,

_____ 5 Everyone in the audience was impressed by

_____ 6 In order to complete the project accurately and on time,

a many of the activities were already **underway**.

b **abundant** natural resources, particularly minerals and precious metals.

c you will get a sense of its **versatility** and value.

d will offer scientific and intellectual **insight** into some of the world's most urgent challenges.

e **insert** two batteries into the compartment at the back.

f but has the **density** of a liquid.

_____ 7 South Africa is a country of

_____ 8 This new and exciting project

_____ 9 He was feeling dizzy
        and confused

_____ 10 Before beginning to operate
        the unit,

g we needed to use a knife to **pry** it open.

h as a result of a **blow** to the head.

i we will need to **seek** additional funding
  from the government.

j his **humble** origins and his perseverance in
  the face of hardship.

Academic Word List

The following are Academic Word List words from Readings 1 and 2 of this unit. Use these words to complete the sentences. (For more on the Academic Word List, see page 299.)

collapsed (v)	exhibit (v)	inserted (v)	modified (v)	retained (v)
distinct (adj)	inherent (adj)	insight (n)	poses (v)	unparalleled (adj)

1 The study suggests that two _____ patterns of behavior have emerged.

2 During the operation, surgeons _____ the devices into the
patient's chest.

3 The restaurant at the top of the mountain offers a / an _____ view of the
valley below.

4 The new law _____ a challenge to schools who are already struggling to
meet other requirements.

5 Although he left his hometown many years ago, he has _____ his ties to
the community.

6 We often feel uncomfortable when other people _____ unusual or
inappropriate behavior.

7 The design of the car has been _____ to meet the new stricter pollution
control standards.

8 Certain risks are _____ to space exploration projects.

9 Several of the older homes _____ during violent storms last week.

10 The new book provides valuable _____ into how the brain works.

Critical Thinking

Reading 1 presents basic information about materials and their properties. Reading 2 offers insights into nature's designs and materials and discusses developments in the field of biomimetics. Based on what you have read in this unit and your own knowledge, answer the questions below. Review the readings if necessary.

> **APPLYING INFORMATION**
>
> You use critical thinking skills when you apply information you have just learned to new situations.

1 In what ways do nature's designs and materials exceed what humans have been able to create?

2 One of the goals of materials scientists has been to optimize more than one desirable property in a single material. How successful have they been? What are some examples in nature of this type of optimization?

3 What advantages might nature's designs have over man-made designs?

4 How do you think scientists seek out examples from nature for inspiration? Do you think their discoveries are all accidental?

5 Have you heard or read about any other examples of biomimetics in the creation of new materials? The design of buildings? Energy solutions? Explain your answers.

Research

You have read about just a few examples of the role of biomimetics in materials science. Investigate other examples of biomimetic research and applications. Consider the physical and design properties that the researchers in this field are pursuing. Find out about the work of one of the researchers listed below or find one on your own.

- Joanna Aizenberg
- Janine Benyus
- Michael Pawlyn

Writing

Your assignment is to write about a design or material that optimizes properties found in nature. Your report should be based on your investigation of biomimetic research.

A Preparing to Write

1 Look over your notes from your research.

2 Review Readings 1 and 2. Highlight any information you think you would like to include in your report.

3 Organize your notes into an outline for the report. It should include the following sections:

- What is the material or design?
- What was the inspiration from nature? Was it an animal? A plant?
- How does it work?
- How does it optimize properties found in nature?
- What are the prospects for this material or design? Is it being used now? Is it likely to be used in the future?

B Writing

1 Write your report. Write one paragraph for each of the points in your outline.

2 Begin each paragraph with a general sentence that tells your reader what the paragraph will be about.

3 Conclude with the prospects of this material or design for future use.

4 When you have finished your report, check it for grammar and spelling errors.

Improving Your Reading Speed

Good readers read quickly and still understand most of what they read.

A Read the instructions and strategies for Improving Your Reading Speed in Appendix 3 on page 316.

B Choose one of the readings in this unit. Read it without stopping. Time how long it takes you to finish the text in minutes and seconds. Enter the time in the chart on page 318. Then calculate your reading speed in number of words per minute.

Retaining Vocabulary

In reading academic texts, you will often encounter unfamiliar words. You are likely to find many of these new words, especially the words from the Academic Word List, again in other readings. It is important to develop strategies for remembering these new words. What should you do when you come across new words that you want to learn and remember? In general, the more often you read, hear, and use a word, the more likely you are to retain it. However, there are some methods you can use to improve your retention.

Examples & Explanations

Key Word Method
Target English word: *barb*
Spanish key word: *barba* =
English *barb*

The key word method is useful for words that you find especially challenging. It is one of the more difficult techniques, so it is not efficient to use for all words. Try to build an association between the new word and a word in your own language. For example, think of a word in your language (*barba*, Spanish for *beard*) that sounds like the word you are trying to learn (*barb*, in English). Then create a picture in your mind in which both appear (e.g., a beard with barbs, or hooks).

Retrieval

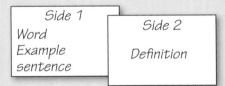

Retrieval is an effective technique for retaining new vocabulary. When you learn a new word, write the word and the sentence in which you found it on one side of a notecard. On the other side, write the definition. You can also write a key word, draw a picture, or include any other information that will help you remember. When you can't remember a word or you give the wrong definition, put that card in a different pile. Study the words in that pile more often. Shuffle your cards so that you study your words in a different order each time. Some websites can also help you create cards. These sites will shuffle the cards for you and present you with words that you got wrong, so you can study them more frequently.

Expanded Rehearsal

Expanded rehearsal means to study something for a long time when you first learn it, then expand the time between the study sessions and make them shorter.

Elaboration
*You should go inside when there is **lightning** because it can be dangerous.*

Elaboration is a technique that helps you learn and remember new vocabulary through active use. After you have studied new words, try to use them: say them out loud, write them in a sentence, think about the different parts of the word, or picture them.

Strategies

These strategies will help you study new vocabulary words.

- For new words you choose to study, make vocabulary cards or use a website as a resource. Include information like an example, a sentence that includes the word, or the definition of the word in English or in your own language. Add any other information you think will help you remember the word.
- Don't review your cards in the same order. Shuffle them, and study them in a different order each time, or use the computer to shuffle them for you.
- Test yourself on a word often right after you learn it. Keep testing yourself regularly, but make the time between your test sessions a little longer each time.
- To help you remember a new word, try to use it. For example, say the word aloud, write it down, or use it in a new sentence.
- If there are words that you are having particular trouble remembering, develop a key word strategy to help you.

Skill Practice 1

Read the following paragraphs. Some of the words may be unfamiliar to you. Choose five words that you think are important for you to learn. Make a card for each word or use a computer website to create them for you.

Solar Power

1   Engineers will play a crucial role in meeting the grand challenges that confront us today and will continue into the future. A committee of respected engineers has drafted a list of the challenges that they see as the most pressing; these are the challenges that future engineers will need to prepare for. With energy topping their list, they offer the following thoughts.

2   Without a doubt, energy is our most urgent challenge. We can no longer rely on conventional, nonrenewable sources of energy that damage the environment and will soon be exhausted. As a source of energy, nothing rivals the sun in its power and availability, but we have been unable to harness solar power efficiently at a reasonable cost. As a result, solar power's share of the energy market is minuscule – just one percent, compared to oil and gas at 85 percent.

3   Current commercial solar cells are not efficient; they convert solar energy at a maximum rate of only about 20 percent. They are limited by their primary component – silicon. Fortunately, promising new materials that can exceed this limit are already in development. Optimizing our storage capacity for solar energy must be our next priority. While all of this new technology is tantalizing, it will not trickle down to affect the lives of ordinary people until its cost drops. For solar energy to have a role in

solving our energy crisis, the cost must be at least equivalent to the cost of fossil fuels. This will be a task for engineers of the future.

Skill Practice 2

Read the following paragraphs. Some of the words may be unfamiliar to you. Choose three words that you think will be particularly difficult for you to remember. Apply the key word strategy to remember them.

Hyperloop – The Future Face of Transportation?

1   Inventor and entrepreneur Elon Musk wants everyone to move a little faster than contemporary trains permit. His futuristic *Hyperloop* transportation system would move twice as fast as the current speed champion, Shanghai's Maglev train, which chugs along at about 250 miles per hour. Musk's efforts have not yet reached fruition, but he has published elaborate plans for his system: it would carry people in pressurized capsules through giant steel vacuum tubes at 700 miles per hour.

2   He wants to demonstrate his project first in California, where he envisions the approximately 350-mile trip between Los Angeles and San Francisco would take about 35 minutes. He proposes to build the tube above ground in proximity to a highway that links the two cities. Each capsule would carry 28 passengers from one city to other and to destinations along the way. Eventually, Musk says, there would also be capsules large enough to carry vehicles. One day there might also be a tube across the country to carry passengers from New York to Los Angeles in less than an hour. For now though, Musk is sticking with the smaller project, which he estimates would cost about 6 billion dollars.

3   Critics question Musk's cost estimate as well as the feasibility of the project itself. Musk acknowledges that the project is still in the design stage but maintains that it is viable. One might be tempted to dismiss this kind of project as just the dream of an eccentric inventor. However, Musk also happens to be the head of a company that made history by designing and constructing the first and still only commercial vehicle to dock at the International Space Station. So even critics are taking him seriously.

Skill Practice 3

Reread the texts in Skill Practices 1 and 2. Choose four more words to study. Make cards for them and study them for a few minutes. Then work with a partner and test each other on your twelve new vocabulary words.

Connecting to the Topic

Discuss the following questions with a partner.

1 Where do new ideas come from?

2 How is innovation different from invention?

3 What are some examples of innovation that you are familiar with?

4 What are some examples of past innovations that have become part of our everyday lives?

5 How important is innovation for our future? Explain your answer.

Previewing and Predicting

> Reading the title and the first sentence of each paragraph can help you predict what the reading will be about.

A Read the first sentences of paragraphs 2–7 in Reading 3 and think about the title of the reading. Then read the following topics. Write the number of the paragraph where you think each topic will be discussed.

PARAGRAPH	TOPIC
	Blue-sky research and innovation
	Why basic research is important
	A description of basic research
	A description of the International Space Station
	An example of blue-sky research
	International Big Science projects

B Compare your answers with a partner's.

While You Read

As you read, stop at the end of each sentence that contains words in **bold**. Then follow the instructions in the box in the margin.

⏺) Blue-sky Research

1   **Very** little science happens in basements and garages anymore; modern science is expensive. Scientific research is a multimillion dollar enterprise with thousands of participants, both in the private[1] and public sectors[2]. There is enormous competition for funding, whether it comes from government agencies or private companies. As one might expect, those who fund research are looking for results, and they don't want to wait for decades to get them. This kind of pressure often controls the course of research, most recently, nudging it in the direction of goal-directed and translational research, that is, research that has explicit, practical, and generally, immediate applications that can enhance the health of the planet and the lives of the organisms that inhabit it. The contention that this kind of research is a good use of often scarce resources seems hard to refute, but many scientists insist that a national research program that is limited to applied science is shortsighted and unwise.

I. Blue-sky Science

2   Basic science, in contrast to applied research, is not directed toward any particular practical or commercial goal; rather, it is driven by curiosity. It seeks answers to some of the world's most fundamental questions about matter[3], nature, and the rules that govern them: What is the origin of our universe? How did life begin? What is the most distant star? The smallest particle of matter? It also targets smaller questions: How does a snail move? What is the function of a particular protein? What explains an element's properties? The goal of a great deal of basic research is simply knowledge for its own sake; it is not **shackled** by the need to solve practical problems.

3   Most of the scientific community acknowledges the need for both of these types of research. Translational research, which aims to facilitate the application of scientific discoveries to practical forms of innovation, is of immense value, but it relies on a substantial initial foundation in basic research. Indeed, it is the results of basic research that provide the raw material for translation and application. Eminent scientist and former editor of the journal *Science,* the late Daniel Koshland, described basic research and translational research as "revolutionary" and "evolutionary," respectively, in the following way: "Basic research is the type that is not always practical but often leads to great discoveries. Applied research refines these discoveries into useful products." The kind of basic research described by Koshland has acquired the nickname "blue-sky science," a term that has come to mean different things to different people. To some,

WHILE YOU READ ❶

As you read, choose words for vocabulary cards. Underline them so you can return to them when you have finished reading.

WHILE YOU READ ❷

Use context and your knowledge of word parts to guess the meaning of the word *shackled*. Does it mean (a) promoted, or (b) restricted?

---

[1] *private sector:* businesses that operate for a profit and are privately owned
[2] *public sector:* businesses, organizations, and services that are run by the government
[3] *matter:* a physical substance

blue-sky means impractical, unprofitable, even unachievable, but to others, it means visionary, innovative, and unrestricted by current beliefs.

II. Unexpected Directions

4   Blue-sky research can lead in unforeseen directions, which, in the view of many scientists, is its greatest strength. They stress the necessity of remaining flexible and open during the research process, and sometimes even the need to ignore the goals you have set and instead, follow a new path. Some of the most significant – and ultimately useful – discoveries have emerged from research that began with very different goals. This circuitous route is often the path to **innovation**.

5   Probably the foremost example of blue-sky research is quantum physics, an esoteric field that is about as far from everyday practicalities as one could imagine. The original quest for knowledge of the subatomic structure of matter had no immediate practical goal. Nevertheless, it was this knowledge that provided the foundation upon which all modern electronics, from the transistor to integrated circuits, was built. Without it, communications networks, high-speed computing, medical technology, and space exploration would never have become a reality. Yet, the physicists involved in the original discoveries had no idea of the magnitude of the economic and even social changes that would result from their research, or how long that process would take – a period of nearly a century. Similarly, curiosity drove physicists and engineers to investigate the unexpected changes in the conductivity of some elements under specific, controlled conditions. Today, we know these elements as semiconductors, also essential components of the electronics industry, without which, life today would be unrecognizable. In both cases, the extensions of blue-sky research that began with no discernible practical goal have led to innovations that ultimately landed in kitchens, hospitals, and schoolrooms all over the world.

III. Big Science

6   Some blue-sky research projects are so big that their implementation requires the cooperation of many organizations and multiple countries. Two such projects are the Large Hadron Collider and the International Space Station, both examples of what physicist Alvin Weinberg dubbed *Big Science*. The Large Hadron Collider in Switzerland is the world's largest and most powerful atomic particle accelerator. Its construction involved more than 10,000 scientists and engineers from over 100 countries, took more than 10 years, and cost more than $6 billion. Its tunnels, located deep below ground, extend more than 16 miles (27 kilometers). The collider accelerates subatomic particles into two beams traveling in opposite directions until they collide. The immediate goal of this crash is to see what kinds of smaller subatomic particles will emerge, but the larger goal of the project is to understand the fundamental forces of the universe. No one is

WHILE YOU READ ❸
Read ahead to the next paragraph to find support for this claim. Underline the supporting details.

The Large
Hadron Collider

certain of the extent of the eventual practical applications of this project, but findings from the collider's predecessors led to major innovations in **technology**.

7   The International Space Station (ISS), a joint project of the space agencies of Canada, Europe, Japan, Russia, and the United States, is even more ambitious. The station, a habitable satellite large enough to be occasionally

WHILE YOU READ

Scan paragraphs 6 and 7. What is the text organization of this part of the reading?

The International
Space Station

visible **with the naked eye** from Earth, has been continuously occupied since 2000. Astronauts on the ISS collect data and perform a wide range of experiments in the natural and physical sciences, focusing in particular on the impact of the microgravity[4] environment. For example, scientists are interested in how weightlessness affects everything from the growth of cells and crystals to conductivity. Much of this research falls into the blue-sky category, but some of it is already yielding practical applications, particularly in materials science. Research findings about the effects of microgravity have helped engineers understand how to optimize major industrial processes, knowledge that may lead to the development of new production methods and materials. Because the ISS uses public funds, there is considerable pressure to show a return on this investment[5], with practical results like these.

WHILE YOU READ 5

Use context to guess the meaning of the phrase *with the naked eye*.

8   The public tends to be more supportive of applied science than basic science perhaps, in part, because they understand it better. This tension between basic and applied science has a long history and is likely to continue. Since as far back as 1945, it has been the center of debate. In a special report to U.S. President Truman on the status of scientific research, the Director of the Office of Scientific Research wrote,

> Basic research leads to new knowledge. It provides scientific capital. It creates the fund from which the practical applications of knowledge must be drawn. New products and new processes do not appear full-grown. They are founded on new principles and new conceptions, which in turn are painstakingly developed by research in the purest realms of science. Today, it is truer than ever that basic research is the pacemaker[6] of technological progress (Bush, 1945).

9   Scientists continue to echo these sentiments, arguing that innovations of the future require us to maintain an active pipeline of basic research today.

---

[4] *microgravity:* a condition in which there is very little gravitational force
[5] *return on investment:* the profit from an activity compared to the amount of investment in it
[6] *pacemaker:* a small electronic device inserted into the body to control heart rate

Main Idea Check

Match the main ideas below to five of the paragraphs in Reading 3. Write the number of the paragraph on the blank line.

_____ A Basic research can lead to unpredictable innovation.

_____ B The role and relative importance of basic and translational research have been debated for a long time.

_____ C Blue-sky research in physics has led to enormously important applications.

_____ D There is competition for funding between the applied and basic sciences.

_____ E Current basic research in physics may lead to future important applications.

A Closer Look

Look back at Reading 3 to answer the following questions.

1 In the first paragraph of Reading 3, what information can be inferred, but is not directly stated?
   a Scientific research is very competitive.
   b Scientific discovery was once more of an individual activity.
   c Many scientists are supportive of basic research even though it is expensive.
   d Very few scientists are engaged in scientific research anymore.

2 The determination of the basic structure of DNA is an example of basic research. **True or False?**

3 Why has the term *blue-sky* been applied to some basic research?
   a Most of the research is focus on advanced physics.
   b It is very expensive.
   c It is rarely profitable.
   d It has no limits.

4 In what way is quantum physics research a good example of the value of blue-sky research?
   a It shows that curiosity-driven research can have practical results.
   b It demonstrates that valuable research can be done when countries cooperate.
   c It shows that the hardest questions take the longest to answer.
   d It demonstrates the importance of beginning research with a clear goal.

5 Why did the author include the example of the Large Hadron Collider?
   a To point to the necessity of international cooperation
   b To give the most extreme example of Big Science
   c To suggest that this blue-sky project may eventually lead to practical findings
   d To demonstrate the importance of basic research for our understanding of the most fundamental issues in science

6 Research at the Large Hadron Collider has already led to important everyday applications. **True or False?**

7 What special feature of the International Space Station may yield important practical applications?

    a Its superconductivity

    b Its low-gravity environment

    c Its international staff of scientists

    d Its low temperature and lack of natural oxygen

Skill Review

In Skills and Strategies 11, you learned about different strategies for vocabulary retention. Checking your understanding of new words can help you remember them better.

A All of the words in the table below appear in Reading 3. Use a (✓) to rank each word according to how much knowledge you have of its meaning. Some of the words may have more than one meaning. Review Reading 3 to see how they are used in context.

WORD	KNOWLEDGE OF WORD		
	A I know the meaning of this word.	B I have an idea of what this word means.	C I do not know what this word means.
acknowledge			
circuitous			
collide			
discernible			
drive			
enhance			
esoteric			
explicit			
founded			
magnitude			
optimize			
predecessor			
quest			
refine			

refute			
scarce			
shortsighted			
stress			
unforeseen			
visionary			

B Now do the Vocabulary Development exercises below. After you have finished, look at the chart in **A** again. Make or use a computer website to create cards for half of the words from columns B or C that you are still not sure about. Review your cards using an expanded rehearsal schedule.

C In two weeks, return to the chart in **A**. Consider the words you chose in **B**. Compare your knowledge of the words for which you created cards to your knowledge of the words for which you did *not* create cards. Complete the blanks below.

1 How many ✓s did you write in columns B and C? _____

2 From the list of words for which you created cards, how many would you now put in column A? _____

3 From the words for which you did not create cards, how many would you now put in column A? _____

Vocabulary Development

Definitions

Find the words in Reading 3 that are similar to the definitions below.

1 very clear and direct (*adj*) Par. 1

2 to improve the quality of something (*v*) Par. 1

3 to prove that something is false (*v*) Par. 1

4 to make something move toward a specific goal (*v*) Par. 2

5 to improve something by making changes, usually small ones (*v*) Par. 3

6 having clear and inspired ideas about what the future should be (*adj*) Par. 3

7 a long and difficult search for something (*n*) Par. 5

8 large size or great importance (*n*) Par. 5

9 able to be seen or recognized (*adj*) Par. 5

10 to make something as effective as possible (*v*) Par. 7

Words in Context

Complete the sentences with words from Reading 3 in the box below.

acknowledged	collided	founded	scarce	stressed
circuitous	esoteric	predecessor	shortsighted	unforeseen

1 The decision to cut the budget is _____. We will all regret it in the future.

2 The new head of the company plans to follow many of the policies established by his _____.

3 Unless we encounter some _____ problems, I believe we will be able to finish the project on time.

4 Because of extensive construction around the city, the taxi had to take a / an _____ route to the airport.

5 When resources are _____, it is important to conserve them and use them wisely.

6 The driver lost control of his motorcycle and _____ with a tree.

7 The hypothesis of her experiment was _____ on a widely accepted theory.

8 Instead of emphasizing the many negative findings of the study, the politician _____ only the few positive results.

9 The professor presented a long, _____ argument about the economic basis of self-government, which none of the students could follow.

10 At the beginning of the talk, the president _____ that the government had made a lot of mistakes in the past.

Critical Thinking

Reading 3 described the goals of and differences between basic and applied research.

A **With a partner, discuss the questions below.**

1 What do you think the relationship between blue-sky science and big science is?

2 In what way is basic research "the pacemaker of technological progress"?

3 What might the consequences of suspending support for basic research be?

4 Do you think scientific research should have practical real-world goals?

5 Is some basic research not worthwhile? On what basis would you judge the value of basic research?

B **Share your answers with the rest of the class.**

> **ANALYZING INFORMATION**
>
> Critical thinking involves thinking carefully about important topics that the writer has not completely explained.

Research

Research a past or present big science program. You can choose one of the projects in Reading 3 or choose one below:

- The Hubble Telescope
- Super Kamiokande
- Very Large Array
- Neptune
- The National Ignition Facility
- Juno
- A project of your choice

Consider the following questions in your research.

- What are its goals?
- How much does it cost?
- Have there already been some benefits from this project?
- What might some future benefits be?

Writing

Write a report about the program that you researched. Your report should have three paragraphs. In the first paragraph, explain the project and its goals. In the second paragraph, describe the results of the project so far. In the final paragraph, give your view of the project. Do you think the research is valuable? Should governments continue to provide funding for it?

Connecting to the Topic

Read the definition of *frugal,* **and then discuss the following questions with a partner.**

> **frugal** (*adj*) careful in the use of money, energy, or other resources

1 Is frugality something positive?

2 Can you give an example of frugality?

3 Are you frugal? Or is someone you know frugal? Give an example that illustrates this frugality.

Previewing and Predicting

Reading the title and section headings can help you predict what a reading will be about.

A **Read the title of Reading 4. What do you think** *frugal innovation* **means?**

_____

B **Read the section headings (*I–V*). Then read the questions below. Write the number of the section in which you are likely to find the answer to each question.**

SECTION	QUESTION
	How does keeping an open mind promote innovation?
	How do obstacles and challenges lead to innovation?
	What is frugal innovation?
	Can reusing resources spur innovation?
	In what parts of the world can we find examples of frugal innovation?
	What part can consumers play in frugal innovation?
	What can we learn from recycling?

C **Compare your answers with a partner's.**

While You Read

As you read, stop at the end of each sentence that contains words in **bold**. Then follow the instructions in the box in the margin.

Frugal Innovation

I. Innovation – a Global Phenomenon

1   **Moving** human knowledge ever forward involves two crucial and related processes: invention, generally considered to be the creation of new ideas and processes, and innovation, the recruitment and refinement of existing ideas and processes in novel contexts or applications. Whereas invention is comparatively rare, the demand for innovation is constant, as scientists, engineers, and businesses, in a never-ending search for newer, better, and faster technology, fuel efforts in research and development[1]. Global expenditures on research and development, most of which take place in fully industrialized nations, topped U.S. $1.5 trillion in 2013. (See Figure 4.6.) Yet some economists argue the return on this enormous investment is not what it could, and perhaps, should be. This trend may

WHILE YOU READ 1

As you read, choose words for vocabulary cards. Underline them so you can return to them when you have finished reading.

Figure 4.6 R&D Expenditures 2013 (in billions)

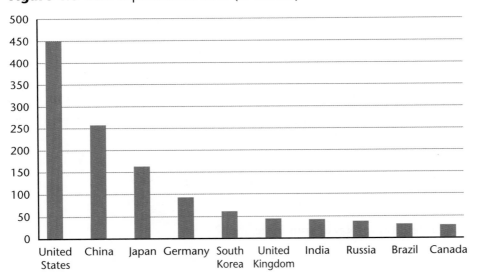

Source: Batelle

be about to change, with a significant amount of innovation expected to come from other parts of the world, where the context for innovation is very different than in industrialized countries like the United States and Japan. Innovation experts like Carlos Ghosn, CEO of Renault-Nissan, say the time has come for a dynamic new perspective on science and engineering; the time is ripe for frugal innovation. Frugal innovation is already practiced all over the world under many different names: *zizhu chuanxin* in Mandarin, *jua kali* in Swahili, *Système D* in French, and *gambiarra* in

---

[1] *research and development:* the part of an organization that works to improve existing products and develop new ones

Brazilian Portuguese, but the phenomenon is probably best known by its Hindi name: *jugaad*. *Jugaad* means the application of available resources and human ingenuity to the solution of a local problem in a way that is appropriate for that context. Proponents of frugal innovation maintain that a highly structured, top-down[2], and often, expensive approach to innovation cannot solve all of the world's complex problems, especially those that plague the developing world. They believe that the principles of jugaad show the best path for innovation in a diverse and changing global environment (Radjou et al., 2012).

II. Opportunity in Adversity

2   Frugal innovation is based on a set of principles, the most important of which is to treat adversity and scarcity not just as challenges to be overcome, but as opportunities, indeed, as the inspiration for innovation. Clean water provides one good example of this. About 780 million people in the world live without access to clean water. About 3.4 million people die every year from water-related illness, many of them babies and young children, who are particularly susceptible to these diseases. Most water purification systems require electricity, yet a substantial number of communities with no source of clean water also have no access to reliable power. The Tata Group in India has met this challenge with a water filter that kills about 80 percent of **waterborne bacteria** in 792.5 gallons (3000 liters) of water, yet costs only about U.S. $16. This is far cheaper than the electricity that would be needed to boil and sterilize the water. The filter offers the additional advantage that it is made from a common waste product in India – the burned husks of rice.

> **WHILE YOU READ** 2
> Use context to guess the meaning of the phrase *waterborne bacteria*.

Water purifier

---

[2] *top-down:* originating in the highest levels of an organization

3   Frugal innovation develops not only in powerful multinational companies like Tata; frugal ideas often begin on a small scale. A group of students in Peru have come up with a different solution to the water shortage in their city, Lima. The students have erected condensers, much like those in air conditioners, inside a billboard[3] that stands above the city skyline. When air comes in contact with the condensers, the vapor in the air turns into water, which then flows into a tank below. Advertisements on the billboard pay for installation and other energy costs. This is a small-scale, bottom-up project, addressing a local problem by providing a local solution. Although it is not yet clear if it could be scaled up to a regional or even national level, it is an exemplary model of jugaad.

III. Reuse, Recycle, Repurpose

4   To do more with less is another fundamental principle of the jugaad philosophy. The goal is to use available materials and technology that already exist and to use them in innovative ways, a mindset that has led to what has been called **leapfrog technology** in some parts of the world. In developed countries, engineers can assume access to a reliable power source, giving them no impetus to innovate beyond it. In contrast, many communities in developing countries are not on a power grid[4], motivating engineers and planners to think creatively. One asset that has been widely embraced by jugaad thinkers is a technology many such communities do have access to: a robust mobile phone network. Innovators have used this network to bring information, education, and even banking service to rural areas. There are no ATMs or debit cards[5] in such communities, but a mobile phone and a portable fingerprint scanner[6] allow people in remote villages to withdraw money at small shops that serve as mobile banks. This type of innovation demonstrates the application of leapfrog technology, but there are also jugaad efforts that utilize almost no new technology, requiring instead only the simplest of materials. One famous example of this lower-tech jugaad thinking is the Liter of Light, pioneered in Brazil and popularized in the Philippines. A one-liter plastic bottle of water installed in the roof refracts sunlight, bringing as much illumination as a 50-watt bulb but with no need for electricity.

IV. Be Flexible

5   Frugal innovators need to be flexible and adapt their ideas as the context requires. Many of the customers at Haier, a huge Chinese company that manufactures consumer products like washing machines, are first-time

---

[3] *billboard:* a very large sign with an advertisement at the side of the road or above a building
[4] *power grid:* the network of electricity wires that connect power stations
[5] *debit card:* a small plastic card that allows people to withdraw and pay with money from their bank account
[6] *fingerprint scanner:* a device that takes images of the patterns on people's fingertips

buyers. One such customer, a farmer, complained that his new machine stopped functioning. The repairman who responded to his complaint discovered that the farmer had not been washing clothes; instead, he had been washing potatoes from his fields and, as a result, the dirt was clogging the pipes. The repairman fixed the machine, but Haier also responded to the broader need. It turned out that thousands of farmers were using their washing machines in the same way, so Haier developed a machine with bigger pipes that doesn't just wash potatoes; it peels them as well.

V. Keep the Needs of the User in Mind

6   C. K. Prahalad, an author and business professor, urged engineers and business leaders to consider the "bottom of the pyramid." Products are often designed with affluent consumers in mind; however, there are also 4 to 5 billion consumers around the world with low incomes but high aspirations. Their combined spending power is enormous, so paying attention to their needs can be profitable. The Nokia 1100 mobile phone, which the journal *Foreign Policy* called the most important phone on the planet, provides ample evidence of this concept. The Nokia 1100 is not a smartphone; it can only make and receive calls and texts, but that is exactly what this market **demands**. In addition, the phone is moisture and dust resistant and includes a light, in the event of power outages, but perhaps most important, it costs only about U.S. $20. It is the best-selling phone of all time, having passed the 250 million mark in 2013.

7   The proponents of jugaad innovation are quick to acknowledge that this approach alone will not solve the world's most pressing problems, but it is an important tool, particularly in a climate of scarce **resources**.

WHILE YOU READ 4

Which definition of *demands* matches the meaning in this sentence?
(a) Ask for in a very strong, forceful way
(b) Need

WHILE YOU READ 5

Go back and skim Reading 4. What is the text organization?

Main Idea Check

Match the main ideas below to five of the paragraphs in Reading 4. Write the number of the paragraph on the blank line.

_____ **A** Frugal innovation utilizes leapfrog technology.

_____ **B** Low income consumers have massive buying power.

_____ **C** Jugaad thinking requires flexibility.

_____ **D** Jugaad approaches to clean water exemplify the principle of opportunity in adversity.

_____ **E** Frugal innovation has the potential to meet many enduring challenges in the developing world.

A Closer Look

Look back at Reading 4 to answer the following questions.

1 U.S. research and development expenditures account for about a third of such spending worldwide. (See Figure 4.6.) **True or False?**

2 Jugaad is presented as a novel concept in Reading 4, so why might so many countries already have their own name for it?

   a Jugaad is a universal concept that everyone can take advantage of.

   b People in the developing world have more ingenious ways of solving their own problems.

   c People in those countries have already been practicing frugal innovation out of necessity.

   d It is unlikely that people around the world would adopt the Hindi term for this approach to innovation.

3 Which statements are consistent with jugaad thinking? Choose all that apply.

   a Adapt your ideas to fit local needs.

   b Use materials that are locally available.

   c Keep your profit margins low.

   d Avoid the use of the newest technology.

4 The Peruvian students' billboard idea for increasing access to water is not being used throughout the country. **True or False?**

5 Which of the following is an example of leapfrog technology?

   a People in a village in Thailand exchange goods instead of using money.

   b A city requires cars to install pollution controls.

   c A national government invests in research and development in mobile technology.

   d A remote village in China uses solar energy to heat water.

6 List three ways in which the Liter of Light project exemplifies frugal innovation.

_____

_____

_____

7 Which of the following would be an example of a product that considers consumers at the bottom of the pyramid?
   a Washing machines that can peel potatoes
   b Bicycles that can move quickly in heavy traffic
   c Small bottles of shampoo that work best in cold water
   d Solar heaters that do not require electricity

Skill Review

In Skills and Strategies 11, you learned about different strategies for vocabulary retention. Checking your understanding of new words can help you remember them better.

A **All of the words in the table below appear in Reading 4. Use a (✓) to rank each word according to how much knowledge you have of its meaning. Some of the words may have more than one meaning. Review Reading 4 to see how they are used in context.**

WORD	KNOWLEDGE OF WORD		
	A I know the meaning of this word.	**B** I have an idea of what this word means.	**C** I do not know what this word means.
adversity			
affluent			
ample			
climate			
clog			
dynamic			
exemplary			
illumination			
impetus			
in the event of			

ingenuity			
installation			
mindset			
novel			
phenomenon			
plague			
proponent			
robust			
sterilize			
susceptible			

B Now do the Vocabulary Development exercises below. After you have finished, look at the chart in **A** again. Make or use a computer website to create cards for half of the words from columns B or C that you are still not sure about. Review your cards using an expanded rehearsal schedule.

C In two weeks, return to the chart in **A**. Consider the words you chose in **B**. Compare your knowledge of the words for which you created cards to your knowledge of the words for which you did *not* create cards. Complete the blanks below.

1 How many ✓s did you write in columns B and C? _____

2 From the list of words for which you created cards, how many would you now put in column A? _____

3 From the words for which you did not create cards, how many would you now put in column A? _____

Definitions

Find the words in Reading 4 that are similar to the definitions below.

1 to be ready for something to happen (*v phrase*) Par. 1

2 inventiveness; cleverness (*n*) Par. 1

3 something that is unusual or new (*n*) Par. 1

4 rules that controls or explains something (*n pl*) Par. 1

5 easily affected by; vulnerable (*adj*) Par. 2

6 a piece of equipment that removes something from water or air (*n*) Par. 2

7 to clean something so that it is free of bacteria (*v*) Par. 2

8 the act of putting something in place so it can be used (*n*) Par. 3

9 attitudes and opinions (*n*) Par. 4

10 a force that makes something happen; motivation (*n*) Par. 4

11 able to be carried (*adj*) Par. 4

12 to block so that movement is stopped or slowed (*v*) Par. 5

13 more than sufficient (*adj*) Par. 6

14 in case of (*idiom*) Par. 6

15 situation (*n*) Par. 7

Synonyms

Complete the sentences with words from Reading 4 in the box below. These words replace the words in parentheses, which are similar in meaning.

adversity	dynamic	illumination	perspective	proponent
affluent	exemplary	novel	plagued	robust

1 There was so little (light) _____ in the room that it was difficult to see.

2 The company conducts business in a / an (ideal) _____ fashion, which is why it is respected worldwide.

3 The book presents a fresh new (viewpoint) _____ on the role of education in economic development.

4 The town by the river has been (troubled) _____ by floods for decades.

5 He is a / an (supporter) _____ of a higher budget for the military.

6 The government predicts (strong) _____ economic growth for the next year.

7 Many people believe that (difficulty) _____ builds character and makes us stronger.

8 Barcelona is a / an (lively) _____ city with an active arts community.

9 This school uses a / an (new) _____ approach to working with children who have failed in the past.

10 Most of the residents of the northern part of the city are (rich) _____; in contrast, the neighborhoods in the south tend to be poorer.

Academic Word List

The following are Academic Word List words from Readings 3 and 4 of this unit. Use these words to complete the sentences. (For more on the Academic Word List, see page 299.)

acknowledge (*v*)	enhance (*v*)	founded (*v*)	phenomenon (*n*)	refine (*v*)
dynamic (*adj*)	explicit (*adj*)	perspective (*n*)	principle (*n*)	stress (*v*)

1 The program will feature interesting guests with _____ personalities.

2 This new method of assessment provides _____ indicators of air and water quality so that authorities can take immediate action.

3 Global warming is a / an _____ on which there is increasing agreement among both scientists and the public.

4 Even critics of the new program _____ that something must be done to ensure that schools are safe for children.

5 A story in today's newspaper reports on the war from the _____ of those who are most deeply affected by it.

6 Members of the committee met to _____ the report that they will present to the public next week.

7 The organization was _____ on the idea that everyone should have a chance at success.

8 The camera is designed on the same _____ as the human eye.

9 Hiring a local guide can _____ your experience when you take a vacation in an unfamiliar place.

10 We cannot _____ enough the importance of research and development.

Critical Thinking

Reading 3 presented innovation on a macro level; you learned about major projects in basic and applied research, usually funded by governments. Reading 4 turns the focus on the micro level, exploring smaller-scale innovative projects that can still have a major impact.

EXPLORING OPINIONS

Critical readers form their own opinions about important topics in a text.

Work with a classmate. Based on what you have read in this unit and your own knowledge, answer questions below. Review the readings if necessary.

1 You have learned about basic and translational research. How do you think that jugaad projects fit into this relationship, if at all?

2 Large-scale research is usually funded by governments, whereas jugaad projects are usually supported by philanthropic and nongovernment organizations. Why do you think this is the case?

3 Do you think governments should provide money for frugal innovations?

4 Most of the jugaad projects you have read about are found in non-industrialized countries. Do you think this should change? Do you think it will?

5 In what ways to do you think "the bottom of the pyramid" will control the future of global innovation?

Research

Research a jugaad innovation that you think will have a major impact on the lives of a large number of people. You may concentrate on a project in your own country or community or choose another community that is of interest to you. (You can search for "jugaad innovation" or "frugal innovation.")

- Has it been used already?
- Has it been successful? Describe the impact it has had.
- What are the costs associated with the innovation? Of development? To the users?
- Do you think it is likely that its use will spread? Why or why not?
- In addition, consider the country where the innovation has been or will be introduced. What are the expenditures of research and development in that country? You can find some of the figures for specific countries at the World Bank and the Organisation for Economic Development and Cooperation.

Writing

Your assignment is to recommend funding the jugaad project you have researched. You will make the recommendation to the government where the project is currently located. In doing so, you should situate the project within the larger context of research and development in that country.

1 Preparing to Write

- Look over your notes from your research.
- Review Readings 3 and 4. Highlight any information you think you would like to include in your report.
- Organize your notes into an outline for the report. It should include the following sections:
  - What is the project?
  - What has been or what could be its impact on the community where it is used?
  - What is its cost? (You do not need to provide exact amounts. You can describe the costs in general.)
  - How much does this country spend on R&D in general?

2 Writing

- Write your report.
  - In the first paragraph, describe the project.
  - In the second paragraph, discuss the project's impact.
  - In the third paragraph, discuss costs and expenditures.
- Begin each paragraph with a general sentence that tells the reader what the paragraph will be about.
- Conclude with your recommendation for funding your jugaad project.

3 When you have finished your report, check it for grammar and spelling errors.

Improving Your Reading Speed

Good readers read quickly and still understand most of what they read.

A Read the instructions and strategies for Improving Your Reading Speed in Appendix 3 on page 316.

B Choose one of the readings in this unit. Read it without stopping. Time how long it takes you to finish the text in minutes and seconds. Enter the time in the chart on page 318. Then calculate your reading speed in number of words per minute.

Preparing for a Test

Academic courses require a lot of reading. Instructors give tests to find out if students have learned, remembered, and understood the reading. There are many different kinds of test questions, but tests on readings usually include short or long answer questions, that is, questions that require answers of several sentences or paragraphs. For any kind of test, preparation will increase your chances of doing well. Many of the strategies that you have learned so far in this book will help you prepare for tests: finding main ideas and supporting details, highlighting key words, taking notes, and using graphic organizers. Probably the most important strategy is predicting what questions will be on the test and practicing how you would answer them.

Examples & Explanations

On January 28, 1989, 73 seconds after it lifted off the ground, the spacecraft *Challenger* exploded in the sky, killing everyone aboard, including a teacher. This disaster could have been prevented.

The launch had been delayed for six days because of rain and technical problems. The morning of the launch was very cold, much colder than normal, a development that concerned the engineers on the project. They had warned the project directors that the O-rings, a rubber part crucial to the first stage of the *Challenger*'s journey, might fail at such low temperatures. [1]They said they didn't have enough data on the performance of the O-rings in the cold. [2]In addition, although many systems in space programs had back-up procedures in case the first system failed, the O-rings had no backup. Unfortunately, the project directors dismissed the engineers' concerns, with tragic results.

Before making predictions about the questions they will encounter, students must have a good understanding of the text. This student has used a system of marking up the text to help her prepare.

She has highlighted the main idea and circled key words.
She has underlined the parts she thinks are important: the reasons for the disaster, a description of the actual events, and some concluding thoughts. She has used numbers to show the specific reasons the disaster occurred.

Then, based on the parts of the text that she has annotated, the student predicted some questions.

What were the causes of the Challenger disaster?
Were they the result of human error, mechanical problems, or other factors?

What actually happened? Describe the events that led to the explosion of the spacecraft.

What is an O-ring? What is its purpose? Why was it so critical?

What lessons can we learn from this disaster?

On that unusually cold and icy morning, the O-rings indeed became too brittle to hold their seal, allowing hot gasses to flow through the hole they created. Flames broke out and damaged the fuel tank, resulting in the destruction of the spacecraft. An investigation after the disaster concluded that managers at the top level had failed. In their eagerness for success, they had ignored engineering procedures and basic safety concerns.

After you have predicted test questions, use your notes to write answers to them. You could also exchange questions with a classmate.

Strategies

These strategies will help you prepare for a test.

- Highlight important information, make notes on the reading or on a separate paper, and review them when you study. Don't reread everything. It takes too much time.
- Review the definitions of key terms and concepts. If the reading does not include them, write your own.
- Based on your notes, try to predict what questions will be on the test.
- Consider questions that go beyond the facts in the reading and questions that require critical thinking.
- Practice answering the questions in writing before the test.

Skill Practice 1

Read the following paragraph that a student has highlighted and annotated. Use this information to predict three questions that might be on a test about this reading.

People are often afraid to make mistakes, but in fact, they are a crucial part of the learning process. Business professor Paul Schoemaker says the same is true for business. He claims that ①99 percent of big business successes arise from previous failure. Therefore, he reasons, it makes sense to study failures for clues to success. Schoemaker calls this "mining failure." He argues that businesses should take a forensic approach to mining failure, similar to the approach that detectives take when they investigate crimes. ②A detailed understanding of why the mistake occurred is the key to growth and innovation, according to Schoemaker. He also stresses that employees should be encouraged to experiment and also allowed to fail. One company, 3M, the company that brought the world Post-It Notes, has established a program that called *Time to Think*. The company encourages its scientists and engineers to spend up to 15 percent of their time exploring new ideas, solving problems, and – failing. Some of 3M's most innovative products, including (Post-it Notes), have come from this program.

Predicted test questions:

1 _____

2 _____

3 _____

Skill Practice 2

Read the following paragraphs that a student has annotated. Then read the answers to the three questions that the student predicted might be on a test. On the blank lines below, write three questions for the three answers.

1   Sometimes innovative design gets ahead of the engineering knowledge that is needed to support it. The Hancock Tower, Boston's tallest building, was designed as a monument of (minimalist, modern architecture). A shimmering tower of reflective glass, it opened five years behind schedule and was plagued with numerous problems. Although the design complied with all building regulations that were in place in the 1970s, by the time it was built, unanticipated problems emerged as a result of the size and novel shape of the building. It was exceptionally tall for the time, with a shape like a parallelogram, which caught passing gusts of wind, <u>causing the building to twist and sway.</u> The movement was strongest on the top floors, causing occupants to feel motion sickness at times, as if they were on a ship. Even more alarming was the fact that during construction, many of the <u>500-pound windows became detached from the building and came crashing down to the ground below.</u> Eventually, all of the more than 10,000 windows had to be replaced.

2   As one might expect, many people were unhappy about the flaws in the building, and there were multiple lawsuits against the parties who designed and built it. All of the flaws were eventually corrected, and today the Hancock Tower is acknowledged as an architectural treasure. The lawsuits were all settled; however, as part of the

settlements, all of the parties involved were required to remain forever silent about what had happened. Sadly, as a result, architects, engineers, and designers since that time have been unable to gain from the lessons learned from the Hancock Tower.

Predicted test questions:

1 _____

2 _____

3 _____

Answers:

1 The Hancock Tower was important because it was a large and beautiful example of the minimalist modern style.

2 There were two major design problems. First, the building swayed in strong wind and made people feel sick. Second, the windows proposed in the original design fell off the building.

3 Architects learned about the limits of the size and shape that a building could take using the engineering technology of the time, but they were unable to learn more about the mistakes that had been made because the lawsuit required those involved to remain silent.

Skill Practice 3

Work with a partner. Read and take notes on the following paragraphs. Then write three questions that you think could be on a test based on the reading. Exchange questions with your partner and write the answers to each other's questions.

1   For most of us, the mistakes we make are something we have to live with. We don't like them, but they are a part of life. Learning from mistakes can be valuable. For instance, there is one place in which mistakes can be really valuable and even priceless – in philately, otherwise known as stamp collecting. Among stamp collectors, mistakes are often prized possessions because the mistakes are generally caught before a large number of stamps containing them are printed and distributed. Printers destroy the faulty stamps that have not been sold. As a result, stamps with errors are usually rare, and rarity translates to value.

2   There are many possible error types, including the use of the wrong color, upside down images, the wrong image, or two images on top of each other. Not all stamps with such errors are valuable, but some are, especially if they are old and in good condition. Probably the most famous stamp error is on the inverted Jenny, a 1918 stamp with an image of an airplane that is upside-down. One sold for U.S. $825,000 in 2007. Even rarer is the 1855 Swedish Teskilling Yellow, which was printed with yellow ink instead of the normal blue. Its last known sale price was U.S. $2.3 million in 2010.

Questions:

1 _____

2 _____

3 _____

Answers:

1 _____

2 _____

3 _____

Connecting to the Topic

Discuss the following questions with a partner.

1 How would you describe the difference between scientists and engineers?

2 What are some major engineering failures or even engineering disasters that you know of (for example, the collapse of a bridge or building, the failure of a major project)? Describe one of them.

3 What do you think the causes of such failures might have been?

4 It has often been said that failure is the best teacher. Do you agree? Why or why not?

Previewing and Predicting

> Reading the title, section headings, and the first sentence of each section can help you predict what the reading will be about.

A Read the section headings and first sentences of sections I–IV in Reading 5, and think about the title of the reading. Then read the following topics. Write the number of the section where you think each topic will be discussed.

SECTION	TOPIC
	Successful engineering projects that are built on failures
	A history of design problems based on overconfidence
	The contrasting roles of scientists and engineers on design projects
	Examples of good designs that do not need improvement
	Failures that occurred as a result of ambitious but unrealistic designs
	The importance of failure in engineering success
	Problems with pursuing perfection in designs

B Compare your answers with a partner's.

While You Read

As you read, stop at the end of each sentence that contains words in **bold**. Then follow the instructions in the box in the margin.

◀» Selections from *An Engineer's Alphabet*

by Henry Petroski

I. Failure

1   Understanding the concept of failure is central to understanding engineering and the engineering design process. In fact, an operational definition of engineering could be that engineering is simply the avoidance of unintended failure. The results of the calculations engineers carry out and the data they collect and analyze in experiments would be virtually meaningless without a sense of how those results or data compare with the critical, or failure values. Whenever engineers work with a steel structure, an electronic device, or a machine, they need to know, for example, the maximum load the structure can support, the maximum current it can take, the maximum rainfall it can accommodate, or the maximum temperature at which it can operate. Without such knowledge, there is no understanding of the limits within which the system can operate without **failure**.

2   Although often associated with the catastrophic collapse of a structure or the total breakdown of a system, the term "failure" can also mean the inability of design to fulfill completely its intended function. Thus, a skyscraper that is in no danger of collapsing, yet is so flexible that the occupants of its upper floors get queasy[1] when moderate winds blow in a certain direction, could be considered a design failure. The **excessive** flexibility of the structure should have been anticipated and the design modified.

3   There is also a paradox associated with design: that failures, through the lessons learned from them, provide invaluable information on how to achieve subsequent successful designs. An example of failure leading to success is the history of the repeated failures of suspension bridges in the early nineteenth century. By studying those failures and their causes, the engineer John Roebling came to understand what was needed in the design in order to achieve a successful suspension bridge, which he did, most famously the Brooklyn Bridge that spans the East River in New York City to this day.

The Brooklyn Bridge

---

[1] *queasy:* feeling as if you are going to vomit

> **WHILE YOU READ ❶**
> As you read this paragraph, choose three words for vocabulary cards. Underline them so you can return to them when you have finished reading.

> **WHILE YOU READ ❷**
> Use context and your knowledge of word parts to guess the meaning of *excessive*. Does it mean (a) dangerous or (b) more than expected?

II. "The Perfect Is the Enemy of the Good"

4   This familiar saying is frequently repeated when a satisfactory – that is, a good – engineering design is unnecessarily and continuously revised with the stated purpose of improving it. The ultimate goal is often stated to be the achievement of the perfect design. However, what "perfect" means depends on many factors, including appearance, constructability, economics, durability, and usability. Because no design can ever be expected to be truly perfect in even one category, the process is **effectively** endless. The elusive "perfect" design can keep "good" designs from being accepted for what they are – simply good, workable designs. The principle of this saying was applied during NASA's Apollo program and was carried over to the agency's development of the space shuttle. It was imperative to discourage design changes once thoughtful decisions had been made, so that the program wouldn't get delayed by unnecessary modifications and their implications for the entire complex system. The philosophy followed at NASA was captured in the dictum, "better is the enemy of good." Or, as the French philosopher Voltaire wrote in the eighteenth century, "the perfect is the enemy of the good."

WHILE YOU READ ❸

Which definition of *effectively* matches the meaning in this sentence? (a) In reality (b) Successfully

5   While a better design can always be achieved, it is not always prudent or necessary to seek **one**. Consider the invention of the World Wide Web, which is attributed to the British engineer and computer scientist Tim Berners-Lee. He developed the web-site making tool known as HTML, which stands for hypertext markup language. The language's focus simply on text made it relatively easy to learn and use. In time, however, its shortcomings with regard to incorporating images and other media onto web sites became clear. Nevertheless, HTML is credited with the rapid growth of web sites, from the 130 in 1993 to more than 23,000 within less than two years. Although far from perfect for creating web sites, HTML's ease of use earned it widespread early adoption and established it as the language of choice.

WHILE YOU READ ❹

In this sentence, the author makes a claim. Scan the next two paragraphs to find supporting details for this claim. Highlight them.

6   Likewise, when Larry Page and Sergey Brin were working on the search engine that became Google, they were not alone. Others were seeking the same objective, and the race was on to be the first to develop a good – not a perfect – product. According to one account, "time mattered more than money" and "innovation mattered more than perfection." Among the characteristics of the Google model was "innovate first, perfect later." (Edwards, 21–22)

7   Another interesting example of this process is the steel-wire paper clip[2]. The familiar loop-within-a-loop design, created by making three 180-degree bends in a four-inch length of wire, is formally known as the Gem. It dates from the late nineteenth century, and though a very good design, is not perfect. Over the course of the following century, hundreds

---

[2] *paper clip*: a piece of wire bent into a shape that will hold papers together

of patents[3] were granted for paper clips that were arguably improvements on the Gem. However, none of these displaced the classic form. In fact, the more inventors tried to achieve perfection, the less likely they seemed to be able to produce a viable competitor of the Gem. In the case of the paper clip, the supposedly better has been repeatedly defeated by the good.

III. Scientists vs. Engineers

8   There have been many attempts to clarify distinctions between scientists and engineers. Perhaps the most widely quoted is the one attributed to aerospace engineer and scientist Theodore von Kármán: "Scientists seek to understand what is; engineers seek to create what has not yet been." Similar ideas have been expressed in numerous ways, including: "Scientists understand the world, but engineers make it work" and "Scientists make it known; engineers make it useful."

A paper clip

9   It is a common complaint among engineers that the news media tends to attribute successful technological endeavors and achievements to science and scientists, whereas technological problems and failures are blamed on engineering and engineers. Thus, landing astronauts on the Moon was hailed as a scientific achievement, but when a test rocket exploded before its launch[4], it was described as an engineering **failure**.

WHILE YOU READ 5

Underline key words in this paragraph that suggest the author's view about the public opinion of engineers.

10   Moreover, after the explosion on the *Deepwater Horizon* oil rig[5] and the subsequent extensive oil leak in the Gulf of Mexico in 2010, there were many instances of action and reporting in which the roles of engineers and scientists were confused. As a result, the public was given misleading pictures of both. At one point, the White House sent the Secretary of Energy, a Nobel-prize winning physicist, to the oil-spill command center in Houston to direct what clearly should have been an engineering effort under the direction of an engineer to stop the leaking well[6]. In the end, it was not scientific knowledge and achievement that ended the leak but engineering experience and technological skill.

An oil rig

---

[3] *patent:* the legal right to be the only person to profit from an invention for a specific number of years
[4] *launch:* the act of sending something into the water or into space
[5] *oil rig:* a structure or platform from which equipment can drill for oil
[6] *well:* a deep hole in the ground from which water, oil, or gas can be extracted

11   Blaming the engineer is not a modern phenomenon. In his first-century essay on the water supply system of Rome, the water commissioner Frontinus described an incident that he experienced at the site of the construction of a tunnel to carry water to the Algerian seaport of Saldae. "There I found everybody sad and despondent; they had given up all hopes that the two opposite sections of the tunnel would meet, because each section had already been excavated beyond the middle of the mountain, and the junction had not yet been effected. As always happens in these cases, the fault was attributed to the engineer, as though he had not taken all precautions to insure the success of the work." (151–152)

IV. Hubris[7] in Engineering

12   The Ancient Greek engineer Archimedes claimed he could move the earth with a lever[8], if only he could locate a suitable fulcrum[9] and place on which to stand. By the Renaissance, engineers generally knew that as with ships and many other forms of construction, there was a limit to the size of levers before they broke under their own weight. However, it took Galileo to explain how and why physical considerations that may be ignored on a small scale can dominate the behavior of a larger but geometrically similar design. Unfortunately, what Galileo knew in the Renaissance was not always remembered in subsequent centuries.

13   With the development of large-scale iron production technologies, it became possible for engineers not only to dream of larger and larger structures, but also to realize them. Isambard Kingdom Brunel, the Victorian engineer known as the "little giant," was famous for his expansive thinking. Although his contemporaries saw the Great Western Railway terminating at Land's End, in southwestern England, Brunel saw it continuing on in the form of a steamship carrying passengers and cargo across the Atlantic Ocean to America. His *Great Western* became one of the first ships to disprove the conventional scientific wisdom of the time: that it would be impossible to build a steamship large enough to carry sufficient coal for such a voyage.

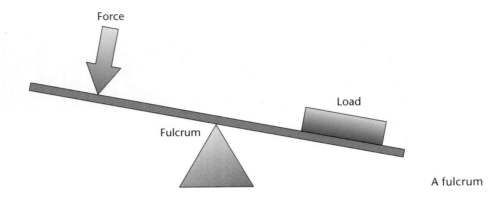

A fulcrum

---

[7] *hubris:* extreme and unreasonable confidence in oneself
[8] *lever:* a bar that, when pressed down on one side, moves something up on the other side
[9] *fulcrum:* the point of support under a lever

WHILE YOU READ ⑥

As you read section IV, think of three questions that might be on a test.

14   If the Atlantic could be crossed, why couldn't greater expanses of sea? Brunel's enormous steamship, the *Great Eastern*, was large enough to carry all the coal it would need to sail from England to the Indian Ocean. Although the 692-foot-long ship was structurally sound, it proved to be too large for most harbors and thus was a commercial failure that would eventually be cut up for scrap[10]. A larger ship would not be built for almost half a century.

15   The design and development of the supersonic[11] Concorde airliner repeated a similar pattern, with the technologically advanced aircraft seeing limited service because its sonic boom[12] made it unwelcome over the populous areas surrounding major airports. Other supersonic projects were abandoned as a result. Clearly, the designs of engineers must be more than just strong enough and fast enough. They must also be compatible with the existing physical, social, and political infrastructure.

Concorde

16   Engineers do not demonstrate their hubris only in great ships, planes, and long-span bridges. Over the years they have proposed such grand schemes as damming the Congo River to create the largest lake in Africa. They have recommended draining the Mediterranean Sea to reclaim the land for crowded Europe. They have dreamed of building a tunnel between England and France. This last scheme was, of course, realized when the Channel Tunnel opened in 1994, two centuries after the idea was first considered. While the Congo is not likely to be dammed in the foreseeable future, the Three Gorges Dam in China has been backing up water on the Yangtze River for almost 400 miles, making Chongqing accessible to oceangoing shipping since 2003. The decision about whether to dam a river is more often political than technical. Engineers can dream, but it takes political skill and determination, as well as money, to start the machinery that will reshape the earth.

17   The ultimate success of grand engineering schemes is frequently limited by factors unrelated to the main idea – by details that are decidedly low tech or even **nontechnical**. This was the case with the Concorde jet. When engineers ignore these factors or treat them as not deserving of the same careful analysis as the main technological challenge, disaster can occur. The sinking of the *Titanic* might not have resulted in such a tragic loss of life had the ship's vulnerability been acknowledged by having enough lifeboats for all on board. The space shuttle *Challenger* might not

WHILE YOU READ 7

In this sentence, the author makes a claim. Scan ahead to find supporting examples for this claim. Highlight them.

---

[10] *scrap:* old or used material, usually metal

[11] *supersonic:* faster than the speed of sound

[12] *sonic boom:* a loud sound that is made when something moves faster than the speed of sound

have exploded had managers paid attention to engineers' warnings about the behavior of O-rings in cold weather. And the space shuttle *Columbia* may not have disintegrated during reentry if trouble with insulating foam[13] had been acknowledged as a critical failing within the shuttle program. In short, catastrophic accidents tend to happen when overconfidence and complacency prevail.

18   Engineers and managers of technology, being human, can come to believe in themselves and their creations beyond reasonable limits. When failures occur, they naturally cause setbacks. However, as soon as the cause of a failed attempt is sufficiently understood and the sting of its tragedy is sufficiently remote, engineers tend to renew their pursuit of ever greater goals. This is as it should be in engineering as in life. For it is as much a part of the human spirit to build longer and to fly faster as it is to probe deeper into the atom and further into the universe than our predecessors. Just as scientists advance their knowledge by standing on the shoulders of giants, so it is that by climbing onto the tops of existing skyscrapers, engineers reach for ever taller heights in their own skyscrapers. If this is hubris, it is an admirable trait that has, on balance, led to cumulative progress in which engineers and non-engineers alike take **pride**.

WHILE YOU READ ⑧

Find an idiom that means *taking everything into consideration* in this sentence. Underline it.

---

[13] *insulating foam:* a soft, light material that covers something to prevent heat or electricity from coming in or out

Main Idea Check

For sections I–IV of Reading 5, match the main ideas to three of the paragraphs in each section. Write the number of the paragraph on the blank line.

SECTION I: Failure

_____ A Design failures provide invaluable lessons for engineers.

_____ B The central job of engineers is to understand the limits, or failure values, of their designs.

_____ C Engineering failures also include designs that do not meet the needs of their users.

SECTION II: "The Perfect Is the Enemy of the Good"

_____ A The search for a perfect design may waste valuable time.

_____ B The original design may end up exceeding future versions of it.

_____ C Inventing something for the sake of innovation does not necessarily lead to a good design

SECTION III: Scientists vs. Engineers

_____ A Not only modern-day engineers have been unfairly blamed for design failures.

_____ B In general, scientists engage in discovery whereas engineers make these discoveries useful.

_____ C There is confusion among the public about the roles that engineers and scientists play.

SECTION IV: Hubris in Engineering

_____ A Engineers' dreams are limited by political and social considerations as well physical laws.

_____ B The development of new materials and technology has allowed engineers to attempt more ambitious designs.

_____ C When engineers pursue their dreams without paying attention to potential problems, the consequences can be disastrous.

A Closer Look

Look back at Reading 5 to answer the following questions.

1 Why does the writer give the example of the flexible building in paragraph 2?
   a To demonstrate the significance of failure
   b To give an example of poor design
   c To show that there are different kinds of failure
   d To show the importance of planning

2 What might be another way of expressing the idea "the perfect is the enemy of the good?

   a Never stop improving.
   b Good is good enough.
   c Perfection is true success.
   d A perfect design is not a good design.

3 What does the author imply might have happened if Tim Berners-Lee had tried to make his web design tool perfect? Choose all that apply.

   a HTML might not be the standard language of the web today.
   b It would have become too difficult for average users to understand.
   c There would be more images and videos on the web.
   d Other people would have quickly discovered problems with his tool.

4 The highest priority for the Google founders was speed, not perfection. **True or False?**

5 What is the main point the author is making in section III?

   a Scientists and engineers are very different.
   b Many people do not respect engineers.
   c People have been complaining about engineers for hundreds of years.
   d The general public does not understand the work of engineers.

6 Greek engineer Archimedes understood the importance of scale in design. **True or False?**

7 Why did the ship the *Great Eastern* fail?

   a Brunel was too ambitious in his design and the ship was too big to sail.
   b The ship could not carry enough fuel to complete long journeys.
   c Brunel did not think about other practical issues when he designed the ship.
   d Many countries refused to have such a large ship in their harbors.

8 In the final paragraph, why does the writer refer to engineers as human?

   a They believe they can accomplish greater feats than is realistic.
   b Their unrealistic dreams do not allow them to recognize failure.
   c Being human, they must adjust their expectations to fit realistic goals.
   d Human nature does not allow them to strive for unrealistic goals.

Skill Review

In Skills and Strategies 12, you learned about preparing for a test. Predicting and answering questions is one of the most effective ways to do this.

A Read section I of Reading 5 again. Then read the questions below that a student predicted might be on a test. Write answers to these questions on the blank lines.

1 Why is understanding failure crucial to engineering success?

_____

2 What are two functions of engineering failure?

_____

3 Why does the author describe engineering failure as a "paradox"?

_____

B At the beginning of section IV, While You Read 6 asks you to predict three questions about this section. Work with a partner and ask each other your questions. Answer them in writing.

Vocabulary Development

Definitions

Find the words in Reading 5 that are similar to the definitions below.

1 to provide space or volume for something (*v*) Par. 1

2 to make something happen as intended or promised (*v*) Par. 2

3 a situation that seems impossible because it includes opposite facts (*n*) Par. 3

4 final; highest (*adj*) Par. 4

5 difficult or impossible to achieve (*adj*) Par. 4

6 sensible (*adj*) Par. 5

7 faults (*n pl*) Par. 5

8 causing someone to believe something that is not true (*adj*) Par. 10

9 people living in the same time period as someone else (*n pl*) Par. 13

10 following the usual practices of the past (*adj*) Par. 13

11 a state in which something or someone can easily be hurt (*n*) Par. 17

12 a feeling of satisfaction with yourself that prevents you from working harder (*n*) Par. 17

13 to be accepted without consideration or to be in a dominant position (*v*) Par. 17

14 the act of following or searching for something (*n*) Par. 18

15 after everything has been considered (*phrase*) Par. 18

Words in Context

A **Use context clues to match the first part of each sentence to its correct second part and to understand the meaning of the words in bold.**

_____ 1 The most fragile objects from the ancient community

_____ 2 As the residents of the village raced to avoid the storm, they

_____ 3 The professor used visuals and practical examples

_____ 4 It is unlikely that there will be regular travel to Mars

_____ 5 After years of research and development, solar energy

_____ 6 Their loss in last week's election

_____ 7 The new owners of the building discovered

a to **clarify** the concept for her students.

b in the **foreseeable** future.

c was a major **setback** for the opposition party.

d it is essential to take **precautions**.

e had **disintegrated** into dust years ago.

f the consequences will be **catastrophic**.

g some things that one cannot **anticipate**.

_____ 8 If firefighters cannot stop the wildfire in the mountains,

_____ 9 If you plan to travel in these dangerous areas,

_____ 10 We tried to plan for everything, but there are

h **abandoned** their homes and animals.

i that a **leak** under the sink had caused water damage.

j is finally a **viable** alternative to coal and oil.

B Compare your answers with a partner's. Discuss what clues helped you match the parts of the sentences and helped you understand what the words in **bold** mean.

Same or Different

The following pairs of sentences contain vocabulary from all the readings in this unit. Write *S* on the blank lines if the two sentences have the same meaning. Write *D* if the meanings are different.

_____ 1 We will need to **modify** our **template** by **inserting** clear instructions for each step.

We will have to **refine** the model by including **explicit** directions for each step in the process.

_____ 2 It will be **nothing short of catastrophic** if supporters of this new law are successful.

It is important to **vigorously** support the **proponents** of the new law.

_____ 3 We have **abundant** proof of the **brilliance** of the engineers in ancient Greece and Rome.

There is an **ample** record of the **ingenuity** of the engineers who worked in Greece and Rome during the classical period.

_____ 4 New technology has provided **impetus** for the development of **portable** devices.

Developments in technology have **spurred** growth in the mobile device industry.

_____ 5 The rescue team always takes **prudent precautions** before they enter buildings after a natural disaster.

The emergency rescue workers **exhibit** courage before they enter buildings that **collapse** in natural disasters.

_____ 6 The new health-care program is **shortsighted** and **plagued** with problems.

The government health care program that is now **underway** will be able to **accommodate** everyone who needs services.

_____ 7 A team of scientists and engineers is working on plans that will remain **viable** as our **climate** continues to change.

A group of scientists and engineers says the **vulnerability** of coastal cities **poses** major challenges for the future.

_____ 8 Unfortunately, it was impossible to **anticipate** the **shortcomings** of the design.

It is regrettable that the **drawbacks** in the design were not **foreseeable**.

Disciplinary Vocabulary

The following words are from all the readings of this unit. Research shows that they frequently appear in academic texts related to engineering. Complete the sentences with these words.

climate (*n*)	consists (*v*)	displace (*v*)	flexible (*adj*)	principles (*n*)
collapsed (*v*)	density (*n*)	dynamic (*adj*)	modified (*v*)	resistance (*n*)
components (*n*)	disintegrate (*v*)	extraction (*n*)	phenomenon (*n*)	sterilize (*v*)

1 Only the strongest buildings survived the earthquake; all of the others _____ immediately.

2 The architects _____ their plans for the new university in order to include more parks and green spaces.

3 It is important for blood vessels to remain _____. When they become hard, it is more difficult for blood to flow through them.

4 Ice floats because it has a lower _____ than water.

5 New techniques that facilitate the _____ of oil from rocks have led to a decrease in the price of oil.

6 Hurricanes are a rare _____ in Australia. They are much more common in other parts of the world.

7 This type of rice has shown remarkable _____ to both disease and very dry conditions.

8 It is unlikely that any language will _____ English as the global language any time soon.

9 The study has three different _____, each of which showed significant results.

10 A very powerful explosion caused the foundation of the bridge to _____ within seconds.

11 The main street of the tiny town _____ of a small store, a café, a post office, and a gas station.

12 Most scientists agree that Earth's _____ is gradually becoming warmer.

13 Isaac Newton established the basic _____ of motion in the seventeenth century.

14 It is important to _____ all of the equipment before you begin in order to kill any bacteria that are present.

15 This is a strong, _____ company that can respond quickly to changes in the industry.

Critical Thinking

In Reading 5, *An Engineer's Alphabet*, you learned about the importance of failure in understanding engineering. You also learned about the sources of failure in a variety of construction, transportation, and exploration projects.

APPLYING INFORMATION

You use critical thinking skills when you apply information you have just learned to new situations.

A With a small group of classmates, consider the three dimensions of failure described in Reading 5 and listed in the chart below. Review the reading and write at least one example of each in the top half of the chart. Then brainstorm with your classmates about other examples of engineering failures that you know about. Write them in the appropriate column in the bottom of the chart.

REASONS FOR FAILURE IN ENGINEERING DESIGNS OR PROCESS		
Not understanding the physical limitations of a project	Not accounting for forces that are external to the process	Hubris and/or complacency

B Compare your charts with charts from other groups. Based on the information that you and your classmates compiled, discuss which source of failure seems to be the most frequent and why.

Research

There have been many engineering failures throughout history. Choose one that you would like to research. It could be a failure that you listed in **A** or another of your choice. Below are some categories you might consider.

- aviation
- bridges
- ships
- space exploration
- factories/industrial sites
- dams
- mines
- buildings

Writing

Write two paragraphs. In the first paragraph, describe what happened in the failure. The second paragraph should explain why it occurred, in other words, what the source of the failure was.

Exercise 1

Writers may connect ideas between sentences in many different ways. The second sentence may:

a describe a **result** or **effect** of what is reported in the first sentence
b provide a **solution** to a problem described in the first sentence
c provide a **contrast** to what is described in the first sentence
d add a **detail** or details to support the more general information in the first sentence

How does the second sentence in each pair of sentences below connect to the first sentence? Write *a, b, c,* or *d* on the line depending on whether it is a result, a solution, a contrast, or a supporting detail.

_____ 1 Only 24 percent of the population of Sub-Saharan Africa has access to electricity. Even those fortunate enough to have such access often experience highly unreliable service with outages more than 50 days a year.

_____ 2 Tariffs on power in most countries in the developing world range from U.S. $.04 to U.S. $.08 per kilowatt hour. In spite of the poor service, the cost in Sub-Saharan Africa can be more than double the rate of neighboring countries.

_____ 3 Efforts to stabilize and rehabilitate dilapidated power grids and scale up power generation capacity are likely to take many years and millions of dollars. Ultimately, an alternative path – the use of leapfrog technology and the development of local solutions – may be a preferable option.

_____ 4 Communities that are not connected to a power grid or have no access to a consistent source of electricity often rely on kerosene. This is hardly an ideal alternative as it is a major source of home fires, and its noxious fumes contribute to the two million annual deaths from indoor air pollution.

_____ 5 Alfredo Moser, a mechanic in São Paolo, Brazil, had to endure constant power blackouts, which had a very negative impact on his business. In response, in 2002, he invented the bottle bulb – a plastic bottle of water with bleach mounted in the roof, which gives 50 watts of illumination at no cost.

Exercise 2

Make a clear paragraph by putting sentences A, B, and C into the best order after the numbered sentence. Write the letters in the correct order on the blank lines.

1 Customers in mature markets have come to expect a continuous parade of new features on their products. ____ ____ ____

A	B	C
However, to customers in emerging markets, such options appear to be instances of over-engineering, when they would prefer simpler, more practical approaches.	These include options like the integration of their social networking sites into their cars' communication systems, and smart options for their household appliances.	One example is the smartphone, which for all of its advanced features, can be brought to a standstill by a speck of dust or a drop of moisture.

2 The late C. K. Prahalad urged multinational corporations to turn their attention to the burgeoning market at the bottom of the pyramid. ____ ____ ____

A	B	C
These are new consumers whose purchasing power as individuals is minimal, but in the aggregate is staggering.	This power will continue to grow, and it is only a matter of time before it will begin to overshadow that of mature markets.	The market is made up of between four and five billion people – more than half of the world's population.

3 Companies who make the switch from mature to emerging markets should be prepared for challenges. ____ ____ ____

A	B	C
The first is undoubtedly the customers themselves, who are often more demanding than the customers in mature markets.	Because they have less to spend, they spend less easily.	They also require different kinds of products with different kinds of features, but they are no less insistent on high quality.

4 One of the biggest challenges for future engineers will be improving and expanding access to clean water. ____ ____ ____

A	B	C
For example, Canada has an abundant supply of water, while countries in the Middle East and many areas of Africa live in a perpetual state of drought, a conditional often made more serious by human activity.	This figure reflects the global situation, but access to water varies tremendously from one region to another.	About 1 out of every 6 people in the world lacks adequate access to water, with more than double that number lacking the basic sanitation services that require water.

5 It may seem that water is all around us. After all, about 70 percent of the earth's surface is covered by water. _____ _____ _____

| **A** However, the vast majority of the water found on Earth is in the form of salt water from the ocean, with only three percent in the form of fresh water. | **B** The remaining fresh water is found in aquifers located underground, which are being drained at an alarming rate by the world's thirsty population. | **C** Of that small percentage, most is locked into snow and ice and is not immediately accessible to large population centers. |

6 Engineers have always played an important role in meeting the world's water needs.
_____ _____ _____

| **A** For example, projects that involve the diversion of precious water resources to large urban centers may harm the environment and, therefore, cannot be considered as long-term solutions. | **B** In the past, their role was to construct wells, dams, and water treatment plants. | **C** In the coming years, engineers working to preserve and enhance our water supply will need to employ increasingly sophisticated approaches that include steps to protect the environment. |

Key Vocabulary

The Academic Word List is a list of words that are particularly important to study. Research shows that these words frequently appear in many different types of academic texts. Words that are part of the Academic Word List are noted with an Ⓐ in this appendix.

UNIT 1 • READING 1

Technology and the Individual

anonymity *n* a situation in which a person is not known by or spoken of by name • *The newspaper promised to protect her **anonymity** so that no one could ever find her.*

assert *v* to state an opinion or claim a right forcefully • *The reporter continues to **assert** that his information is accurate.*

attribute Ⓐ *v* to say or think that something is the result or work of something or someone else • *He **attributes** his fame to hard work and good luck.*

autonomous *adj* existing or acting separately from other things or people • *There are several **autonomous** regions in India, which have some degree of independence from the central government.*

convey *v* to take or carry someone or something to a particular place • *Please **convey** this important information to all of your employees.*

guideline Ⓐ *n* a piece of information that suggests how something should be done • *The company headquarters has issued **guidelines** regarding energy and sustainability.*

head start *n* the advantage of beginning before others in a competition or other situation • *The after-school program provides a **head start** to children who are interested in computer programming.*

imitate *v* to copy someone's speech or behavior, or to copy something as a model • *Children often **imitate** the behavior of their parents.*

impact Ⓐ *n* the strong effect or influence that something has on a situation or person • *The new law will have an especially negative **impact** on the poor.*

impediment *n* something that makes progress or movement difficult or impossible • *The high unemployment rate will be an **impediment** to economic growth.*

innovation Ⓐ *n* a new idea or method, or the use of new ideas and methods • *You can see all of the latest **innovations** in electronics at the technology convention.*

network Ⓐ *n* a group formed from parts that are connected together; also, a group of computers that are connected and can share information • *People who are in your social **network** may be able to help you when you are looking for a job.*

precursor *n* something that comes before another and may lead to it or influence its development • *This model from ten years ago was the **precursor** to today's smartphones.*

revolutionary Ⓐ *adj* relating to a complete change in a system of government, or bringing or causing great change • *In the nineteenth century, the idea of women voting was **revolutionary**.*

rule of thumb *n* a method of judging a situation or condition that is not exact but is based on experience • *As a **rule of thumb**, a man of average weight who walks one mile will burn 100 calories.*

simultaneously *adv* at exactly the same time • *It is difficult to send a text message and talk on the phone **simultaneously**.*

stereotypical *adj* an idea that is used to describe a particular type of person or thing, or a person or thing that is thought to represent such an idea • *The director is looking for an actor with a **stereotypical** Brooklyn accent.*

target audience *n* the particular group of people to which an advertisement, a product, a website, or a television or radio program is directed • *The **target audience** for the new magazine is women in their twenties and thirties.*

transmission Ⓐ *n* the act of sending or giving something • *The **transmission** of disease from one person to another can be reduced by simple hand washing.*

undertaking Ⓐ *n* an effort to do something, especially to do a large or difficult job • *The construction of the bridge was a huge **undertaking** that took five years.*

UNIT 1 • READING 2

Virtual Reality and Its Real-World Applications

afford *v* to supply or provide something to someone • *The new computers **afford** students the opportunity to use the latest technology.*

application *n* a particular use • *This technology will have **applications** in healthcare and education.*

contradiction Ⓐ *n* a fact or statement that is the opposite of what someone has said or that is so different from another fact or statement that one of them must be wrong • *There seems to be a **contradiction** between what he says and what he actually does.*

coordination Ⓐ *n* the ability to make all the parts of your body work together • *Table tennis requires excellent **coordination** between the eyes and the hands.*

countless *adj* very many; too many to be counted • *There have been **countless** efforts to solve the problem but none has been successful.*

discomfort *n* the feeling of not being comfortable, either from a physical cause or from a situation • *You will experience some discomfort after the surgery for about 24 hours.*

draw *v* to pull or direct something or someone in a particular direction, or attract someone toward a particular place • *The movie quickly draws the audience into the action.*

echo *v* to fill a place with repeated sounds, or to be filled with these sounds • *A voice will echo off the walls of an empty room.*

embedded *adj* existing or firmly attached within something or under a surface • *Links to important websites were embedded in the document.*

evolve Ⓐ *v* to change or develop gradually • *We have an initial design for our new product but I am sure it will evolve over the next few months.*

heightened *adj* increased, especially an emotion or effect • *There has been a heightened level of security on the border between the two nations.*

immersion *n* the complete involvement of someone in an activity • *During her immersion course in Italian, she lived with an Italian family and spoke no English.*

mirror *v* to be a copy of something; to be similar to something • *Results from the study mirror observations that have been made about animal behavior in the past.*

morph *v* to change gradually in appearance or form • *Police are concerned that this small disturbance will morph into something more dangerous.*

motion sensor *n* a device that discovers and reacts to changes in movement • *A motion sensor above the door indicates when someone enters.*

platform *n* a particular computer technology that can be used with some types of software programs but not with others • *The company is moving its website to a different platform that has more flexibility.*

practical *adj* effective or suitable • *Early laptop computers were not very practical because they were so heavy.*

rationale *n* the reasons or intentions for a particular set of thoughts or actions • *The rationale for beginning the school day later is that students will be more alert.*

rehabilitation *n* the process of returning someone to a healthy or normal condition • *After surgery on his knee, the soccer player needed months of intensive rehabilitation before he could start playing again.*

repetitive *adj* expressed or happening in the same way many times • *I hate to be repetitive, but I need to say this one more time.*

scenario Ⓐ *n* a description of possible events • *We need to prepare even for scenarios that seem very unlikely.*

scratch the surface *idiom* to deal with only a small part of a subject or a problem • *In the first course, we can only scratch the surface of what you will eventually need to learn.*

simulation Ⓐ *n* a model of a real activity, created for training purposes or to solve a problem • *This simulation of traffic patterns lets us predict when and where the heaviest volume will be.*

stationary *adj* not moving, or not changing • *The horses remained stationary for a few minutes and then ran away.*

virtual Ⓐ *adj* almost, but not exactly or in every way; "virtual reality" is a set of images and sounds produced by a computer that seem to represent a real place or situation • *Some video game players spend more time in their virtual worlds than in the real world.*

UNIT 1 • READING 3

Life in 3D

algorithm *n* a list of instructions for solving a problem, especially relating to mathematics • *Google uses a special algorithm to provide the most relevant responses to searches.*

alter Ⓐ *v* to change a characteristic, often slightly, or to cause this to happen • *Plastic surgery can dramatically alter a person's appearance.*

artificial intelligence *n* the use of computer programs that have some of the qualities of the human mind, such as the ability to understand language, recognize pictures, and learn from experience • *Doctors are using artificial intelligence to help make more accurate diagnoses.*

component Ⓐ *n* one of the parts of a system, process, or machine • *Some of the components of computers contain dangerous chemicals.*

correspond *v* to be similar or the same in some way • *In the secret code, each letter corresponds to a number or symbol.*

emerge Ⓐ *v* to appear by coming out of something or out from behind something • *The sun will emerge from behind the clouds when the rain ends.*

entail *v* to involve or make something necessary • *This project entails careful attention to small details.*

implausible *adj* difficult to believe; not probable • *The story she told the police seems implausible so they are going to investigate the matter further.*

input *n* information, money, or energy that is put into a system, organization, or machine so that it can operate • *We have asked the community for their input about the proposal to build a subway system.*

intersecting *adj* (of a line or surface) crossing at a point or set of points • *Intersecting lines can never be parallel.*

juxtaposition *n* the act of putting things or people next to each other, especially in order to compare them • *Critics did not like the juxtaposition of modern and classical styles in a single building.*

manipulate Ⓐ *v* to control something by using the hands or a machine • *Users can manipulate objects on the screen simply by touching them.*

mechanism Ⓐ *n* a part of a machine, or a set of parts that work together • *A **mechanism** within the equipment controls pressure and temperature.*

mimic *v* to copy the way that someone speaks and moves • *The actor could **mimic** famous people's voices perfectly.*

pave the way *v phr* to make it possible or easier for something or someone to follow • *As the first female prime minister, she was able to **pave the way** for many other women in politics.*

perspective Ⓐ *n* the method used to give objects drawn or painted on a flat surface the appearance of depth and distance • *Renaissance artists like Raphael used the rules of **perspective** to make their paintings appear more three-dimensional.*

plane *n* a flat surface that continues in all directions • *You need to remember the equation for the line where two **planes** intersect.*

proportion *n* the relationship between one thing and another in size, amount, or degree • *Your weight increases in **proportion** to the number of calories you eat.*

replica *n* a copy of an object • *This painting is a **replica** of one that hangs in the Louvre Museum in Paris.*

trick *v* to make someone believe something that is not true or real • *This mirror can **trick** you into thinking that things are farther away.*

UNIT 1 • READING 4

Mapmaking in the Digital Age

aerial *adj* of, from, or in the air • *An **aerial** photograph can show you just how big this city is.*

amorphous *adj* having no fixed shape; not clear or determined • *Through the rain and fog, the buildings appeared as **amorphous** shapes in the distance.*

approximation Ⓐ *n* the act of coming near in quality, amount, value, or character • *I am not sure of the exact amount; this is just an **approximation**.* **approximate** *adj* almost exact • *The **approximate** distance between Los Angeles and New York is 4,000 kilometer.* **approximate** *v* to come near in quality, amount, value, or character • *I don't have a ruler so I can only **approximate** the height of the table.*

chart Ⓐ *n* a way of presenting information, usually by putting it into vertical rows and boxes on a sheet of paper, so it can be easily understood • *There is a **chart** on the wall that lists all the irregular verbs.*

collaborative *adj* working together or with someone else for a special purpose • *This project has been a **collaborative** effort so we should all be very proud.* **collaboration** *n* the act of working together or with someone else for a special purpose • *The after-school program was developed in **collaboration** with several local artists.* **collaborate** *v* to work together or with someone else for a special purpose • *The university encourages the faculty to **collaborate** in their research.*

disclose *v* to give information to the public that was not previously known • *The newspaper did not **disclose** the name of the man who was arrested.*

dominate Ⓐ *v* to have control over a place or a person, or to be the most important person or thing • *Just a few media companies **dominate** the entire market.*

fragment *n* a small piece or part, especially one that is broken off of something • *The glass broke into tiny **fragments** when she dropped it.*

glimpse *n* a brief look at someone or something • *She got a **glimpse** of the famous movie star as he was leaving the restaurant.*

gratification *n* pleasure; satisfaction • *I wrote this book for personal **gratification**, not money.* **gratify** *v* to please someone, or to satisfy a wish or need • *I believe this story will **gratify** the public's appetite for news about the rich and famous.*

incorporate Ⓐ *v* to include something within something else • *The report **incorporates** the ideas and contributions of many different people.*

indicate Ⓐ *v* to show or signal a direction or warning, or to make something clear • *The results **indicate** that the number of plant species is declining.*

instant *n* happening immediately • *Many children can't wait for a reward; they want **instant** gratification.*

margin of error Ⓐ *n phr* the amount by which a set of data might not be accurate • *This survey has a **margin of error** of +/− five percent.*

masterpiece *n* something made or done with great skill, especially an artist's greatest work • *The Mona Lisa is considered Da Vinci's **masterpiece**.*

navigator *n* a person in a vehicle who decides on the direction in which the vehicle travels • *Whenever we go on trips, I am usually the driver, and my husband is the **navigator**.* **navigate** *v* to direct the way a vehicle, especially a ship or aircraft, will travel • *Long ago, sailors would **navigate** using the stars as their guide.* **navigable** *adj* deep and wide enough for a ship to go through • *There has been no rain all year so the rivers are no longer **navigable**.*

pervasive *adj* present or noticeable in every part of a thing or place • *Smartphones have become **pervasive** in modern society.*

premier *adj* best or most important • *This is the city's **premier** hotel, where kings and presidents stay when they visit.*

speculate *v* to form opinions about something without having the necessary information or facts; to make guesses • *The plane simply disappeared, and now we can only **speculate** about what happened to it.* **speculation** *n* a guess about something without having enough information to be certain Some people say he made is money selling weapons but that is just **speculation**.* **speculative** *adj* based on a guess and not on information • *This claim is highly **speculative** and is not based on facts or evidence.*

superimpose *v* to put a picture, words, etc., on top of something else, especially another picture, words, etc., so that what is in the lower position can still be seen, heard, etc. • *For the poster, let's* **superimpose** *our names over this photograph.*

UNIT 1 • READING 5

How Information Got Smart

absolute *adj* complete; without limit or to the largest degree possible • *There was* **absolute** *silence in the room as the test began.*

amass *v* to gather a large amount of something, especially money, by collecting it over a period of time • *Rebel soldiers are trying to* **amass** *a large supply of guns.*

capacious *adj* having a lot of space and able to contain a lot • *The* **capacious** *room could hold more than 200 people.*

compound *v* to make something worse by increasing or adding to it • *The recent rain will* **compound** *the suffering of the earthquake survivors.*

constraint *n* something that limits the range of a person's actions or freedom • *We will have to work within the* **constraints** *of our budget.*

contract *v* to catch or become ill with a disease • *The news report says that more people are likely to* **contract** *the new form of the disease in coming months.*

correlate *v* to have a connection between two or more things • *Good nutrition and an active lifestyle generally* **correlate** *with good health.*

critique *n* a report that discusses a situation or the writings or ideas of someone and offers a judgment about them • *I am reading a magazine article that offers a* **critique** *of our national energy policy.*

discoverable *adj* able to be found or learned for the first time • *With the right tools, the patterns in the records are all* **discoverable**.

exponentially *adv* if something increases exponentially, it increases at a quicker and quicker rate as the thing that increases becomes larger • *The global use of cell phones has increased* **exponentially** *in the last five years.*

imperative *adj* extremely important or urgent • *Choosing a strong password is* **imperative** *in order to protect your personal information.*

increment *n* one of a series of amounts that increase a total • *The daily temperature increased in* **increments** *of five degrees.*

inexplicable *adj* that cannot be explained or understood • *Her disappearance is* **inexplicable**; *no one can think of a reason for it.*

information overload *n* a situation in which you receive too much information at one time and cannot think about it in a clear way • *I experience* **information overload** *if I listen to people talk about technology for too long.*

inhibitor *n* something that stops or slows down a process • *This substance is an* **inhibitor** *of human growth so should not be given to children.*

interrelated *adj* connected in such a way that each thing has an effect on the others • *Intelligence and language ability are* **interrelated**.

mash up *phr v* to combine information or technology from different sources • *He is going to* **mash up** *music from different artists to create a new song.*

open-ended *adj* without an end date or planned way of ending • *Our vacation is* **open-ended**; *we may be gone for months.*

oppressive *adj* causing people to feel worried and uncomfortable; cruel and unfair • *The* **oppressive** *new laws led to protests in the streets.*

pare down *phr v* to reduce something to a level at which only what is absolutely necessary is left • *I have to* **pare down** *my clothes so I can fit them all into the suitcase.*

promulgate *v* to spread beliefs or ideas among a lot of people • *Next week the government will* **promulgate** *the new guidelines for early childhood education.*

relevant Ⓐ *adj* related to a subject or to something happening or being discussed • *You should include only information that is* **relevant** *and will support your argument.*

tantamount *adj* equal • *The working conditions at the factory were* **tantamount** *to slavery.*

traverse *v* to move or travel through an area • *Two major highways* **traverse** *the city, from east to west and north to south.*

widespread *adj* existing or happening in many places or among many people • *There is a* **widespread** *confusion over the new parking rules.*

UNIT 2 • READING 1

Health and Wellness on the Go

avert *v* to prevent something bad from happening; avoid • *In order to* **avert** *future disasters, we must be better prepared for extreme weather.*

capability Ⓐ *n* the skill, ability, or strength to do something • *Students' success depends, in part, on the* **capability** *of their teachers.*

chronic *adj* (especially of a disease or something bad) continuing for a long time • *He smoked his whole life, and now he suffers from* **chronic** *lung disease.*

comply *v* to obey an order, rule, or request • *Doctors are required to* **comply** *with government rules and regulations.*

consult Ⓐ *v* to get information or advice from a person, especially an expert, or to look at written material in order to get information • *You should* **consult** *a financial professional before you invest your money.*

Outsourcing: Managing Labor Needs

assemble Ⓐ *v* to put together the parts of something • *We bought the bookshelf in a big box; now we just have to assemble it.*

automate Ⓐ *v* to make something operate automatically by using machines or computers • *New technology has allowed businesses to automate many of the processes in their operations.*

backlash *n* a strong, negative reaction to something, especially to change • *There has been a backlash against the new rules, and many people are refusing to follow them.*

consolidate *v* to bring together or unite things that were separate • *He plans to consolidate what he owes on all of his credit cards into a single payment.*

core Ⓐ *adj* the most important or most basic part of something • *In this first course, we will study core concepts in the field.*

delegate *v* to give a particular job, duty, etc., to someone in a lower position so that they will do it for you • *As a leader, it is important to learn to delegate responsibility to others.*

downsize *v* (of a company) to reduce the number of employees, usually as part of a larger change in the structure of an organization • *After several years of disappointing profits, the company decided to downsize its operations.*

entity Ⓐ *n* an organization or a business that has its own separate legal and financial existence • *The international division of the company has been operating as a separate entity.*

execution *n* the act of doing or performing something in a planned way • *The design and execution of the plan will take place over a period of four years.*

foothold *n* a situation in which someone has obtained the power or influence needed to get what is wanted • *Invasive species have gained a foothold in the national park.*

frustrated *adj* annoyed, disappointed, or discouraged • *We are becoming very frustrated at all of the delays.*

hindrance *n* a person or thing that makes a situation difficult; the act of making it difficult for someone to act or for something to be done • *Worrying too much about grammar can actually be a hindrance in learning a new language.*

merchandise *n* goods that are bought and sold • *After the big sale, there was very little merchandise left on the shelves.*

patriotism *n* love that people feel for their country • *Some people fly the flag of their country in front of their homes to show their patriotism.*

prevalent *adj* existing commonly or happening frequently • *The mosquito that carries malaria is prevalent in large parts of Africa, as well as areas of South and Southeast Asia.*

provoke *v* to cause a particular reaction or feeling • *The attack is likely to provoke anger as well as sorrow.*

regulation *n* an official rule or law • *The government has issued new regulations that banks will need to follow beginning January 1.*

reverse Ⓐ *v* to cause something to go in the opposite direction, order, or position • *The candidate has promised to reverse the tax increases if he is elected.*

secure *v* to obtain something, sometimes with difficulty • *In order to stay in business, the company will need to secure a loan of $10 million.*

security Ⓐ *n* freedom from risk and the threat of change for the worse • *The new rules for airline passengers will help protect national security.*

standardized *adj* made so that one thing is the same as others of that type • *Most manufacturers use standardized measurements in their products.*

streamline *v* to change something so that it works better, especially by making it simpler • *In order to increase our productivity, we need to streamline our operations and make them more efficient.*

subsidiary Ⓐ *n* a company that is owned by a larger company • *The company sold several of its subsidiaries that had not been profitable.*

unresolved Ⓐ *adj* (especially of a problem or difficulty) not solved or ended • *At the end of the meeting, several important issues remained unresolved.*

valid Ⓐ *adj* based on truth or reason; able to be accepted • *Give me a valid reason why we should continue with this strategy.*

The Language of Twenty-First-Century Business

converse Ⓐ *v* to talk with someone • *My Portuguese is good enough to converse about everyday topics.*

counterpart *n* a person or thing that has the same position or purpose as another person or thing in a different place or organization • *The ambassador will meet with his counterpart from Turkey.*

debate Ⓐ *n* a discussion, especially one in which several people with different opinions about something discuss them seriously, or the process of discussing something • *It is time for a national debate on how to decrease unemployment among young people.*

devise *v* to invent something, especially with intelligence or imagination • *We need to devise a plan to beat our competitors.*

eloquence *n* the use of language to express ideas or opinions clearly and well, so that they have a strong effect on others • *Martin Luther King, Jr. was famous for the eloquence of his speeches.*

exclusively Ⓐ *adv* limited to a specific thing or group • *This product is available exclusively from our website.*

expansion Ⓐ *n* the increase of something in size, number, or importance • An **expansion** *of the transit system to the suburbs is planned for next year.*

foster *v* to encourage the development or growth of ideas or feelings • *The Olympic Games can* **foster** *a positive image for the host country.*

impose Ⓐ *v* to establish something as a rule to be obeyed, or to force the acceptance of something • *Western nations often tried to* **impose** *their values on the countries that they colonized.*

inevitable Ⓐ *adj* certain to happen • *When her child came home from school with a cold, it seemed* **inevitable** *that she would catch it.*

intelligible *adj* (of speech and writing) clear enough to be understood • *The man had a very heavy accent so his voice message was not* **intelligible**.

mutually Ⓐ *adv* in a way that shows that two or more people or groups feel the same emotion or do the same thing with or for each other • *If we discuss this calmly, I am sure we can decide on a* **mutually** *agreeable solution.*

neutral Ⓐ *adj* not expressing an opinion or taking actions that support either side in a disagreement or war • *Switzerland took a* **neutral** *position during the war.*

nuance *n* a quality of something that is not easy to notice but may be important • *He has been watching basketball since he was a boy so he understands all the* **nuances** *of the game.*

outnumber *v* to be greater in number than someone or something • *Latinos now* **outnumber** *African Americans in most U.S. cities.*

simplistic *adj* simple but not effectively dealing with a real situation or problem, which is more complicated • *This analysis reflects a* **simplistic** *understanding of the issues.*

supervisor *n* a person responsible for the good performance of an activity or job • *I have a meeting with my* **supervisor** *to discuss my job performance.*

troubleshoot *v* to try to find the cause of a product or system not working correctly, especially one involving a piece of equipment or machine, and try to find the solution • *An engineer came from the company's main office to* **troubleshoot** *the computer problems we have been having.*

utilitarian *adj* designed to be useful rather than decorative • *The room had simple,* **utilitarian** *furniture that met our basic needs.*

vastly *adv* extremely; largely • *They have* **vastly** *different tastes in music; she like rap and he prefers opera.*

Disruptive Innovation and the Challenges of Social Media

accelerate *v* to make something happen faster or sooner • *A comfortable environment and the presence of family can* **accelerate** *a patient's recovery.* **acceleration** *n* an increase in the speed or rate of something • *The* **acceleration** *in the disappearance of sea ice has alarmed scientists.*

charity *n* an organization that gives money, food, or help to people who need it • *The students raised $2,000 for a local* **charity**.

connotation *n* a feeling or idea that is suggested by a word in addition to its basic meaning, or something suggested by an object or situation • *In many parts of the world today, the word* fat *has a negative* **connotation**, *but this was not always the case.*

cumbersome *adj* difficult to do or manage and taking a lot of time and effort • *The new online system for taking orders is very efficient and will replace the old,* **cumbersome** *system that used paper.*

currency Ⓐ *n* the money in use in a particular country • *All of the paper* **currency** *in the United States is the same color.*

customize *v* to make or change something according to a customer's or user's particular needs • *A travel company can* **customize** *a trip to meet your needs and fit your budget.*

demise *n* the end of the operation or existence of something • *Some people predicted that the Internet would result in the* **demise** *of television, but that has not occurred.*

displace Ⓐ *v* to force something or someone out of its usual or original place • *Some media experts believe that Bollywood will* **displace** *Hollywood as the movie center of the world.*

disruptive *adj* tending to damage the orderly control of a situation • *A ringing cell phone can be very* **disruptive** *in a meeting.* **disruption** *n* an interruption in the usual way that a system, process, or event works • *The cable company reported that the storm caused a brief* **disruption** *in its service.* **disrupt** *v* to prevent something, especially a system, process, or event, from continuing as usual or expected • *Next week's strike is likely to* **disrupt** *public services.*

embrace *v* to accept something with great interest or enthusiasm • *The public is often slow to* **embrace** *new ideas.*

erode Ⓐ *v* to weaken or damage something by taking away parts of it gradually • *In the second half of his term, support for the president began to* **erode**. **erosion** Ⓐ *n* the weakening or damage done to something by a series of gradual losses or parts of it • *News of bad behavior by athletes has led to an* **erosion** *of fan's trust and support.*

integral Ⓐ *adj* necessary and important as a part of a whole, or contained within it • *The music is an* **integral** *part of the film.*

obsolete *adj* no longer used or needed, usually because something newer and better has replaced it • *I buy a new computer every five years because old models quickly become* **obsolete**.

preference *n* the fact of liking or wanting one thing more than another • *Twenty percent of the people in the survey indicated a* **preference** *for shopping online.* **preferable** *adj* better or more suitable • *If you wish to contact our office, email is* **preferable**. **prefer** *v* to like, choose, or want one thing rather than another • *Do you* **prefer** *to exercise in the morning or in the evening?*

premise *n* an idea or theory on which a statement or action is based • *National education policy is based on the* **premise** *that all children deserve a good education.*

recruit *v* to persuade someone to become a new member of an organization • *In the U.S., the top college football programs try to* **recruit** *the same high school players.*

subtle *adj* not loud, bright, noticeable, or obvious; also, small but important • *It is difficult to see the* **subtle** *differences without a magnifying glass.*

thumb through *phr v* to turn the pages of a book or magazine quickly and read only small parts • *I usually* **thumb through** *magazines at the supermarket before I buy them.*

underestimate **Ⓐ** *v* to think that something is less or lower than it really is • *Never* **underestimate** *the determination and strength of your enemies.* **underestimation** **Ⓐ** *n* the opinion that something is smaller, easier, less important, or less extreme than it actually is • *This figure is probably an* **underestimation** *of the number of different species in the world.*

utilize **Ⓐ** *v* to make use of something • *The new parking garage* **utilizes** *the available space in a very efficient way.*

UNIT 3 • READING 5

New Thinking About the Right to Copy Art

advent *n* the beginning of an event, the invention of something, or the arrival of a person • *With the* **advent** *of digital technology, the home entertainment industry exploded.*

around the clock *idiom* all day and all night without stopping • *Hospitals provide emergency assistance* **around the clock**.

artisan *n* a person who does skilled work with his or her hands • *It is much more expensive to buy furniture from an* **artisan** *than a department store.*

broaden *v* to increase the range of something • *After focusing on the downtown area, police began to* **broaden** *their search for the missing boy.*

clamor *n* a loud complaint or demand • *The* **clamor** *from business groups for fewer regulations has increased with the weakening economy.*

commence **Ⓐ** *v* to begin something • *The performance will* **commence** *as soon as the sun sets.*

constitute **Ⓐ** *v* to be equal to or considered as • *These actions* **constitute** *a threat to national security.*

copyright-protected *adj* protected under the legal right to control the production and selling of a book, film, photograph, piece of music, etc., for a particular period of time • *This material is* **copyright-protected,** *so you may not use it without permission from the author.*

dangle *v* to hang loosely, or to cause something to hang • *Her long earrings* **dangled** *just above her shoulder.*

detriment *n* harm or damage • *We need to make choices today that are not to the* **detriment** *of future generations.*

diminution **Ⓐ** *n* a reduction in size or importance • *By next year there will be a visible* **diminution** *in our military presence.*

dissenting *adj* (law) having a legal opinion that differs from the opinion of most of the other judges of the court • *In last week's court ruling, there was just one* **dissenting** *vote.*

infringement *n* the action of breaking the terms of a law or agreement; violation • *Many people oppose the new law as an* **infringement** *on their right to free speech.*

interference *n* an attempt to spoil or prevent the progress of a situation or event • *The candidate argued that there is too much government* **interference** *in our private lives.*

liberalization *n* the process of allowing changes in the ways things are done • *Economic* **liberalization** *resulted in an increase in small private businesses.*

luxury *n* great comfort, especially as provided by expensive and beautiful possessions, surroundings, or food, or something enjoyable and often expensive but not necessary • *Many people around the world live in poverty while a privileged few live in* **luxury**.

motif *n* an idea that appears repeatedly in the work of an artist or in a piece of writing or music • *Fish and birds are a frequent* **motif** *in the artist's work.*

recognizably *adv* identifiably; distinguishably • *Although the bones in the ground were very old, they were* **recognizably** *human.*

remand *v* to send a case back to another court to be tried or dealt with again • *The judge will probably* **remand** *the case because of technical errors in the procedure.*

retrospective *n* an exhibition of work that an artist has done in the past • *There were more than 100,000 visitors during the first month of the museum's Picasso* **retrospective**.

sue *v* to take legal action against a person or organization, especially by making a legal claim for money because of some harm that the person or organization has caused you • *Several workers plan to* **sue** *their employer for injuries they suffered at the factory.*

twist of fate *idiom* a strange or unexpected event that has serious consequences • *In a cruel* **twist of fate**, *the men who went into the disaster area to rescue survivors became victims themselves.*

unauthorized *adj* without official permission • *Police are investigating an **unauthorized** entry into the building last night to determine if anything was taken.*

uninspired *adj* not exciting or interesting • *According to the critic, the presentation of the food at the new restaurant was **uninspired**.*

well-disposed *adj* willing or likely to do something • *I explained my plan to the rest of the group and most of them seemed **well-disposed** toward my ideas.*

UNIT 4 • READING 1

The Pursuit of Strength

array *n* a large number of similar things • *There was a huge **array** of fruits and vegetables at the outdoor market.*

attain Ⓐ *v* to achieve something difficult to do or obtain • *It took her five years to **attain** fluency in French.*

collapse Ⓐ *v* to fall down suddenly • *Most of the buildings in the village are likely to **collapse** if there is an earthquake.*

confer Ⓐ *v* to give an ability, honor, etc., to someone or something • *Sunlight **confers** important health benefits but can also be harmful.*

distinct Ⓐ *adj* clearly separate and different • *The styles of the two artists are quite **distinct**, so they are not easily confused.*

distribute Ⓐ *v* to divide something among several or many people, or to spread or scatter something over an area • *The city has a program that **distributes** meals to elderly residents who live alone.*

drawback *n* a disadvantage or problem; the negative part of a situation • *I love my new apartment, but one **drawback** is the traffic noise.*

endeavor *n* an effort or attempt to do something • *Climbing a mountain is a risky **endeavor**.*

exhibit Ⓐ *v* to show something in public • *Local artists **exhibit** their work at City Hall.*

inherent Ⓐ *adj* existing as a natural and permanent quality of something or someone • *A certain level of risk is **inherent** to most forms of investment.*

modify Ⓐ *v* to change something slightly, especially to improve it or make it more acceptable or less extreme • *We will have to **modify** the design to fit the smaller budget.*

nothing short of *idiom* strongly showing this quality • *Her quick recovery was **nothing short of** a miracle!*

pose Ⓐ *v* to cause something, especially a problem or difficulty • *City engineers believe the bridge is too old and **poses** a risk to public safety.*

resistance *n* the state of not being easily changed or damaged by something • *This type of carpet shows a high level of **resistance** to stains and can be cleaned easily.*

retain *v* to keep or continue to have something • *An apple will **retain** its shape even after cooking.*

rupture *v* to burst or break, or to cause something to burst or break • *If the pressure gets too high, the gas pipeline might **rupture**.*

spur *v* to encourage an activity or development, or to cause something to develop faster • *Higher oil prices are likely to **spur** the development of other forms of energy.*

tradeoff *n* a situation in which the achieving of something you want involves the loss of something else which is also desirable, but less so • *There is often a **tradeoff** between price and quality.*

unparalleled Ⓐ *adj* having no equal; better or greater than any other • *The 1950s was a period of **unparalleled** growth and prosperity in this country.*

vigorously *adv* very forcefully or energetically • *Authorities will **vigorously** enforce the new parking regulations.*

UNIT 4 • READING 2

Biomimetics

abundant *adj* more than enough; a lot of • *In the past, fish were **abundant** in this river, but now there are very few.*

blow *n* a hard hit with a hand or heavy object • *The force of the **blow** was strong enough to break one of his ribs.*

brilliance *n* great intelligence or skill • *Einstein was known for his intellectual **brilliance**.*

code Ⓐ *n* (genetics) a set of symbols the pattern of chemicals made in the genes which controls the characteristics and qualities of a living thing • *Scientists are working to determine the genetic **code** of this type of cancer.*

commercial *adj* intended to make money, or relating to a business intended to make money • *These materials are for educational, not **commercial**, purposes.*

consist of *phr v* to be made or formed of various specific things • *The test **consists of** 20 multiple-choice questions and 20 true-false questions.*

decipher *v* to discover the meaning of something hard to understand or which contains a hidden message • *The handwriting is very messy, so it is difficult to **decipher** the message.*

density *n* (physics) the relationship between the mass of a substance and its size • *The **density** of our bones decreases as we age.*

extraction Ⓐ *n* the process of removing or taking out something • *The **extraction** of coal from the earth is difficult and dangerous work.*

flexible Ⓐ *adj* able to bend or be bent easily without breaking • *Some new smartphones have a **flexible** screen that will not crack if you bend it.*

humble *adj* low in rank or position; poor • *The company's director is very successful now, but his career had a very **humble** beginning with a job in the factory.*

insert Ⓐ *v* to put something in something else • *To open the door, you must **insert** your card into the slot.*

insight Ⓐ *n* a clear, deep, and sometimes sudden understanding of a complicated problem or situation, or the ability to have such an understanding • *The new studies offer insight into the origins of the universe.*

labor Ⓐ *n* practical work, especially work that involves physical effort; also, the workers themselves, especially those who do practical work with their hands • *The creation of this garden required a great deal of labor.*

mainstay *n* the most important part of something, providing support for everything else • *Tourism has become a mainstay in the nation's economy.*

probe *v* to search into or examine something • *The article probes important issues in greater depth than television news.*

propagate *v* to reproduce or spread • *This genetic mutation may eventually propagate across the population.*

pry *v* to open, move, or lift something by putting one end of a tool under it and pushing down on the other end • *At first we could not open the door, but we were finally able to pry it open with a screwdriver.*

reproduce *v* to produce a copy of something • *Scientists must be able to reproduce the results of an experiment for a discovery to be considered valid.*

rival *v* to be equal or as good as • *Although most people download their music today, some people believe that nothing rivals the sound of old-fashioned vinyl records.*

seek *v* to search for something or try to find or obtain something • *A new government program seeks to help children who have run away from their homes.*

snap *v* to break something quickly with a cracking sound • *As she was falling, she could hear a bone in her arm snap.*

template *n* a method or model that can be copied and used by others • *You can use the report that I wrote as a template when you write your own.*

underway *adj* beginning to exist or is happening now • *The celebration is already underway and will continue through the night.*

versatility *n* the state of being able to be used for many different purposes • *He is a very valuable player because of his versatility; he can catch, hit, and throw the ball equally well.*

UNIT 4 • READING 3

Blue-sky Research

acknowledge Ⓐ *v* to accept the truth or recognize the existence of something • *He needs to acknowledge that he is not as strong as he once was.*

circuitous *adj* not straight or direct; roundabout • *We took a rather circuitous route to our destination, but we finally arrived.*

collide *v* (especially of moving objects) to hit something violently • *If you text while walking, at some point you will collide with another person or object.*

discernible *adj* able to be seen, recognized, or understood • *The tops of the buildings were barely discernible in the heavy fog.*

drive *v* to cause something to progress, develop, or become stronger • *Manufacturing no longer drives the economy; today technology is more important.*

enhance Ⓐ *v* to improve the quality, amount, or strength of something • *The sunlight enhances the beauty of the house and garden.*

esoteric *adj* intended for or understood by only a few people who have special knowledge • *For most people, high-energy physics is an esoteric field beyond their understanding.*

explicit Ⓐ *adj* very clear and complete • *I gave you explicit instructions to be home by midnight.*

found *v* to base a belief, claim, idea, etc., on something • *The country was founded on the belief that everyone is born equal.*

magnitude *n* large size or great importance • *The magnitude of the storm was much greater than anyone had predicted.*

optimize *v* to make something as good or effective as possible • *The software allows us to optimize our use of material and minimize waste.*

predecessor *n* a thing that comes before another in time or in a series, or a person who had a job or position before someone else • *Unlike his predecessor, the new university president will live on campus.*

quest *n* a long search for something that is difficult to find • *The quest to extend the human lifespan has been going in for centuries.*

refine Ⓐ *v* to improve something by making small changes • *We need to refine our advertisements in order to attract more customers.*

refute *v* to prove a statement, opinion, or belief to be wrong or false • *In a speech later today, the mayor will refute claims that he has wasted government funds.*

scarce *adj* not available in necessary amount, or rare • *In many parts of the world, fresh water has become a scarce resource.*

shortsighted *adj* showing a lack of thought for what might happen in the future • *Destroying our forests is shortsighted; we should be planning for the long-term future.*

stress Ⓐ *v* to give special importance or emphasis to something • *The schools stresses basic skills, like reading, writing, and math.*

unforeseen *adj* unexpected and often unwanted • *Sometimes even small changes can have unforeseen consequences.*

visionary *adj* being able to envision how a country, society, industry, etc. will or should develop in the future and to plan in a suitable way • *The public is looking for a visionary leader, someone who can help improve their lives and make them proud of their country.*

Frugal Innovation

adversity n a difficult or unlucky situation or event • *The founders of the company faced considerable **adversity** when they started their business.*

affluent adj having a lot of money or possessions; rich • *As they become more successful, many people move out of the city to more **affluent** suburbs.*

ample adj enough, or more than enough, or (especially of body size) large • *I was worried that there would not be enough food, but now I see that there is an **ample** amount.*

climate n a general attitude, opinion, or feeling • *With soldiers and police on every street, there is a **climate** of fear in the city.*

clog v to become blocked or filled so that movement or activity is slowed or stopped, or to cause this to happen • *Hair and pieces of food can **clog** your sink.*

dynamic Ⓐ adj having a lot of ideas and enthusiasm; energetic and forceful • *She is a **dynamic** leader, with lots of energy and new ideas.*

exemplary adj extremely good of its type so that it might serve as a model for others • *The soldier was awarded a medal for her **exemplary** behavior during the rescue operation.*

filter n a piece of equipment or a device for removing solids from liquids or gases • *The water is not safe, so you should boil it or use a **filter** before you drink it.*

illumination n light • *With little or no **illumination** on the street, we had to drive slowly and carefully.*

impetus n a force that encourages a particular action or makes it more energetic or effective • *The primary **impetus** for his decision to study medicine was the death of his mother when he was a teenager.*

in the event of idiom if something should happen • *In the **event of** an accident, his insurance will cover most of the costs.*

ingenuity n the skill of thinking, performing, or using things in new ways, especially to solve problems • *You will need to use all of your **ingenuity** to solve this problem.*

installation n the act of putting something in place so that it is ready for use • *The **installation** of the new carpet is scheduled for next Tuesday.*

mindset n a person's attitudes or opinions resulting from earlier experiences • *When you come to work for this company, you have to change your **mindset** because it operates very differently.*

novel adj new and original; not like anything seen before • *The movie breaks tradition and takes a **novel** approach to the crime story.*

perspective Ⓐ n a particular way of viewing things that depends on one's experience and personality • *Sometimes it is useful to look at the situation from a different **perspective** before you make up your mind.*

phenomenon Ⓐ n anything that is or can be experienced or felt, especially something that is noticed because it is unusual or new • *In the 1980s, the Sony Walkman became a cultural **phenomenon**.*

plague v to cause someone or something difficulty or suffering, especially repeatedly or continually • *Although the situation has improved somewhat, violent crime continues to **plague** the neighborhood.*

portable adj small and light enough to be carried or moved easily, and not attached by electric wires • *Transistor radios made music and news **portable** for the first time.*

principle Ⓐ n a basic truth that explains or controls how something happens or works • *You should study the basic **principles**, not all of the minor details.*

proponent n a person who supports an idea, plan, or cause • *The candidate has always been a **proponent** of workers' rights.*

ripe for adj phr ready or in good condition for something to happen • *Surveys of public opinion suggest that the time is **ripe for** change.*

robust adj strong and healthy • *The economy has demonstrated three straight years of **robust** growth.*

sterilize v to make something completely clean and free of bacteria • *Hospitals have equipment to **sterilize** medical tools after use.*

susceptible adj easily influenced or likely to be hurt by something • *You are more **susceptible** to infection if you are tired and under a lot of stress.*

Selections from *An Engineer's Alphabet*

abandon Ⓐ v to leave behind or run away from someone or something; to give up something • *She had to **abandon** her university studies when her father lost his job and could not pay the fees.*

accommodate Ⓐ v to provide space or a place for a group or things • *The restaurant can **accommodate** about 50 guests in one evening.*

anticipate Ⓐ v to imagine or expect that something will happen, sometimes taking action in preparation for it • *The city **anticipates** a large crowd to celebrate the team's victory.*

catastrophic n involving or resulting in great suffering or destruction • *After weeks of rain, another storm could be **catastrophic** for the area.*

clarify Ⓐ v to make something clearer or easier to understand • *When I am reading difficult material, sometimes reading aloud helps to **clarify** it for me.*

complacency n a feeling of calm satisfaction with your own abilities or situation that prevents you from trying harder • *The biggest danger in preventing the spread of disease is **complacency**; people think they are safe so they are not careful.*

contemporary Ⓐ *n* a person living in the same time period as someone else • *The artists Picasso and Dali were **contemporaries**; both lived through most of the twentieth century.*

conventional Ⓐ *adj* following the usual practices of the past • ***Conventional** therapy has not been effective, so doctors are going to try an experimental treatment.*

disintegrate *v* to become weaker or be destroyed by breaking into small pieces • *Ancient bones that have been buried underground will start to **disintegrate** when exposed to air.*

elusive *adj* hard to describe, find, achieve, catch, or remember • *Officials are investigating the explosion, but the cause remains **elusive**.*

foreseeable *adj* able to be understood in advance • *The negative impact of the change in policy was not **foreseeable**.*

fulfill *v* to do something as promised or intended, or to satisfy your hopes or expectations • *The government hopes to **fulfill** its promise of free education within five years.*

leak *n* the act of a liquid or gas escaping from a hole or crack in a pipe or container, or (of a container) of allowing liquid or gas to escape • *A **leak** in the gas pipeline caused an explosion.*

misleading *adj* causing someone to believe something that is not true • *The newspaper article contained some truth but also **misleading** information.*

on balance *idiom* with all things considered • *There were a few problems, but **on balance**, the program has been a great success.*

paradox *n* a statement or situation that may be true but seems impossible or difficult to understand because it contains two opposite facts or characteristics • *It is a **paradox** that so many people are overweight at the same time others are starving.*

precaution *n* an action taken to prevent something unpleasant or dangerous from happening • *As a **precaution**, you should make a copy of your passport before you travel internationally.*

prevail *v* to exist and be accepted among a large number of people • *In the end, I hope that common sense will **prevail** over emotion.*

prudent *adj* showing good judgment in avoiding risks and uncertainties; careful • *It is not **prudent** to carry a lot of cash; credit and debit cards are safer.*

pursuit Ⓐ *n* the act of following or searching for someone or something • *Several police officers ran in **pursuit** of the man with the gun.*

setback Ⓐ *n* something that causes delay or stops progress • *Losing one game was a **setback**, but the team still hopes to win the series.*

shortcoming *n* a fault of someone or something • *The new cell phone model is a major improvement, but it still has a few **shortcomings**.*

ultimate Ⓐ *adj* most important, highest, last, or final • *The **ultimate** goal of the organization is to eliminate hunger.*

viable *adj* able to exist, perform as intended, or succeed • *I do not believe that the candidate's plan is economically **viable**.*

vulnerability *n* the ability to be easily hurt, influenced, or attacked • *The soldiers' position in an open field increased their **vulnerability** to enemy attacks.*

Index to Key Vocabulary

Words that are part of the Academic Word List are noted with an Ⓐ in this appendix.

abandon Ⓐ **4.5**
absolute **1.5**
abundant **4.2**
accelerate **3.4**
acceleration **3.4**
accommodate Ⓐ **4.5**
acknowledge Ⓐ **4.3**
advent **3.5**
adversity **4.4**
advocate Ⓐ **3.1**
aerial **1.4**
affluent **4.4**
afford **1.2**
aggressive **2.4**
alarmed **2.4**
algorithm **1.3**
alter Ⓐ **1.3**
alternatively Ⓐ **2.5**
amass **1.5**
amorphous **1.4**
ample **4.4**
analogy Ⓐ **2.5**
anonymity **1.1**
anticipate Ⓐ **4.5**
application **1.2**
appreciate Ⓐ **2.5**
approximate **1.4**
approximation Ⓐ **1.4**
around the clock **3.5**
array **4.1**
artificial intelligence **1.3**
artisan **3.5**
ascertain **2.4**
aspiration Ⓐ **2.3**
assemble Ⓐ **3.2**
assert **1.1**
assume Ⓐ **2.2**
attain Ⓐ **4.1**
attribute Ⓐ **1.1**
automate Ⓐ **3.2**
autonomous **1.1**
avert **2.1**
backlash **3.2**
bind **2.3**
blow **4.2**
brilliance **4.2**
broaden **3.5**
capability Ⓐ **2.1**

capacious **1.5**
capital **3.1**
catastrophic **4.5**
charity **3.4**
chart Ⓐ **1.4**
chronic **2.1**
circuitous **4.3**
clamor **3.5**
clarify Ⓐ **4.5**
climate **4.4**
clinical **2.4**
clog **4.4**
code Ⓐ **4.2**
collaborate **1.4**
collaboration **1.4**
collaborative **1.4**
collapse Ⓐ **4.1**
collide **4.3**
commence Ⓐ **3.5**
commercial **4.2**
compile Ⓐ **2.2**
complacency **4.5**
comply **2.1**
component Ⓐ **1.3**
compound Ⓐ **1.5**
compound Ⓐ **2.5**
confer Ⓐ **4.1**
confines **3.1**
connotation **3.4**
consist of **4.2**
consolidate **3.2**
constitute Ⓐ **3.5**
constraint **1.5**
consult Ⓐ **2.1**
contaminate **2.5**
contemporary Ⓐ **4.5**
contract **1.5**
contradiction Ⓐ **1.2**
conventional Ⓐ **4.5**
converse Ⓐ **3.3**
convert Ⓐ **3.1**
convey **1.1**
coordination Ⓐ **1.2**
copyright-protected **3.5**
core Ⓐ **3.2**
correlate **1.5**
correspond **1.3**
counterpart **3.3**

countless **1.2**
criteria Ⓐ **2.5**
critique **1.5**
cross one's fingers **2.4**
cumbersome **3.4**
currency Ⓐ **3.4**
customize **3.4**
dangle **3.5**
debate Ⓐ **3.3**
decipher **4.2**
defective **2.3**
delegate **3.2**
demise **3.4**
density **4.2**
derive Ⓐ **2.2**
detect Ⓐ **2.1**
deteriorate **2.4**
detriment **3.5**
devastating **2.3**
devise **3.3**
diagnosis **2.1**
diminution Ⓐ **3.5**
discernible **4.3**
disclose **1.4**
discomfort **1.2**
discoverable **1.5**
disintegrate **4.5**
disorder **2.3**
displace Ⓐ **3.4**
disrupt **3.4**
disruption **3.4**
disruptive **3.4**
disseminate **2.2**
dissenting **3.5**
distinct Ⓐ **4.1**
distress **2.1**
distribute Ⓐ **4.1**
dominate Ⓐ **1.4**
downsize **3.2**
draw **1.2**
drawback **4.1**
drive **4.3**
dynamic Ⓐ **4.4**
echo **1.2**
elated **2.4**
eliminate Ⓐ **2.2**
eloquence **3.3**
elusive **4.5**

embedded **1.2**
embrace **3.4**
exemplary **4.4**
emerge Ⓐ **1.3**
endeavor **4.1**
enhance Ⓐ **4.3**
entail **1.3**
enterprise **3.1**
entity Ⓐ **3.2**
entrepreneur **3.1**
equivalent Ⓐ **2.5**
erode Ⓐ **3.4**
erosion Ⓐ **3.4**
esoteric **4.3**
ethical **2.3**
evolve Ⓐ **1.2**
exceed Ⓐ **2.1**
exclusively Ⓐ **3.3**
execution **3.2**
exhibit Ⓐ **4.1**
expansion Ⓐ **3.3**
explicit Ⓐ **4.3**
exponentially **1.5**
extraction Ⓐ **4.2**
facilitate Ⓐ **2.2**
fatigue **2.4**
feasibility **2.2**
filter **4.4**
flexible Ⓐ **4.2**
flounder **3.1**
foothold **3.2**
for good **2.4**
foreseeable **4.5**
formula Ⓐ **2.5**
foster **3.3**
found **4.3**
fragment **1.4**
frustrated **3.2**
fulfill **4.5**
fund **2.2**
gamble **2.5**
glimpse **1.4**
gratification **1.4**
gratify **1.4**
guideline Ⓐ **1.1**
haphazard **2.5**
head start **1.1**
heightened **1.2**

herald **2.2**
hindrance **3.2**
humble **4.2**
hurdle **2.5**
illumination **4.4**
imitate **1.1**
immensely **2.5**
immersion **1.2**
impact Ⓐ **1.1**
impediment **1.1**
imperative **1.5**
impetus **4.4**
implausible **1.3**
implementation Ⓐ **2.2**
implication Ⓐ **2.4**
impose Ⓐ **3.3**
in conjunction with **2.1**
in the event of **4.4**
incentive Ⓐ **2.5**
incidence Ⓐ **2.1**
inconsequential **2.3**
incorporate Ⓐ **1.4**
increment **1.5**
indicate Ⓐ **1.4**
inevitably Ⓐ **2.3**
inevitable Ⓐ **3.3**
inexplicable **1.5**
information overload **1.5**
infrastructure Ⓐ **2.2**
infringement **3.5**
ingenuity **4.4**
inherent Ⓐ **4.1**
inherit **2.3**
inhibitor **1.5**
initiate Ⓐ **2.2**
initiative Ⓐ **3.1**
innovation Ⓐ **1.1**
input **1.3**
insert Ⓐ **4.2**
insight Ⓐ **4.2**
installation **4.4**
instant **1.4**
integral Ⓐ **3.4**
integrate Ⓐ **2.2**
intelligible **3.3**
interference **3.5**
interrelated **1.5**
intersecting **1.3**

intervention (A) 2.3
intuition 2.5
invasive 2.4
ironically 2.4
isolated (A) 2.2
juxtaposition 1.3
labor (A) 4.2
leak 4.5
leverage 3.1
liberalization 3.5
luxury 3.5
magnitude 4.3
mainstay 4.2
manipulate (A) 1.3
margin of error (A) 1.4
mash up 1.5
masterpiece 1.4
mechanism (A) 1.3
merchandise 3.2
mimic 1.3
mindset 4.4
minimize (A) 2.1
mirrored 1.2
misleading 4.5
modify (A) 4.1
monitor (A) 2.1
morph 1.2
motif 3.5
motion sensor 1.2
motivate (A) 2.3
mutually (A) 3.3
navigable 1.4
navigate 1.4
navigator 1.4
network (A) 1.1
neutral (A) 3.3
nothing short of 4.1
novel 4.4
nuance 3.3
obsolete 3.4
obstacle 2.2
odds (A) 2.3
on balance 4.5
onset 2.3
open-ended 1.5

oppressive 1.5
opt for 2.4
optimize 4.3
outbreak 2.2
outcome (A) 2.2
outlook 2.4
outnumber 3.3
overlook 2.2
overwhelmingly 2.4
paradigm (A) 3.1
paradox 4.5
pare down 1.5
patriotism 3.2
pave the way 1.3
perilous 2.5
perspective (A) 1.3
perspective (A) 4.4
pervasive 1.4
phase (A) 2.5
phenomenon (A) 4.4
pioneering 2.4
pivotal 3.1
plague 4.4
plane 1.3
platform 1.2
portable 4.4
pose (A) 4.1
practical 1.2
precaution 4.5
precursor 1.1
predecessor 4.3
predominant (A) 2.2
prefer 3.4
preferable 3.4
preference 3.4
preliminary (A) 2.2
premier 1.4
premise 3.4
prevail 4.5
prevalent 3.2
principle (A) 4.4
prioritize (A) 2.5
probe 4.2
procure 3.1
productivity 3.1

profound 2.5
promote (A) 2.1
promulgate 1.5
propagate 4.2
proponent 4.4
proportion 1.3
prospective 2.1
provoke 3.2
prudent 4.5
pry 4.2
pursuit (A) 4.5
quest 4.3
radical (A) 2.4
rally 2.4
rationale 1.2
reception 2.1
recognizably 3.5
recruit 3.4
recurrence 2.4
refine (A) 4.3
refute 4.3
regulation 3.2
rehabilitation 1.2
relapse 2.4
relevant (A) 1.5
reliance 3.1
remand 3.5
remote 2.2
repetitive 1.2
replica 1.3
reproduce (A) 4.2
resistance 4.1
resolution 3.1
retain 4.1
retrospective 3.5
reverse (A) 3.2
revolutionary (A) 1.1
ripe for 4.4
rival 4.2
robust 4.4
routine 2.2
rule of thumb 1.1
rule out 2.3
rupture 4.1
scarce 4.3

scenario (A) 1.2
scratch the surface 1.2
screen 2.3
sector (A) 3.1
secure 3.2
security (A) 3.2
seek 4.2
sequence (A) 2.3
serendipity 2.5
setback (A) 4.5
shortcoming 4.5
shortsighted 4.3
side effect 2.5
sift 2.5
simplistic 3.3
simulation (A) 1.2
simultaneously 1.1
snap 4.2
solicit 3.1
speculate 1.4
speculation 1.4
speculative 1.4
spur 4.1
stable (A) 2.5
standardized 3.2
stationary 1.2
status (A) 2.3
stereotypical 1.1
sterilize 4.4
streamline 3.2
stress (A) 4.3
subsequent (A) 2.3
subsidiary (A) 3.2
subtle 3.4
sue 3.5
superimpose 1.4
supervisor 3.3
susceptible 4.4
sustain (A) 2.1
synthesize 2.5
tantamount 1.5
target audience 1.1
tantamount 1.5
template 4.2
therapeutic 2.3

threshold 2.2
thrive 3.1
thumb through 3.4
to no avail 2.4
toxic 2.5
track 2.1
tradeoff 4.1
trajectory 2.3
transcribe 3.1
transformation (A) 2.1
transmission (A) 1.1
transmit (A) 2.1
traverse 1.5
trick 1.3
trigger (A) 2.2
troubleshoot 3.3
twist of fate 3.5
ultimate (A) 4.5
ultimately (A) 2.5
unauthorized 3.5
underestimate (A) 3.4
underestimation (A) 3.4
undergo (A) 2.4
undertaking (A) 1.1
underway 4.2
unforeseen 4.3
uniformly (A) 2.4
uninspired 3.5
unparalleled (A) 4.1
unresolved (A) 3.2
utilitarian 3.3
utilize (A) 3.4
utmost 2.4
valid (A) 3.2
vastly 3.3
vehicle (A) 2.2
venture 3.1
versatility 4.2
viable 4.5
vigorously 4.1
virtual (A) 1.2
visionary 4.3
vulnerability 4.5
well-disposed 3.5
widespread 1.5
yield 2.4

Improving Your Reading Speed

Good readers read quickly and understand most of what they read. However, like other skills, reading faster is a skill that requires good technique and practice. One way to practice is to read frequently. Read about topics you are interested in, not just topics from your academic courses. Reading for pleasure will improve your reading speed and understanding.

Another way to practice is to choose a text you have already read and read it again without stopping. Time yourself, record the time, and keep a record of how your reading speed is increasing.

These strategies will help you improve your reading speed:

- Before you read a text, look at the title and any illustrations. Ask yourself, *What is this reading about?* This will help you figure out the general topic of the reading.
- Read words in groups instead of reading every single word. Focus on the most important words in a sentence – usually the nouns, verbs, adjectives, and adverbs.
- Don't pronounce each word as you read. Pronouncing words will slow you down and does not help you to understand the text.
- Don't use a pencil or your finger to point to the words as you read. This will also slow you down.
- Continue reading even if you come to an unfamiliar word. Good readers know that they can skip unfamiliar words as long as they understand the general meaning of the text.

Calculating Your Reading Speed

After you have completed a unit in this book, reread one of the readings. Use your cellphone or your watch to time how long it takes you to complete the reading. Write down the number of minutes and seconds it took you in the chart on the following pages.

You can figure out your reading speed; that is your words per minute (wpm) rate by doing the following calculation:

First, convert the seconds of your reading time to decimals using the table to the right.

Next, divide the number of words per reading by the time it took you to complete the reading. For example, if the reading is 525 words, and it took you 5 minutes 50 seconds, your reading speed is about 90 words per minute (525 ÷ 5.83 = 90).

Record your wpm rate in the chart on the following pages.

Seconds	Decimal
:05	.08
:10	.17
:15	.25
:20	.33
:25	.42
:30	.50
:35	.58
:40	.67
:45	.75
:50	.83
:55	.92

UNIT	READING TITLE	NUMBER OF WORDS IN READING	YOUR READING TIME minutes:seconds 00:00	READING SPEED (WPM)
Unit 1 Technology	Technology and the Individual	1480	9 : 01	12 : 61
	Virtual Reality and Its Real-World Applications	1394	____ : ____	
	Life in 3D	1388	____ : ____	
	Mapmaking in the Digital Age	1177	____ : ____	
	How Information Got Smart	2484	____ : ____	
Unit 2 Biomedical Science	Health and Wellness on the Go	1296	____ : ____	
	Funding Global mHealth Projects	1332	____ : ____	
	Genomics	1356	____ : ____	
	A Case Study in Genomics	1252	____ : ____	
	Drug Discovery in the Twenty-First-Century	2060	____ : ____	

UNIT	READING TITLE	NUMBER OF WORDS IN READING	YOUR READING TIME minutes:seconds 00:00	READING SPEED (WPM)
Unit 3 Business	Crowdsourcing and Crowdfunding	1427	8:20	174.02
	Outsourcing: Managing Labor Needs	1602	9:40	1781
	The Language of Twenty-First-Century Business	1387	6:15	225.52
	Disruptive Innovation and the Challenges of Social Media	1438	7:00	205.42
	New Thinking About the Right to Copy Art	2127	13:20	961.136
Unit 4 Science and Engineering	The Pursuit of Strength	1332	___:___	
	Biomimetics	1063	___:___	
	Blue-sky Research	1220	___:___	
	Frugal Innovation	1194	___:___	
	Selections from *An Engineer's Alphabet*	2053	___:___	

REFERENCES

Unit 1, Reading 1

Boden, Margaret A. *The Creative Mind: Myths and Mechanisms*. London: Routledge, 2004. Print.

Chafuen, Alejandro. "Thinking About Think Tanks: Which Ones Are the Best? *Forbes*. Forbes, 23 Jan. 2013. Web. 13 Aug. 2015.

Johnson, Steve. *Where Good Ideas Come From: The Natural History of Innovation*. Riverhead Books: New York, 2010. Print.

Lieberman, Jodi. "The Garage Innovation Myth." *Thebreakthrough.org*. The Breakthrough Institute, 04 Dec. 2012. Web. 13 Aug. 2015.

Moretti, Enrico. *The New Geography of Jobs*. Boston: Houghton Mifflin Harcourt, 2012. Print.

Novak, Matt. "Tesla and the Lone Inventor Myth." *BBC*. BBC, 18 Nov. 2014. Web. 13 Aug. 2015.

Olink, Troy. "The New Geography of Jobs: Where You Live Matters More Than Ever." *Forbes*. Forbes, 22 May 2012. Web. 13 Aug 2015.

Piiparinen, Richey, Charles Post, and Jim Russell. "A Newer Geography of Jobs: Where Workers with Advanced Degrees Are Concentrating the Fastest" *Urban Publications*. Paper 1190, 2014. Web. 14 Aug. 2015.

Popova, Maria. "Combinatorial Creativity and the Myth of Originality." *Smithsonianmag.org*. Smithsonian, 12 Jun. 2012. Web. 13 Aug. 2015.

Schwartz, Evan I. *The Last Lone Inventor: A Tale of Genius, Deceit & the Birth of Television*. Harper Collins: New York, 2003.

"Stanford Professor A.J. Paulraj Wins the 2014 Marconi Prize." Press release. *Marconisociety*. The Marconi Society, 21 Jan. 2014. Web. 13 Aug. 2015.

Unit 1, Reading 2

Frank, Meghan and Neal Carter. "Groundbreaking Experiment in Virtual Reality Uses Video Game to Treat Pain." Video. *Rockcenter.NBCNews*. NBC News, 24 Oct. 2012. 13 Aug. 2015.

Ohannessian, Kevin. "Oculus Rift, Sony, and the Coming Virtual Reality Revolution." *fastcompany.com*. Fast Company, 19 Mar. 2014. Web. 14 Aug. 2015.

O'Raw, Paul. "An Evaluation of Virtual Reality Technology as an Occupational Therapy Treatment Tool in Spinal Cord Injury Rehabilitation." *NRH*. National Rehabilitation Hospital, Nov. 2006. Web. 13 Aug 2015.

Sherman, William and Alan B. Craig. *Understanding Virtual Reality*. San Francisco: Morgan Kaufmann Publishers, 2003. Print.

Shuster, Brian. "Virtual Reality and Learning: The Newest Landscape for Higher Education." *Wired.com*. Wired, Dec. 2012. Web. 13 Aug. 2015.

Venables, Michael. "Eve: Valkyrie—The Future of Immersive Virtual Reality Gaming Experience," *Forbes*. Forbes, 20 Nov. 2013. Web. 13 Aug. 2015.

"The Video Game Revolution: History of Gaming." *PBS.org*. PBS, n.d. Web. 13 Aug. 2015.

"Virtual Worlds Online: Living a Second Life." *Economist*. The Economist, 28 Sep. 2006. Web. 13 Aug. 2015.

Unit 1, Reading 3

"3D Printing: The Printed World." *Economist*. The Economist, 10 Feb. 2011. Web. 13 Aug. 2015.

Bargmann, Joe. "Urbee 2, the 3D-Printed Car That Will Drive Across the Country." *Popularmechanics.com*. Popular Mechanics, 04 Nov. 2013. Web. 13 Aug 2015.

Falconer, Jason. "Poppy, a 3D-Printed Humanoid Robot That Defies Conventions." *Gizmag.com*. Gizmag, 22 Oct. 2013. Web. 13 Aug. 2015.

Robarts, Stu. "World's First" 3D Printed Car Created and Driven by Local Motors." *Gizmag.com*. Gizmag, 17 Sep. 2014. Web. 13 Aug 2015.

Russon, Mary-Ann. "Human or Machine? Life-Like Android Robots from Japan Show Glimpses of the Future." *ibtimes.co.uk*. International Business Times, 24 Jun. 2014. Web. 13 Aug 2015.

Unit 1, Reading 4

"Cartographers and Photogrammetrists." *bls.gov*, Bureau of Labor Statistics, 08 Jan. 2014. Web. 13 Aug. 2015.

Cuoghi, Diego. "The Mysteries of The Piri Reis Map." *diegocuoghi.com*, n.d. Web. 13 Aug 2015.

"500-year-old map by Piri Reis on Display at Topkapi Palace." *Istanbulview.com*, 24 Jan. 2013. Web. 13 Aug 2015.

"GPS History: How It All Started." *Maps.gps.info.com*, n.d. Web. 13 Aug. 2015.

Hoye, Paul F. and Paul Lunde. "Piri Reis and the Hapgood Hypotheses." *aramcoworld.com*. Jan/Feb 1980. Web. 13 Aug. 2015.

Kite, Buddy. "Four Innovative Mapmakers Re-inventing the Very Idea of Maps." *Esquire*, Esquire, n.d. Web. 13 Aug. 2015.

Knutsen, Matt. "The New York City Historical GIS Project." *nypl.org*, New York Public Library, 13 Jun. 2012. Web. 13 Aug. 2015.

Lincoln Motor Company. "The New Cartographers." *washingtonpost.com*. The Washington Post, 22 Jul. 2013. Web. 13 Aug. 2015.

Wouters, Flip. "5 Best 3D Video Projection Mapping Magic—It Will Blow You Away." *bestofmarketing.com*, n.d. Web. 13 Aug 2015.

Unit 1, Skills and Strategies 3

Beynon-Davies, Paul.. *Business Information Systems*. Basingstoke, UK: Palgrave, 2009.

Marcus, Gary and Ernest Davis. "Eight (No, Nine!) Problems with Big Data." *NYTimes*. The New York Times, 06 Apr. 2014. Web. 13 Aug 2015.

McAfee, Andrew and Erik Brynjolfsson, "Big Data: The Management Revolution." *hbr.org*. Harvard Business Review, Oct. 2012. Web. 13 Aug. 2015.

Unit 2, Reading 1

"The Market for mHealth App Services Will Reach $26 Billion by 2017." *PRNewswire.com*. PR Newswire, 08 Mar. 2013. Web. 14 Aug. 2015.

Flatow, Ira. "Can Technology Deliver Better Health Care?" *NPR*. NPR, 01 June 2012. Web. 07 Aug. 2015.

Marshall, Matt. "Vinod Khosla Says Technology Will Replace 80 Percent of Doctors — Sparks Indignation." *VentureBeat*, 02 Sept. 2012. Web. 07 Aug. 2015.

Sreenivasan, Hari. "The Quantified Self: Data Gone Wild?" *PBS*. PBS, 23 Sep. 2013. Web. 07 Aug. 2015.

West, Daniel. "How Mobile Devices Are Transforming Healthcare." *Issues in Technology Innovation: 18*. Brookings, May 2012. Web. 14 Aug. 2015.

West, Daniel. *Improving Healthcare through Mobile Medical Devices and Sensors*. Paper. *brookings.edu*. Center for Technology Innovation at Brookings, Oct. 2013. Web. 14 Aug. 2015.

Winslow, Ron. "The Wireless Revolution Hits Medicine." *wsj.com*. The Wall Street Journal, 14 Feb. 2013. Web. 07 Aug. 2015.

Yu Xiaohui, et al. *mHealth in China and the United States*. Report. Center for Technology Innovation at Brookings, 12 Mar. 2014. Web. 13 Aug 2015.

Unit 2, Reading 2

Chhabra, Esha. "Ubiquitous Across Globe, Cellphones Have Become Tool for Doing Good." *NYTimes*. The New York Times, 07 Nov. 2013. Web. 13 Aug. 2015.

Joyce, Christopher. "Cellphones Could Help Doctors Stay Ahead Of An Epidemic." *NPR*. NPR, 31 Aug. 2011. Web. 07 Aug. 2015.

MacPherson, Yvonne and Sarah Chamberlain. *Health on the Move: Can Mobile Phones Save Lives?* Policy Briefing #7. BBC Media Action, Feb. 2013. Web. 13 Aug. 2015.

"mHealth: New Horizons for Health through Mobile Technology." *Global Observatory for eHealth Series— Volume 3*, World Health Organization, 2011. Web. 13 Aug. 2015.

Rosenberg, Tina. "The Benefits of Mobile Health, on Hold." *NYTimes*. The New York Times, 13 Mar. 2013. Web. 07 Aug. 2015.

Vital Wave Consulting. *mHealth for Development: The Opportunity of Mobile Technology for Healthcare in the Developing World*. Washington, D.C. and Berkshire, UK: UN Foundation-Vodafone Foundation Partnership, 2009.

West, Daniel. "How Mobile Devices Are Transforming Healthcare." *Issues in Technology Innovation: 18*, 2012. Brookings.

Unit 2, Reading 3

"Cracking Your Genetic Code." *PBS*. PBS, 28 Mar. 2012. Web. 07 Aug. 2015.

Guttkind, Lee. *An Immense Power to Heal: The Promise of Personalized Medicine*. Pittsburgh: In Fact Books, 2012. Print.

"The Human Genome Project Completion: Frequently Asked Questions." *genome.gov*. National Human Genome Research Institute, 30 Oct. 2010. Web. 14 Aug. 2015.

"Personalized Health: Matching Treatment to Your Genes." *NIH News in Health*, National Institutes of Health, Dec. 2013. Web. 14 Aug. 2015.

Pinker, Steven. "My Genome, My Self." *NYTimes*. The New York Times, 10 Jan. 2009. Web. 07 Aug. 2015.

Timmerman, Luke. "Ready or Not, Genomics Is Coming to a Hospital Near You." *Xconomy RSS*, 11 Jun. 2012. Web. 07 Aug. 2015.

Unit 2, Reading 4

"Cancer Doctor Becomes Cancer Patient." Video. *CBSNews*. CBS, 31 Jul. 2012. Web. 07 Aug. 2015.

Kolata, Gina. "In Treatment for Leukemia, Glimpses of the Future." *Nytimes*. The New York Times, 07 July 2012. Web. 07 Aug. 2015.

Zimmer, Carl. "In a First, Test of DNA Finds Root of Illness." *NYTimes*. The New York Times, 04 Jun. 2014. Web. 07 Aug. 2015.

Unit 3, Skills and Strategies 7

Ha, Thu-Huong. (August 14, 2013) "How Journalist Paul Lewis Helped Solve to Murders Wing Social Media." *Ideas*. *TED.com*, TED, 14 Aug. 2013. Web. 13 Aug. 2015.

Unit 3, Reading 1

Barnett, Chance. "The Top 10 Crowdfunding Sites for Fundraising." *Forbes*. Forbes, 08 May 2013. Web. 13 Aug 2015.

Causer, Tim and Valerie Wallace. "Building A Volunteer Community: Results and Findings" from *Transcribe Bentham*. *Digital Humanities Quarterly*, Vol. 6:2, 2012. Web. 13 Aug. 2015.

Crowdsource. "Crowdsourcing and Verification of data: A Real-World Cost-Effective Solution." *crowdsource.com*, 15 May 2012. Web. 13 Aug. 2015.

"The Crowdsourcing Industry Report." *crowdsourcing.org*. 2015. Web. 13 Aug. 2015.

Morgan, Timothy Prickett. "How Ancestry Branched Out and Embraced Sale." *enterprisetech.com*. 09 Jan. 2014. Web. 13 Aug. 2015.

Morgenegg, Ryan. "Crowdsourcing Effort Helps Millions Identify Ancestors." *Deseret News*. 01 Aug. 2014. Web. 13 Aug. 2015.

Wald, Jeff. "3 Ways Social Networking Is Impacting the Global Economy." *Forbes*. Forbes, 03 Jul. 2014. Web. 13 Aug. 2015.

Unit 3, Reading 2

Beeler, Carolyn. "Outsourced Call Centers Return, to US Homes." *NPR*. NPR, 25 Aug. 2010. Web. 08 May 2015.

Creeden, Aine. "Homeless People and Nonprofits' Increasing Use of Social Media and Mobile Technology to Connect." *NPQ: Nonprofit Quarterly*, 14 Jun. 2014. Web. 13 Aug. 2015.

"Job Outsourcing Statistics." *statisticsbrain.com*. 01 Jan. 2014. Web. 13 Aug. 2015.

"Texas Instruments Outsources More Production to Taiwan's UMC." *WantChinaTimes*, 02 Feb. 2012. Web. 13 Aug. 2015.

Vlasic, Bill and Brett Clanton. "The Fall of Flint." *DetroitNews*. Detroit News, 11 Dec. 2005. Web. 10 May 10 2015.

Wadhwa, Vivek. "Crowdsourcing is Overtaking Outsourcing." *wsj.com*. The Wall Street Journal, 20 Dec. 2013. Web. 13 Aug. 2015.

Witsil, Frank. "Call Center Jobs Increase as More Return From Overseas." *USAToday*. USA Today, 04 Aug. 2014. Web. 09 May 2015.

Zeitlin, Matthew. "Why Call Center Jobs Are Coming Back." *The Daily Beast*, 28 Aug. 2012. Web. 07 May 2015.

Unit 3, Reading 3

Albright, Dann. "Future Communication Devices Everyone Will Want to Own." *makeuseof.com*, 14 Aug. 2014. Web. 13 Aug. 2015.

Allen, Frederick E. "A New International Business Language: Globish." *Forbes*. Forbes, 01 Mar. 2012. Web. 13 Aug. 2015.

Chotiner, Isaac. "Globish for Beginners." *newyorker.com*, 10 May 2010. Web.13 Aug. 2015.

"Esperanto: Simple, Logical and Doomed…" *Economist*. The Economist, Sep. 2013. Web. 13 Aug. 2015.

Nerrière, Jean-Paul and David Hon. *Globish the World Over*. International Globish Institute, 2009.

Caren, Allie. "Redefining What It Means to Talk in the Age of Smartphones." *NPR*. NPR, 22 Jun. 2014. Web. 13 Aug. 2015.

Polack, Gillian. "Languages in Medieval England." *Triviumpublishing.com*, 2009. Web. 13 Aug. 2015.

"Why Use Language Translation Software?" *Systran*, n.d. Web. 13 Aug. 2015.

Unit 3, Reading 4

"AAMI Journal Shines Light on Growing Impact of 3D Printing in Healthcare Technology." *aami.org*, 20 Feb. 2014. Web. 13 Aug. 2015.

Howard, Caroline. "Disruption vs. Innovation: What's the Difference?" *Forbes*. Forbes, March 27, 2013. Web.

Howard, Caroline. "The 12 Most Disruptive Names In Business 2013: The Full List." *Forbes*, Forbes, 2013. Web. 13 Aug. 2015.

Karli, Aulia Maharani. "How Strongly Can Social Media Influence and Control People's Lives?" *voicesofyouth.org*, 2013. *Web*.13 Aug. 2015.

McCarthy, Tom. "*Encyclopedia Britannica* Halts Print Publication after 244 Years." *guardian.com*, The Guardian, 13 Mar. 2012. Web. 13 Aug. 2015.

Nisen, Max. "How 'Disrupt' Got Turned Into an Overused Buzzword." *businessinsider.com*, 28 Sep. 2013. Web. 13 Aug. 2015.

Tartakoff, Joseph. "Victim of Wikipedia, Microsoft to Shut Down Encarta." *gigaom.com*, 20 Mar. 2009. Web. 13 Aug. 2015.

"The Biggest Trends in Business for 2013." *Entrepreneur.com*, 03 Dec. 2012. Web. 13 Aug. 2015.

Unit 3, Skills and Strategies 9

Gladwell, Malcolm. "Creation Myth: Xerox PARC, Apple, and the Truth about Innovation." *New Yorker*, The New Yorker, 16 May 2011. Web. 13 Aug. 2015.

Schissel, Nathan. "3D printing and Implications on Intellectual Property Rights." *technologylawadvisor.com*, 10 Nov. 2014. Web. 13 Aug. 2015.

Triumph of the Nerds: The Television Program Transcripts—Part 3. *PBS*, PBS, n.d. Web. 13 Aug. 2015.

Unit 4, Skills and Strategies 10

Ashley, Steven and Larry Greenemeier. "9 Materials That Will Change the Future of Manufacturing [Slide Show]." *Scientific American*, Scientific American, 22 Apr. 2013. Web. 13 Aug. 2015.

"Collector's Corner: Mohs Scale of Hardness." *minsocam.org*, Mineralogical Society of America, n.d. Web. 07 Aug. 2015.

"Mushroom Material." *Nova*. PBS, 17 Oct. 2013. Web. 13 Aug. 2015.

King, Hobart. "REE—Rare Earth Elements and Their Uses." *Geology.com*, n.d. Web. 13 Aug. 2015.

Unit 4, Reading 1

Bilton, Nick. "Bend It, Charge It, Dunk It: Graphene, the Material of Tomorrow." *NYTimes*, The New York Times, 13 Apr. 2014. Web. 07 Aug. 2015.

Condliffe, Jamie. "5 Crazy New Man-Made Materials That Will Shape the Future." *Gizmodo*, 09 Sep. 2009. Web. 07 Aug. 2015.

Gordon, Jim. *The New Science of Strong Materials*. Princeton: Princeton University Press, 1968. Print.

"Materials: Forging Ahead." *Economist*. The Economist, 21 Apr. 2012. Web. 07 Aug. 2015.

"Nobel Awarded For Thin, Versatile Carbon Material." *NPR*. NPR, 05 Oct. 2010. Web. 07 Aug. 2015.

"Strange Matter: What Is Materials Science?" *StrangeMatterExhibit.com*, N.p., n.d. Web. 07 Aug. 2015.

Webb, Johnathan. "New Family of Recyclable Plastics Created 'by Accident'." *BBC*, BBC News, 15 May 2014. Web. 07 Aug. 2015.

Unit 4, Reading 2

Ashley, Steven. "Future of Substance: New Materials Promise Better Batteries, Stronger Steel." *Scientific American*, v 308:5, 30 Apr. 2013. Web. 13 Aug. 2015.

Gordon, Jim. *The New Science of Strong Materials*. Princeton: Princeton University Press, 1968. Print.

Graber, Cynthia. "Insect Cuticle Inspires New Material." *Scientific American*, 20 Dec. 2010. Web. 07 Aug. 2015.

Ledgett, Hadley. "1 Million Spiders Make Golden Silk for Rare Cloth." *Wired.com*, 23 Sep. 2009. Web. 07 Aug. 2015.

Morgan, James. "New Waterproof Surface Is 'Driest Ever'." *BBC*. BBC News, 21 Nov. 2013. Web. 07 Aug. 2015.

Morgan, James. "Self-healing Plastic Mimics Blood Clotting." *BBC*. BBC News, 09 May 2014. Web. 07 Aug. 2015.

Mueller, Tom. "Biomimetics." *National Geographic*, National Geographic, Apr. 2008. Web. 07 Aug. 2015.

Petit, Charles. "Material as Tough as Steel? The Abalone Fits the Bill." *newyorktimes*, The New York Times, 21 Mar. 2005. Web. 07 Aug. 2015.

"Tough, Light and Strong: Lessons From Nature Could Lead to the Creation of New Materials, Science Study Says." *Jacobs School of Engineering*. 14 Feb. 2013. Web. 13 Aug. 2015.

Unit 4, Reading 3

Bush, Vannevar.. *Science the Endless Frontier*. Washington: U.S. Government Printing Office, 1945.

Fang, Ferric C. and Arturo Casadevall. "Lost in Translation—Basic Science in the Era of Translational Research." *Infection and Immunity*. American Society for Microbiology, 28 Dec. 2009. Web. 07 Aug. 2015.

Karagianis, Liz. "The Brilliance of Basic Research." *Spectrum*. Massachusetts Institute of Technology, Spring 2004. Web. 13 Aug. 2015.

Santoso, Alex. "The Wonderful World of Big Science." *Neatorama*, 15 Jul. 2009. Web. 07 Aug. 2015.

Unit 4, Reading 4

"First Break All the Rules: The Charms of Frugal Innovation." *Economist*. The Economist, Apr. 2010. Web. 13 Aug. 2015.

Grueber, Martin, Tim Studt, et. al. "2014 Global R&D Forecast." Report. *R&D Magazine*. Battelle, Dec. 2013. Web. 13 Aug. 2015.

Ashoka. "Jugaad: The Art of Converting Adversity into Opportunity." *Forbes*. Forbes, 23 Mar. 2013. Web. 07 Aug. 2015.

Keating, Joshua E. "The AK-47 of the Cell-Phone World." *Foreign Policy*. Foreign Policy, 03 Jan. 2011. Web. 14 Aug. 2015.

Orendain, Simone. "In Philippine Slums, Capturing Light in a Bottle." *NPR*. NPR, 28 Dec. 2011. Web. 14 Aug. 2015.

Prahalad, C.K. *The Fortune at the Bottom of the Pyramid*. NJ: Wharton School Publishing, 2006. Print.

Radjou, Navi, Jaideep Pradhu, and Ahuja, Simone. *Jugaad Innovation: Think Frugal, Be Flexible, Generate Breakthrough Growth*. San Franciso: Jossey-Bass, 2012. Print.

Smith-Strickland, Kiona. "A Billboard That Condenses Water from Humidity." *Popular Mechanics*. Popular Mechanics, 25 Apr. 2013. Web. 14 Aug. 2015.

Unit 4, Skills and Strategies 11

"Make Solar Energy Economical." *Grand Challenges for Engineering*. National Academy for Engineering. n.d. Web. 13 Aug. 2015.

Illustrations

Jim Atherton

Photography

T = Top, C = Centre, B = Below, L = Left, R = Right, B/G = background

p.1: ©SOMMAI/Shutterstock; p.11: ©Roger Askew/Alamy; p.19: ©EPA European Pressphoto Agency/Alamy; p.21: ©Valentyna Chukhlyebova/Alamy; p.33: ©Rob Atkins/ Getty Images; p.34: ©Alfred Pasieka/Science Photo Library/ Getty Images; p.35: ©Aflo Co. Ltd./Alamy; p.43: (L) ©Selimaksan/Getty Images; (R) ©Deco/Alamy; p.44: (L) ©Empics/Shutterstock; (R) ©Mechanik/Shutterstock; p.59: (T) ©Padu Foto/Shutterstock; (B) ©USBFCO/Shutterstock; p.60: ©Kim Steele/Getty Images; p.75: ©Ariel Skelley/Getty Images; p.111: (T) ©The Biochemist Artist/Shutterstock; (B) ©LY Photo/Shutterstock; p.113: ©Tribalium/ Shutterstock; p.135: ©Pictorial Press Ltd/Alamy; p.139: ©R. Classen/Shutterstock; p.149: ©Robert S/Shutterstock; p.157: ©EPA European Pressphoto Agency/Alamy; p.158: ©Newsies Media/Alamy; p.194: ©NetPhotos/Alamy; p.195: ©Rawpixel/Shutterstock; p.211: ©Timothy A. Clary/AFP/ Getty Images; p.214: ©Courtesy of the Artist and Petzel, New York; p.227: ©Pranodhm/Shutterstock; p.237: ©Bonnin Studio/Shutterstock; p.244: ©Adrian Dennis/AFP/Getty Images; p.245: ©Freer/Shutterstock; p.258: (T) ©SSSCCC/ Shutterstock; (B) ©Naeblys/Shutterstock; p.267: ©Indranil Mukhergee/Getty Images; p.269: ©Annie Eagle/Alamy; p.283: ©Songquan Deng/Shutterstock; p.285: (T) ©Ilya Akinshin/Shutterstock; (B) ©Photri Images/Alamy; p.287: ©Senohrabek/Shutterstock.

Text

David Weinberger for the text on pp. 59–65 adapted from 'How Information Got Smart' by David Weinberger. Reproduced by kind permission of David Weinberger;

Graph on p. 192 adapted from 'The Crisis at Encyclopaedia Britannica' by Shane Greenstein and Michelle Devereux. Copyright © Kellogg School of Management 2006;

Alan Behr for the text on pp. 210–215 adapted from 'Copyright Law vs. Art and the Papal Censor of the Kissing Nun' by Alan Behr. Reproduced by kind permission of Alan Behr;

Henry Petroski for the text on pp. 283–288 adapted from 'An Engineer's Alphabet' by Henry Petroski. Reproduced by kind permission of Henry Petroski.

Typeset: emc design ltd.

Audio production: John Marshall Media